THE BUZZ ON™

ROMANCE & SEDUCTION

Rusty Fischer

Paul Love

LF LEBHAR-FRIEDMAN BOOKS

NEW YORK · CHICAGO · LOS ANGELES · LONDON · PARIS · TOKYO

The Buzz On Romance & Seduction

Lebhar-Friedman Books
425 Park Avenue
New York, NY 10022

Published by Lebhar-Friedman Books
Lebhar-Friedman Books is a company of Lebhar-Friedman, Inc.

Printed in the United States of America

Library of Congress Cataloging in Publication Data on file at the Library of Congress

ISBN: 0-86730-851-6

Produced by Progressive Publishing (1-888-355-8044) (www.propubltd.com)
Editor: John Craddock; Creative Director: Nancy Lycan
Photo Art Directors: Nancy Lycan, Michele Thomareas, Peter Royland, Rena Seibert
Editorial Contributor: Michele Thomareas
Design Director: Vivian Torres; Designers: Marco Echevarria, Lanette Fitzpatrick, Suzanne Miller, Rena Seibert

Visit our Web site at lfbooks.com

THE BUZZ ON™

ROMANCE & SEDUCTION

ACKNOWLEDGMENTS

The authors dutifully wish to thank the following for their contributions to this book:

Chris White, several of whose Top-5 lists appear in this book and who was a countless inspiration for those that don't! Chris is owner of TopFive.com, at http://www.topfive.com.

Haythum Raafat Khalid, who has graciously allowed us to use the quotes found in this book, which also appear on his Web site, Famous Quotations Network: http://www.famous-quotations.com.

Thanks to the friendly folks at http://www.women.com for providing illuminating survey results on the ongoing battle of the sexes.

We also wish to thank the following for their contributions to this book:

Cheryl Trecoske and Caesars Pocono Resorts; Dara Fujimoto and Kapalua Bay Hotel; Julie Pavao and Princeville Resort; and Shailesh Adalja and Taj Exotica Hotel.

THE BUZZ ON
ROMANCE & SEDUCTION

CONTENTS

ROMANCE WRECKS AT SEDUCTION JUNCTION

Once upon a time, there were blissful days, when men were men, women were women, sabretooth tigers were house pets, and a thunk on the head from a Flinstones club meant getting "lucky." Actually, no one around now can remember those days or wants to repeat them—outside of some over-the-edge rock groups. The world has slowly but surely evolved for the better, but how much? Those handy clubs have been replaced by cyber greeting cards, men cry (a lot), and women work (overtime).

Still, the dreams of romance and seduction are never too far out of mind for the modern man or woman. They just seem harder to fulfill. After all, if you're single, you're still trying to get lucky. Or if you're with someone and want it to stay that way, there seem to be plots hatched to keep you apart and more obstacles than there are to peace in the Middle East.

LESSONS OF LOVE

If you've moved past Jell-O shooters as your attempt at seduction and neon condoms as your nod to romance,

There's a reason that romance and seduction usually go hand in hand: You can't quite have one without the other. First you romance, then you seduce. Right? Of course, it can happen the other way. After all, spewing perky pick-up lines over beer nuts and ordering your date a Kamikaze just before last call worked in your college days. (Wait, you did that last night? Keep reading.) Think of the process now as the difference between Algebra 101 and Calculus 6000. Much like seduction, romance requires an active participation from both parties, whether you are young or old, gay or straight, rich or poor. In truth, neither romance nor seduction requires buckets of money. (Although it helps.) A thoughtful note in your lover's lunchbox or listening to her dreams and desires will go much further in enhancing your relationship than flowers or a trip to the Bahamas. (Okay, the trip is a sure winner.)

and you're ready to put a little time, effort, and creativity into your love life, or even your pursuit of a love life, then it's time for *The Buzz On Romance & Seduction.* Let the games begin!

1 SEDUCTION SECRETS

It's pretty easy to dismiss the classic ploys of lighting a potential lover's cigarette while staring hypnotically into her eyes or spiking his drink as hopelessly dated seduction techniques, especially in an age when evolving love lessons with a technological twist have come into play. From enticing e-mails to mesmerizing messages on your voice mail, the world of romance and seduction requires an electric schematic to aid the lustful in landing the perfect partner.

Still, while there are new ways to seduce, you still want to achieve the old-fashioned result, right? (Though virtual sex is an option.)

So it helps to balance the old with the new. Listening closely in conversation, catching a sexual innuendo, playing hard to get—they all have worked for centuries. While keeping an eye on your e-mail box, consider some of the tried and true seduction secrets.

CASANOVA: THE ORIGINAL BAD BOY

He's either a luscious libertine or a primitive pig, depending on your perspective, but talk about someone who had romance and seduction down to a science, and you're talking about Giacomo Casanova, the legendary seducer. Everywhere he went, and he traveled through Europe extensively, women fell deeply in love with him. Not only that, but he was such a charmer that noblemen welcomed him into their elite circles of society (until he hit on their wives, that is), and even princes and popes opened their doors to a man whose claim to fame was screwing around. Hey, somebody had to do it.

He wasn't born to love, though. This supreme seducer actually began life as a sickly little kid in Venice in 1725. He was forced to be so inactive that he often described the first years of his life as "vegetative." The popular myth of his "gift" is that his loving grandmother took the eight-year-old to a female witch doctor, seeking a magical cure for the boy's chronic nosebleeds. Feeling sorry for the boy's condition and his depressed disposition, the sorceress cast an enchantment over him to both arouse his passions and make him irresistible to women.

Well, whether her spell was potent is debatable, but there are no doubts that Casanova's abilities with women developed quite early. His first sexual experience came when he was just 11 years old, at the hands, so to speak, of Bettina, the sister of the priest who was charged with his education.

With that kind of introduction, he decided on a priestly path himself, entering the Seminary of San Cipriano. Then they started to talk about this celibacy thing, and shortly after joining the seminary in Padua, Casanova was expelled for what history has come to refer to in records as "scandalous behavior." Perhaps another priest's sister was involved this time. Either way, getting expelled was an idea he was going to have to get used to, as he was about to turn pro in the scandalous conduct department.

Yes, Giacomo Casanova was one of the first men in history to prove that women totally dig the "bad boy" image. (It still works: How else do you explain Kid Rock and Eminem?) In fact, it is often noted that Casanova was ardently welcomed by so many powerful people simply because his dubious deeds were so often the gossip of high society throughout Europe. After a string of unsuccessful jobs and a stint in jail, Casanova traveled to Naples and embarked on one of his most torrid and outrageous affairs with Donna Lucrezia. The torrid part simply comes from the fact that they were both extraordinarily passionate people. The scandalous part came later. Ending the affair with Donna, Casanova then was introduced to a young boy named Bellino. Casanova was supposed to be matched up with Bellino's sister, but he couldn't help feeling a stronger attraction to Bellino himself. (Had the ultimate lady's man changed his tune?) In all fairness, Bellino was a very feminine looking singer who was supposed by most to be a eunuch (meaning he had no balls, literally and figuratively).

Confused but undeterred, Casanova set out to determine why his passions would lead him astray. It turned out that his instincts served him well, and Bellino was indeed a girl (kind of like Yentl without all the yelling). They fell in love and planned to marry, but the King balked. He told Bellino (now called Theresa) that he didn't want to interfere with her career because he saw true talent in her singing.

Overall, Casanova observers fall into two camps: There are those who see him as a womanizing pig who used women for his

own pleasure; but there are also those who see him as an ultra-romantic, who actually worshiped women with whom he slept. It's just that his passions were so strong (he was a product of voodoo), he couldn't focus them on any one woman for long.

History shows that many of the women Casanova loved, for however brief the period, remained devoted friends with him. Many times when he was in trouble, whether he was in jail, being banished from a city, or being hunted by government officials, it was often a former lover who bailed him out. Yep, old Cas' sure knew how to make a lasting impression. For anyone trying to be a modern day Casanova, male or female, here's one of his secrets—he built up a mouth-watering mystique around himself. And there was truth in advertising: He actually did most of the things he was rumored to have done.

hard. Feeling differently from the attraction and passions he'd had for women previously, he was actually in love with Henriette. Even love, however, couldn't pacify his promiscuity. It may not sound like much by today's standards, but the way Henriette excited him most was to play her cello for him. At the time, this was the height of impropriety, as a woman was supposed to be concealed when playing the cello, since she had to cradle the instrument between her widely spread legs. Underwear was likely optional at these private concerts.

> *"A good time to keep your mouth shut is when you're in deep water."*
> —Sidney Goff

There were some, though, who even Casanova couldn't charm, namely the State Inquisitors (that's right, the merciless and torturing morality police of the 18th century), who weren't exactly keen on what they considered to be "black magic." With these guys on his tail, the only choice he had was to run, so he did.

Leave it to Casanova to have such luck, though, that while fleeing the authorities of Venice (for the first of many times) he ran right into the arms of Henriette, who would become his greatest love. When Casanova met Henriette, she was dressed like a man, but he saw through the disguise (it helps to have experience with this sort of thing). He fell for her instantly, and he fell

As with any of Casanova's sweethearts, however, the relationship with Henriette was short, lasting less than a year. He got over his most beloved quickly, though, and resumed his debauched lifestyle. Inevitably, though, those killjoys known as Inquisitors caught up with Casanova and put him in a cell for life. Until he escaped, that is. It was an escape that became the talk of European high society, and made him the most sought after dinner guest in the land. After this, some scholars believe that the government wised up and got Casanova on their side.

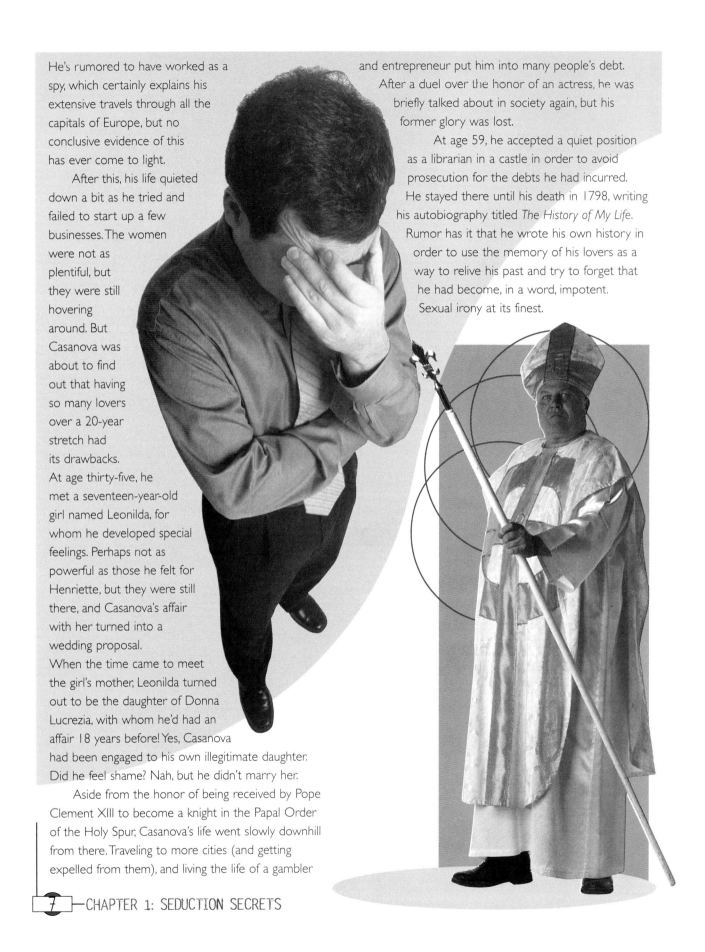

He's rumored to have worked as a spy, which certainly explains his extensive travels through all the capitals of Europe, but no conclusive evidence of this has ever come to light.

After this, his life quieted down a bit as he tried and failed to start up a few businesses. The women were not as plentiful, but they were still hovering around. But Casanova was about to find out that having so many lovers over a 20-year stretch had its drawbacks. At age thirty-five, he met a seventeen-year-old girl named Leonilda, for whom he developed special feelings. Perhaps not as powerful as those he felt for Henriette, but they were still there, and Casanova's affair with her turned into a wedding proposal.

When the time came to meet the girl's mother, Leonilda turned out to be the daughter of Donna Lucrezia, with whom he'd had an affair 18 years before! Yes, Casanova had been engaged to his own illegitimate daughter. Did he feel shame? Nah, but he didn't marry her.

Aside from the honor of being received by Pope Clement XIII to become a knight in the Papal Order of the Holy Spur, Casanova's life went slowly downhill from there. Traveling to more cities (and getting expelled from them), and living the life of a gambler and entrepreneur put him into many people's debt. After a duel over the honor of an actress, he was briefly talked about in society again, but his former glory was lost.

At age 59, he accepted a quiet position as a librarian in a castle in order to avoid prosecution for the debts he had incurred. He stayed there until his death in 1798, writing his autobiography titled *The History of My Life*. Rumor has it that he wrote his own history in order to use the memory of his lovers as a way to relive his past and try to forget that he had become, in a word, impotent. Sexual irony at its finest.

COY CONVERSATION

GET A CLUE

Despite its obvious sultry images of long-stemmed roses, sexy lingerie, and smoldering glances, seduction is often a more subtle art of nuances and hints, suggestions and mystery. Nowhere is that made more evident than in conversation. And whether you're sporting a hip goatee or the latest shade of lipstick, unfortunately it's not what your lips look like that really matters, but what they say.

When you've finally mustered up enough courage to engage in conversation with that hottie in the corner or the hunk at the bar, you may want to listen closely to pick up all those hidden clues your barstool trophy is tossing off.

For instance, you can find out a lot about a person from how he or she answers a simple question. Say a certain Sexy Sally sidles up to your table on the way to the restroom. She sees a long line, makes a crumpled face, and starts to sigh as she turns around to head back from whence she came. To tell if she's really all that crushed, or if she's just looking for a chance to chat you up, why not ask her a simple question, such as "You know, there's never a line in the men's room. Want me to guard the door?"

Okay, some might consider it a little gross, but it shows her a few things. One, you've noticed why she seemed so upset.

Two, you at least offered to stand on the other side of the door, so in bar-speak that makes you a bona fide gentleman. Three, you've opened the lines of communication if, indeed, she wanted to start one. Now the ball's in her court. But how does she answer? Well, just like you, she has three options.

First, she could crinkle her nose, flip back her hair, and sidle off across the floor to diss you to her friends. Second, she could simply sneer and say "No, that's all right, my date will watch the door" before continuing on her way to the bathroom. Or, third, she could laugh and hang out for a while.

APPETIZING ANSWERS

In the previous example, you were forced to, as the Marines say, "improvise, adapt, and overcome." You saw an opportunity that could have gone any of a dozen different ways, and tossed off a quick one-liner that may or may not have gotten Sexy Sally's attention. Hey, at least you tried. Other questions, however, need to be just a little bit more calculated if you want to conquer the next summit, so to speak.

For instance, not everyone on the singles scene is, actually, single. There are only so many bars, clubs, and lounges in town, and couples have to find one somewhere. Perhaps that handsome hunk in the corner is from out of town and waiting on his date, who is carefully lining every square inch of the toilet in the ladies room, before disinfecting the stall with her handy travel size bottle of Lysol. How do you find out?

Well, you could be as unseductive as possible and simply walk up to him and ask if he's single. Or, you could be just a tad bit more seductive and ask if the seat next to him is taken. Or, you could take your time and try to be a little bit more coy.

For instance, if he's wearing a tie, why not sidle up to the bar for a fresh drink and comment on it as you wait: "Nice tie. Did you pick that out yourself?"

If he's there with someone, he'll most likely say, "Naw, my date chose this one," all the while nervously eyeing the restroom door. In that case, grab your fresh drink and head for the other end. If, on the other hand, he

smiles condescendingly and says, "Yes, and I tied my own shoes, too," you might just have found yourself a personable companion for the evening.

Then again, if he says something like, "Yes, I did, but only because it works great in tying up wrists. Are you interested in finding out?" you might want to cool him off with that drink.

SENTENCE STARTERS

Don't stop mining for clues just because you found a Sexy Sally or Terrific Tom to join you at your table, booth, or barstool, however. Now the fun really begins. After all, it wasn't exactly brain surgery figuring out if someone was single in a singles spot, now was it? Now you need to find out how single they are, how long they've been single, how they like being single, and more important why they're single in the first place.

To that effect, here are a few great sentence starters that will help you find out if your potential lover is sincere or a scammer:

Skip the usual "Come here often?" line. If he says "yes," you don't want to know, and if she says "no," she's probably lying. Instead, why not say something like, "Wow, this beer's going right through me. Any idea where the bathroom is?" If she perks up and gives you detailed instructions, such as "turn left at the cigarette machine, take three paces past the Bud Girl poster, and right under the neon Pale Ale sign is a slight dip in the floor, avoid that and keep walking six more paces . . ." you've pretty much got your answer.

TITILLATING TACTICS

There's a great scene in the classic teen movie *Fast Times at Ridgemont High* in which Mike Damone (played by Robert Romanus) is schooling a few newbies at the fine art of picking up chicks. "No matter where you are," he counsels, "act like that's the coolest place in town." It may be simple advice from a simpleton, but it's also effective. As you are about to learn, that's one of only a handful of titillating tactics to help you on your path to seduction.

CROWD CONTROL

Let's face it, to go out and meet people, you almost always have to deal with some kind of crowd. Either there's a wait to get in the club or a line at the theater door. And while it's reassuring to know that you're not alone in this single seduction scene, it would also be nice to have a little elbow room for a change. That's why crowd control is so important. For no matter how crowded your establishment of choice, try to remain in control.

For instance, the dance floor may be hopping, but the lovely lady across from you is forcing a smile, as well as those token dance moves. Start by introducing yourself, and after you've each shouted your name into the other's ear three times, why not suggest going

TOP
Romantic Songs
(You Might Have Forgotten About)

"It Must Have Been Love"	Roxette
"Wind Beneath My Wings"	Bette Midler
"Can't Help Falling..."	Elvis Presley
"More Than Words"	Extreme
"The One"	Elton John
"Here and Now"	Luther Vandross
"Endless Love"	Mariah Carey
"Right Here Waiting"	Richard Marx
"You're Still The One"	Shania Twain
"What a Girl Wants"	Christina Aguilera
"Possession"	Sarah McLachlan
"Somebody"	Depeche Mode
"What a Wonderful World"	Louis Armstrong
"With or Without You"	U2
"Moonlight Serenade"	Glen Miller
"When I Fall in Love"	Celine Dion/Clive Griffin
"True"	Spandau Ballet
"I Swear"	John M. Montgomery
"I'll Make Love to You"	Boyz II Men
"Save the Best for Last"	Vanessa Williams
"Take My Breath Away"	Berlin
"That's What Friends Are For"	Dionne Warwick
"You Sang to Me"	Marc Anthony
"Butterfly Kisses"	Bob Carlisle
"I Need You"	Leann Rimes
"Can You Feel the Love Tonight?"	Elton John
"I Finally Found Someone"	Bryan Adams and Barbra Streisand

happy hour patrons and you and the handsome hunk you've just bumped into are getting a little tired of rubbing elbows, literally. Why not grab his elbow instead and suggest moving out to the patio, back deck, or perhaps even grabbing a beer or two up the street. After all, in the sexy steps of seduction, three hundred sweaty souls is a crowd, but two is just right.

CUTTING IT SHORT

If your true intent is to seduce someone, you must be ever vigilant and always ready to avail yourself of every opportunity. Occasionally, this means cutting the fun short in favor of quitting while you're ahead.

For instance, let's say you've just run into the man of your dreams, or at least your daydreams, at a party of a friend of a friend of a friend.

You've giggled over the host's choice of dated retro music, gagged at the spinach dip, and shared the arm of a particularly large end chair for more than an hour. Everything about your spontaneous combustion is a green light, and that makes it the perfect time to get up and go.

Don't forget, anyone can have a one-night stand with a handsome stranger. Okay, or at least a one-night stand with another human. But the aim of true seduction is a love that lasts, or at least lasts for a while. That means taking extra precautions against falling too quickly for his dazzling eyes and clever patter.

somewhere more "quiet." Not only does this get her out of the way of the other hundred single gents there, but you can get better acquainted.

Or perhaps the bar is wall to wall with grumbling

Passionate Poetry

The First Day

I wish I could remember the first day,
First hour, first moment of your meeting me;
If bright or dim the season, it might be
Summer or winter for aught I can say.
So unrecorded did it slip away,
So blind was I to see and to foresee,
So dull to mark the budding of my tree
That would not blossom yet for many a May.
If only I could recollect it! Such
A day of days! I let it come and go
As traceless as a thaw of bygone snow.
It seemed to mean so little, meant so much!
If only now I could recall that touch,
First touch of hand in hand! - Did one but know!

—Christina Rossetti (1830-1894)

Besides, cutting things short allows you an air of mystery, especially when you don't exactly answer his insistent, "What? But we were having such a great time? What could be so important that you'd have to leave in the middle of the party?"

No matter what you told him, from a helicopter is picking you up to take you to a special audience at the White House to Brad Pitt just pulled up in his limo, nothing is going to be quite like what he imagines in his mind when you tell him, ever so sultrily, that it's "none of his business."

When he asks for your number, you certainly can't

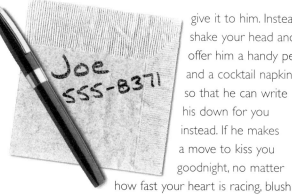

give it to him. Instead, shake your head and offer him a handy pen and a cocktail napkin so that he can write his down for you instead. If he makes a move to kiss you goodnight, no matter how fast your heart is racing, blush accordingly and offer your hand, to shake, instead.

But where will you go when the night is still so young? Straight to your favorite girlfriend's house, of course. After all, you have to decide how long to wait before you call him back!

SHY GUY

Everyone knows girls love the bad boy, that handsome rake who treats them like dirt and enjoys it when they pour buckets of tears out over him. But for every girl who hasn't had her fill of bad boys yet, there's always one who has, and what she wants is the exact opposite: A gentleman who will treat her right and hold the door open while he's doing it. The trick is to not outlast your shyness, or your good boy act will send her running into the arms of the next bad boy she meets.

For instance, if you're looking for something longer than a one-night stand, even if she's offering, why not try resisting for a change. Yes, it's anathema to everything you've been taught by your brothers, your buds, and your hormones, but it just could be the difference between hearing the same old "Don't call me, I'll call you," and "I'm cooking veal piccata next Saturday night, would you like to come over and taste my dish?"

DARING DUDS

Perhaps you've tried every tactic in the book, and even some of your own (can you say "magic potion?"), all to no avail. Perhaps it's time for one of the most drastic tactics of all: a new look. Think about it. If you've had the same old haircut since you were 12, it might be time to say good-bye to Ed, your dear old barber, and splurge on an actual hairstyle at that snooty salon uptown. If you're heading off to happy hour after work every Friday night, why not bring a pair of pleated slacks and a dark turtleneck to change into after work?

For the ladies, if your expensive perfume's driving them away, why not try something different for a change? If your high heels hurt and they're not working anyway, why not be comfortable and check out some of the latest footwear fashions? If you're used to wearing wool and cashmere, grays and blacks, why not throw a splash of color into the ensemble with a scarf or hat?

No one's asking you to be anyone other than who you are, but sometimes even you don't know when you're in a rut. After all, a new turtleneck or a splash of color might just be the confidence booster you need to kick your sexy seduction tactics into overdrive!

PLAYING HARD TO GET

Of all the seduction strategies that have been handed down through time, including the ever-reliable buying of comically named shots, there is probably none more popular than playing hard to get. For those of you who have been living in a cave for the last decade (which would actually be considered at the extreme end of hard to get), the concept of aloofness involves acting all cool and standoffish on the outside when, in reality, you're all shaking knees and sweaty palms.

Over time, of course, women have proved themselves to be much better at playing hard to get than men, if only out of necessity. After all, men have been hitting on women since the Stone Age, when, of course, hitting on women meant actually hitting them. Could this be where the term came from? Slowly, however, as history has proved women to be equal (some would say superior) to men, men have had to catch up in this seductive game as females began hitting on them. Minus the bat, that is. Not because women are any less violent than men, of course, they just care about their fingernails a whole lot more. Nowadays, both sexes equally use this passion ploy to their advantage.

In case you need to play a little catch-up, whether you're a man or a woman, or a girl or a boy, for that matter, here are a few modern twists to this passionate pastime.

ELECTRONIC ORGANIZER

Today's version of the hastily scribbled note left under your windshield or in your mailbox is undoubtedly the hastily keyed in e-mail left in your inbox. We've all received e-mails from those who feel that, if you haven't responded in, say, 15 minutes, it is their right, no, their duty to send you a total of 15 additional e-mails in that 16th minute!

Obviously, those hyper typists have no grasp of the modern art of playing hard to get. Instead, they come off as pathetically desperate. To avoid playing e-mail tag at hyperspeed, there is a new tool at your disposal called an "autoreply."

Consider the following scenario: You and a cute coworker have been involved in a little harmless flirtation for, let's say, the last year or two. You give each other googly eyes at the water cooler, play a little too rough at the employee volleyball game, and are so quick and fast with the sexual innuendoes that other employees within earshot get visibly nauseous.

Naturally, you enjoy the daily flurry of e-mails through the morning and afternoon, which of course goes nowhere. So how do you kick things up a notch when it's ready to take that next step and actually do something about it? Simple, hit them with an autoreply. You've seen these devices. They're usually employed when a coworker or other e-mail contact is going out of town or away from her desk. Like voicemail, they reply with a preprogrammed message, such as "Kimberly is at an optometrists' convention and will be away from her desk all week. She will gladly respond to your e-mail upon her return, if she feels like it. Thanks for your patience."

But who says your autoreply has to be all business? Program your autoreply, or have the geeks down in IT do it, so that your little friend's e-mail is the only one you auto-respond to. Then program the message to say something bogus, such as "Kimberly's computer is being overhauled this week, and is only receiving e-mail intermittently. She apologizes for this hiccup, and will gladly respond to your missed messages sometime next week."

Start your autoreply marathon first thing Monday morning, and your little friend is sure to go stir crazy by lunch! Your water cooler winks will get winkier, your harmless flirtations in the halls will become more dangerous, and by Wednesday your little sexual innuendoes from cubicle to cubicle will become downright erotic. By Friday, he should be eating out of your Palm Pilot!

NOT-SO-NEIGHBORLY

From time to time, couples meet in the same place they occasionally eat, that is, at home. With condo and apartment complex living, it is no longer unnatural or even creepy to date someone you live near, above, or even under. Think about it: Aside from work and the singles bars, where else are you going to meet a potential partner? Compared with hanging out in a dimly lit bar, running into a hottie or a hunk at the sunny community mailbox isn't so bad.

However, the intimacy level (aka surveillance factor) goes way up when you're lusting where you live, as your potential partner can quickly determine your comings and goings, especially if she lives in the same building or unit as you do. With only a minimum of detective work, she can quickly decipher when you leave in the morning, what you wear to the pool, when you get the mail, and what's underneath all those plain brown wrappers.

But there's no reason to let this invasion of privacy work against you. Use those prying eyes as an asset and kick your playing-hard-to-get up a gear with the help of a few female friends.

Sisters work best here, if you've got one. So why not invite yours to stay with you for a while. You know, just to catch up? This way, you can rediscover your family ties and play a few mind games at the same time.

If no sisters are available, why not bribe a leggy coworker to do a little overtime at your house one or two nights a week, for the price of a home cooked meal or even take-out from her favorite restaurant. You can score some brownie points at work and get your future femme fatale all hot and bothered at the same time. After all, nothing ignites the flames of passion quite like the heat that jealousy generates. For instance, if your lady friend is in the habit of cruising by your building around eight each night, why not begin the nightly habit of going for a walk with your sister, coworker, or even paid companion in the evening? Make sure to laugh uproariously as her car drives up, and don't forget to wave as she passes by.

Check the mail together when you know your lady friend is checking hers, and invest in a string bikini for your stand-in and spend hours at the pool on the weekends. Even if she doesn't show up, chances are her telescope is working overtime on her balcony. After a week or

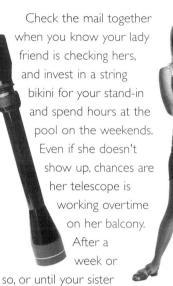

so, or until your sister remembers why she quit talking to you in the first place or your takeout dinner budget dries up, play the part of the wounded boyfriend and lurk at all your usual places, only this time going solo. Strike up a conversation in dulcet tones and don't be surprised if you get a quick invitation to "pour your heart out" by the soda machine or in the gazebo by the mailboxes.

Don't, however, play it as if you and your imposter were going out. Instead, admit that you were so hurt that your lady friend wasn't interested that you were confiding all of your troubles in a friend from work or, better yet, your sister. If that doesn't work, it's time to move!

TABLE FOR ONE

Since food is so often at the center of our modern dating rituals, why don't you take the step of eating one step further and play the fiercely independent single diner who could not care less if she ever has another date in her life. Guys love the thought of seducing the buxom bookworm who takes off her glasses and lets her hair down once the lights go off, so be sure to stop by a bookstore and pick up something appropriate before trying this ploy—like this book.

Hint: To make your reading more pleasurable, splurge on two similarly sized hardbacks. Make one intellectual, such as The Mating Rituals of Papua New Guinea Medicine Men or anything by Stephen Hawking, and the other racy or fun, such as SEX! SEX! SEX! or anything by Jackie Collins (same difference). Then just switch the dust jackets and no one will ever be the wiser!

Next, find a local café or bistro (you don't want to end up dating someone from halfway across town, do you?) with an unusually high ratio of single men dining alone, or handsome waiters without wedding rings. Begin dining there once or twice a week, eating lightly (unless your budget allows for the nightly filet mignon splurge) and lingering over decaf until you start yawning or the pages of your book grow bleary.

Use your book as a crutch, creating the image of a lovely, strong, independent woman who responds politely when spoken to, but is in general alone and aloof. You don't want to come off like an ice queen, but neither should you be Chatty Cathy. There's nothing wrong with a little harmless flirting with the single guy at the table next to you or that waiter with the muscles and the Mohawk, but appearing desperate for either conversation or company isn't what you're shooting for.

In time, other single regulars will slowly make your acquaintance and, hopefully, a move or two, which you will naturally receive politely with a wistful look at your book as you set it aside. (Put it close to you, of course, unless you want to hear your new date say something like, "Hmm, when did Stephen Hawking start writing torrid love scenes about Hollywood wives?")

There are lots of variables to consider with this hard-to-get hijinx, such as how pricey the menu is, what kind of neighborhood you live in, whether the waiters are gay or not, etc. As a general rule, don't try this one for longer than it takes you to read your book. If you finish two novels and still haven't gotten a desirable date out of the deal, you might be better off hitting happy hour with the rest of the girls.

At least that way you'll get to use your mouth for something other than chewing!

"Better to have loved a short man than never to have loved a tall."
—David Chambless

PHONE TAG

Aside from deleted e-mails and the famed cold shoulder, nothing says "I'm playing hard to get" quite like an endlessly ringing telephone. It's hard enough to get those all-important "digits," let alone work up the courage to call in the first place. But to hear nothing but ringing or, even worse, the annoying sound of the callee's voice on the answering machine, over and over and over again, is nothing short of temptation torture. So how do you become the torturer instead of the tortured? Come along and we'll give you the buzz.

OCCUPYING OCCUPATION

The secret to playing a really good game of phone tag is to keep your mind off, what else, the phone. Instead of rushing home to see if he's called, stay busy. After all, if you're outside playing racquetball, it's impossible to wait for a phone that never rings, or better yet, rings off the hook!

For instance, while you're waiting for her to call, or dreading that she won't call, you can avoid the torture of sitting by a dead phone by joining the gym, playing a round of golf, swimming a few hundred laps, taking in a double feature after work, dining out, or simply getting a second job.

After all, nothing says "I'm unavailable" quite like working 90 hours a week!

TECHNOLOGY MATTERS

Once she finally calls, however, you must naturally let the voice mail or answering machine get it. "Must" being the operative word here. Even if you're sitting there while her sultry voice pours out her undying love for you, sit on your hands and avoid picking up the phone! If you're not heavy enough to keep your hands still that way, tie them to your shoelaces or handcuff yourself to a heavy table halfway across the room. Whatever it takes, leave the phone unattended and let the machine get it.

In preparation for this moment, why not change your message completely. Get rid of the sappily sweet no brainer, "I'm not here right now, but if you leave your name and number, I'll be happy to get right back to you." Instead, why not smoke several packs of cigarettes (especially if you've never smoked in your life) and mumble something cryptic such as, "You know what to do" or, "Talk after the beep!"

UNPLUGGED

Another phone tag option is to lose the answering machine altogether and simply let the phone ring and ring and ring and ring. To make this less annoying, of course, you could always turn off the ringer. However, then you'll never know if he called once, twice, 15 times, or never!

Besides, there's something erotic about an endlessly ringing phone. To pass the time more quickly, picture him sitting there suffering endlessly on the other end of the line. He's sitting on pins and needles, wondering where you are, wondering who you're with, wondering what you're doing, wondering who you're doing it with, wondering when you'll get back, wondering if you'll ever get back at all!

Imagine his tapping feet and bobbing head and his fingers flying fast and furious over those seven little numbers. Then imagine him naked! When you can't take it anymore, it's time to pick up the phone! (Who knew phone tag could be this much fun?)

I. D. REQUIRED

Technology is your friend, so embrace it and invest in one of those caller I. D. gadgets that everyone and his mother seem to have. Sure, it costs a little bit more, but what's a few extra bucks in this sweet struggle we call love? Besides, letting the phone ring and ring and ring isn't exactly the best way to keep your mother out of town, especially if it's her on the other end of the line!

This way, each time the phone rings, you can saunter past and revel knowing that Sexy Susie's number keeps popping up, again and again, over and over, all night long. And, when your Mom finally buzzes through, you can joyfully pick up the phone and talk for hours and hours and hours about simply nothing at all. Not only will this earn you immeasurable brownie points with your dear old mom, but it's sure to drive Sexy Susie straight up the wall!

KEEPING BUSY!

Speaking of a busy signal, you don't have to wait for Mom to call to send that sizzling signal to Sexy Steven. You can always just take the darn thing off the hook each night, stowing it in some hallway drawer or under your mattress. However, no matter how deep you bury the offending appliance, that irritating busy signal always seems to penetrate every nook and cranny of the house, buzzing and bleating like some modern tell-tale heart!

To avoid going crazy yourself, why not dust off your address book and hook up with a few old friends while you're busy driving Sexy Steven into a straitjacket at the same time. Why not dial up your old college roommate, just for kicks? See how she's doing, giggle with her kids, even shoot the breeze with her husband if you're feeling froggy. Hey, whatever it takes to keep that phone line tied up.

When you run out of old college buddies and other close friends, why not chat up minor acquaintances, everyone from that boring fellow down the hall at work to the ladies who lunch. Talk as long as you wish, and make sure that you either have a cordless phone, or plenty of food handy as you burn up the lines.

Just make sure to cancel the call waiting first! Otherwise, Sexy Steven will be hearing an endless ring instead of a busy signal, and that three-hour conversation you endured with that heavy woman from human resources will be all for naught. Until she starts stalking you, that is.

FOLLOWING THE E-MAIL TRAIL

DIGITAL DETECTIVES

Love it or hate it, e-mail is here to stay and you might as well just get used to it. Perhaps you already have. After all, for the first time in recent memory, the rise in the cost of postage stamps made about as big a ripple as CBS' *The Mole*, and there's a sneaking suspicion that it was because few of us bother to send personal mail anymore—aside from bills and the spring renewal subscription to *Sports Illustrated*, that is.

Now that even moms and grandmas have personal computers, what's the point? Need a quick recipe? E-mail Nana. Need expert advice on rolling over your 401-K? E-mail Daddy-o. It's as simple as typing in a few grammatically incorrect sentences (just don't e-mail your English teacher) and clicking a button. And best of all, it's free. So is it any surprise that savvy seducers have gone the way of the e-mail trail?

One reason that e-mail enticement has become so popular is the ease with which folks can acquire those handy little addresses. From workplace newsletters to a forwarded message from a friend of a friend of a friend, all it takes is a little cyber snooping before you're in possession of that sexy little redhead's work address or that hunk from the gym's AOL screen name.

From there, a torrid affair is often a simple introduction away: "Don't delete this! I'm not a stalker, just a closet fan of yours from work . . ." If your message manages to avoid the dreaded little trash can icon, the only thing stopping you is your typing speed, or lack thereof.

Hitting the delete button, however, can be mighty tempting. Amid the flurry of junk e-mail, spam, and annoying "Fwd.:" messages from friend and foe alike, it's no great feat for a harried e-mail recipient to trash your merry missive as soon as it has arrived. So how do you get out of the trash and into his heart? Simple: Creativity.

A White Rose

The red rose whispers of passion,
And the white rose breathes of love;
O, the red rose is a falcon,
And the white rose is a dove.
But I send you a cream-white rosebud
With a flush on its petal tips;
For the love that is purest and sweetest
Has a kiss of desire on the lips.

—J.B. O'Reilly (1844-1890)

Passionate Poetry

To a Stranger

Passing stranger! You do not know
How longingly I look upon you,
You must be he I was seeking,
Or she I was seeking
(It comes to me as a dream)

I have somewhere surely
Lived a life of joy with you,
All is recall'd as we flit by each other,
Fluid, affectionate, chaste, matured,

You grew up with me,
Were a boy with me or a girl with me,
I ate with you and slept with you,
your body has become
not yours only nor left my body mine only,

You give me the pleasure of your eyes,
face, flesh as we pass,
You take of my beard, breast, hands,
in return,

I am not to speak to you, I am to think of you
when I sit alone or wake at night, alone
I am to wait, I do not doubt I am to meet you again
I am to see to it that I do not lose you.

— Walt Whitman (1819-1892)

CREATIVITY COUNTS!

The truth is, anyone with an Internet account and a screen name can send an e-mail. And nowadays, both are free. From free Internet service providers such as NoCharge.com and NetZero.com, to free e-mail accounts with everyone from Yahoo! to Hotmail.com, the World Wide Web has never been so inexpensive! Naturally, this makes sending an e-mail as easy as blowing a kiss.

The trick, then, is to have your secret admirer actually read your e-mail. For starters, subject headings are usually the first thing they'll read. Don't lie here, that will just take away from all the time you spent writing the actual message. Saying something like "You've just won a million dollars!" is a quick way to tick off a frustrated secretary who's just fetched her fifth pot of coffee for the day. Not to mention, most folks would simply trash this type of message for fear that a virus was attached!

Try to be coy, instead. A subject heading such as "Drinks tonight? Just a thought" or "Electronically winking at you" is just mysterious enough to catch someone's interest, yet not creepy enough to send them clicking your way into the cyber dump. Also, including their first name in the subject heading may hint to them that it's not junk mail.

Once they've actually opened the message, assure them that you're no creep by introducing yourself and letting them know where you got their

Outlook Express

Print | Delete | Send & Receiv

subject | starts with

Subject

You just won a million dollars!

address. It's definitely not sexy to feel spied upon, so honesty is important here. You've gone to the trouble of tracking down their address, which should get your foot in the door, if only electronically.

If they're still reading by this point, it helps to tell them why you're writing. Does the luster of her hair get you through the afternoon doldrums from eight cubicles away? Does his snazzy tie brighten your every morning? Sometimes it's these little details that keep someone reading, even if they have no intention of acting upon your invitation or enticement. Then again, you could just change your mind.

After the flattering honesty, have a concrete request. Do you want to meet them for lunch in the corporate cafeteria? Or perhaps have a drink or two after work? Don't move too fast, but don't miss your chance, either. Make it simple, make it effortless, and make it something you can do publicly so they don't go calling the cops!

If they bite, your romantic secret admirer image will get you even more attention if nothing pans out in the end.

If they don't bite, though, you have to live with the stalker reputation for a few years.

GOOFY GREETINGS

Perhaps you're the greeting card type. Anyone who is anyone knows that sending an eGreeting is as simple as one, two, three. You can't log on Yahoo! or AOL without being bombarded with opportunities to send a goofy greeting card to one and all. The holidays come and go with pop up windows left and right, so is it any wonder that online lovers have gotten the hint and logged on for love?

Sexy cards are fair game, and even if their cyber graphics aren't all that racy, typing in your own erotic message is as easy as hitting all the right keys. What

Passionate Poetry

Who Ever Loved That Loved Not at First Sight?

It lies not in our power to love or hate,
For will in us is overruled by fate.
When two are stripped, long ere the course begin,
We wish that one should love, the other win;

And one especially do we affect
Of two gold ingots, like in each respect:
The reason no man knows; let it suffice
What we behold is censured by our eyes.
Where both deliberate, the love is slight:
Who ever loved, that loved not at first sight?

—Christopher Marlowe (1564-1593)

Passionate Poetry

To His Coy Love

I pray thee, leave, love me no more,
Call home the heart you gave me!
I but in vain that saint adore
That can but will not save me.
These poor half-kisses kill me quite
Was ever man thus servèd?
Amidst an ocean of delight
For pleasure to be starvèd?
Show me no more those snowy breasts
With azure riverets branchèd,
Where, whilst mine eye with plenty feasts,
Yet is my thirst not stanchèd;
O Tantalus, thy pains ne'er tell!
By me thou art prevented:
'Tis nothing to be plagued in Hell,
But thus in Heaven tormented.
Clip me no more in those dear arms,
Nor thy life's comfort call me,
O these are but too powerful charms,
And do but more enthral me!
But see how patient I am grown
In all this coil about thee:
Come, nice thing, let thy heart alone,
I cannot live without thee!

—Michael Drayton (1563-1631)

better way to ask someone out than to zip them a quick gigabyte greeting card at work requesting a face-to-face at happy hour or a weekend trip to the movies?

READING BETWEEN THE LINES

Watched pots never boil, and neither do watched inboxes. Waiting for a reply to your frisky e-mail can be as trying. Stay busy and don't dwell on it to the point of hating the person you wrote to by the end of the day. People leave their desks for big meetings, conference calls, and personal leave, and the fact that they haven't replied for a couple of hours doesn't mean there's a paddy wagon waiting for you down in the parking lot.

When the reply does come, however, you must read it very carefully to detect hidden meanings. Unless, of course, the subject line says, "KISS OFF!" in all caps. That pretty much says it all. Barring that, however, reading between the lines is your best bet when deciphering a reply to your e-mail.

For instance, perhaps he said something like, "I'd love to meet you for drinks after work, but my girlfriend sort of frowns on stuff like that." Well, this isn't as bad a diss as it sounds. For instance, he said "love," not "like." That's a good thing. He also said "girlfriend," not "wife." That's two for the plus column. Unfortunately, his lady friend isn't into the open

Passionate Poetry

Love Not Me

Love not me for comely grace,
For my pleasing eye or face,

Nor for any outward part:
No, nor for a constant heart!
For these may fail or turn to ill:
Should thou and I sever.

Keep, therefore, a true woman's eye,
And love me still, but know not why!
So hast thou the same reason still
To dote upon me ever.

—John Wilbye (1574-1638)

I'm all booked up for this week." Okay, yes, this does sound like a blow-off. But don't trash the reply in anger just yet. For starters, she did say "too bad," not "thank God!" Also, she's only booked up for the "week," not "forever."

Maybe it was Wednesday afternoon by the time you got the courage to e-mail her, and Thursday morning by the time she wrote back. That's only a day and a half of missed opportunity. Let her stew the rest of the day and then zoom her a message around lunchtime on Friday casually wondering if she "has any room on her dance card for next week."

You never know, she could just be a big fan of the phrase "dance card" and accept!

relationship gig. That's cool. Save the e-mail for later, and look for clues that things aren't exactly blissful on the home front.

After a month or two, hit him with another message asking how things are going. If he replies with a long rant about "all women being crazy," odds are he's fighting with Little Miss Can't Do Drinks After Work Without Me. Offer to prove to him that not all girls are crazy.

Perhaps she replied with something rather more cryptic, such as, "Too bad you didn't write sooner, but

2
SEDUCTION
STRATEGIES

Knowing the many secrets to seduction is one thing, but putting them to use is quite another. Sure, you may know how to flirt, but where do you flirt? You may know what to say, but who do you say it to? (No, not the mirror.) To help you as you strive for seduction perfection, we have compiled a collection of seduction strategies.

After all, seducing someone in a bar is quite different from seducing someone, say, at work. (Unless, that is, you work in a bar.) So whether you're seducing a stranger or a lifelong friend, picking someone up at a coffee shop or sidling up to that handsome hunk next door, the following chapter has a strategy, even for you.

COURTSHIP
COUNTS

No matter what arguments people try to pose, it's understood that chivalry is dead in modern society. Sorry, guys, it doesn't count when you set off the sensor to the automatic door for her. Still, we do have our courtship rituals for today; they're just drastically different from those in days of yore.

The origins of courtship, as we know it today, are hazy but probably are tied to the pagan practice of worshipping multiple goddesses. After the spread of Christianity (which definitely didn't put women on a pedestal, except the Virgin Mary), these beliefs survived in—where else?—France. The stories of devotion to goddesses, stoked with some fresh French wine, emerged from the work of French poets and the songs of troubadours, and from there the romances of courtly love were born.

Inspired by all this flowery poetry floating around, women suddenly became supreme objects of yearning in the middle ages. Women were, indeed, still considered objects, but now their love and affection had to be won rather than taken by force or traded by the family for some cows. Hey, it was a step in the right direction, at least.

All this romance, and it wasn't related to marriage. Marriage, in this period, was about the husband gaining land and political influence from the family of his bride—it was essentially a business deal, into which the woman had little input. Secretly, though, it was thought fashionable for a woman to have a man pining after her. After all, if she had already helped produce a child or two of royal blood (at least one boy), then she had done her duty as a wife, and her life had become boring. So naturally, a woman became the envy of all her married friends if she had a second gallant devotee.

However, in a time when it was legal for a man to kill his wife for even an inkling of infidelity, any affair had to be kept under wraps. Hence, one of the rules of courtship was that a love made public didn't endure. But, to add yet another contradiction, love had become so idealized that it became a belief of knights, those with whom chivalry is often associated, that one who was not in love with a woman was flawed.

Doesn't sound like it would cause any trouble, does it? Well, what it brought about was women having many illicit and passionate affairs with several knights (sometimes concurrently). This, of course, led to knights fighting with spurned nobles or other knights to win the favor of a fine female, sometimes ending in the death of one of the duelers. Guess love *is* a battlefield.

By the Victorian era, courtship became a ritual, which was all about virtue. No longer did a man win a woman with daring deeds of valor. Nope, now the impending issue was who would make the woman seem the most honorable.

This change came about due to the strict moral code of the time, and the idea that courtship should lead directly to a marriage, rather than it being an extramarital affair (though that still happened quite often). And the basic rule was that he who was most respectable (and richest) won. Maintaining a maiden's honor and virtue was also the reason behind the complicated rules of courtship in Victorian times.

The strictest of these rules was that potential young lovers were *never* left alone. In fact, a guy who was interested in courting a girl wasn't even allowed to see her, at first. He had to go to her house and drop off a calling card to her parents. When they were finally permitted to see each other, there had to be a chaperone (usually a married friend of the girl's family, or the girl's mother) present at all times. It was always someone from the girl's side because the beginning of a courtship always took place at the house of the

girl. This was to ensure that the guy wouldn't take any indelicate liberties with her (one push of a button and the Secret Service took him out). Talk about your home-field advantage!

The young couple couldn't even leave the house together until the girl's parents felt sure enough of the boy. Usually, then, they could go on a stroll around the property of the girl's home, then maybe to a social event, such as the theater, but the chaperone always followed.

Even flirting was forbidden in sight of others. Considered rude to be practiced in public, playful flirting was often interpreted through gestures with a fan. For instance, if a woman fanned herself slowly, it meant she was already involved. If she fanned with her right hand in front of her face, she was saying, "come with me." If a lady drew the fan across her forehead, she was warning the boy that they were being watched.

Apparently, the bright orange flags they originally used were a tad too obvious.

The only break young couples ever

got from supervision would be at the end of the night at the doorstep of the girl's house, where the chaperone would turn her head, and the young couple could do whatever they could get away with for about fifteen seconds. Yes, that's where we get the tradition of the end of the night kiss (it would be nice, though, if it would be the girl dropping the guy off once or twice).

Make no mistake, though. No matter how much of the courting ritual revolved around the woman, marriage was almost exclusively set up to subsidize men. Only a man could marry into a family with a higher social status than his, therefore attaining a higher status for himself. Women could only marry on the same level or down the social scale—she couldn't even approach someone of higher rank, unless being introduced by a mutual friend. Nor did a woman's status change upon getting married, she simply went from being supported by her father to being supported by her husband, her husband then getting access to her family's estate. Marriages were rarely prearranged, but, because of what the man often stood to gain, the parents of both sides had to approve of a match before matrimony.

Although things gradually loosened up, courtship didn't leave the hands of the parents until the twentieth century. Actually, it was one invention in particular that played a big part in changing the face of courtship altogether—the car.

Cars turned courtship into dating and gave a young couple the means to get away from the watchful eyes of their elders. Finally, young adults had the independence to act out their dirty desires. It's no accident that the most popular part of a car quickly became the backseat.

With this independence, dating became more casual—a way to test the waters of relationships rather than dive right into marriage. Dating became a recreational activity, as did "parking." Sure, the eventual goal was marriage, but there was no longer any need to rush into it with the first available person. The ability to date also brought the ability to be picky about whom to date, which, at long last, brought love into the picture. America itself had a part in this as well, as marriage was no longer the only way to jump up in social class. The American Dream of becoming successful by applying effort helped bring along the car, and helped bring love into the committed relationship (though, we still haven't managed to get past extramarital affairs).

But someone forgot to check the brakes. That love rode straight on into free love, and the '60s blossomed. With a proliferation of mind-altering drugs and women becoming independent of men, this culture took a look at courtship and dating, and decided to toss it all aside.

Birth control was another pill that became a big

A Code of Honor

"Never approach a friend's girlfriend or wife with mischief as your goal. There are just too many women in the world to justify that sort of dishonorable behavior. Unless she's really attractive."

—Bruce Friedman

factor. With the reduced risk of pregnancy, sex became just as casual as dating. After all, sex was now enjoyed by both men and women, and neither wanted to endure the pain of dating someone for months before getting down to what they really wanted.

Sure, this attitude led to many excesses and had its downfalls, but it also led to where we are today. Courtship is available to those who want it, but optional to those who don't. There are other choices now, too, such as personal ads and chat rooms. Courtship has come a long way over time, but it's still just as exciting now as it was in medieval times to get that first smile—or smiley face :)—from someone.

WORKPLACE SEDUCTION

In this increasingly workaholic world, where young lions spend 12 plus hours a day at work, not including their one-hour lunch hunched over their briefcases and evenings hunched over their laptops, the workplace is fast becoming a popular, if not perfect, place to practice those sultry seductions.

And, while the heady scent of white-out and paperclip residue may not exactly be the equivalent of musky muskrat love, it'll do until the dot.com world sinks completely or both lovers get promoted.

COWORKER COZINESS

One of the high-points of workplace seduction is the inherent coziness factor that comes from toiling alongside your coworkers day and night, night and day and night and night…. From overtime to last minute FedEx runs, you are instantly joined in a team situation that can't help but foster at least a niggling sense of trust, which is always good when starting a relationship.

There is the boss to complain about, or perhaps the client. There are deadlines to bitch about, or perhaps the receptionist. There are late-night pizzas and passing flirtations at the vending machine and planned ambushes at the water cooler each afternoon.

Yet while harmless flirtation is one thing, an all-out seduction plan is quite another.

NOT HOME AWAY FROM HOME

The first step in workplace seduction is to never let work seem like your home away from home. Though it's tempting to bring your entire collection of *Star Wars* men to help you get through the day ("How should I handle this account, Obi-Wan?"), Perky Paula over in marketing might not appreciate your enthusiasm for those little dolls, however valuable they may be one day.

Likewise, your fondness for religious statues and rosaries may not be the best way to convince Totally Ted that you are the tempting seductress he's been searching for. Therefore, stick to the more generic touches of hominess that litter cubicles all across the country, such as a plant or two, the odd family photo, and perhaps the occasional Christmas mug full of pencils and pens. Anything more makes it seem like you don't have a life outside of work. And that's hardly sexy.

THE VENUS CANDY TRAP

To make your cubicle more of a destination than a mere pit stop along the way to the restroom each day, why not invest in a simple candy dish and keep it constantly stocked with "good" candy, such as caramels or Laffy Taffy. (Skip the starlight mints, that's strictly amateur hour.) Not only

will this make you popular with coworkers, but it gives Perky Paula or Totally Ted the perfect opportunity to stop by your cubicle, every day, for that much-needed afternoon pick-me-up, so to speak.

After all, why not take advantage of those overflowing candy endorphins to prompt Paula or Ted to fork over a little brain sugar induced info, such as who they date, if they date, why they don't date, where they live, boxers or briefs, etc. People say the darndest things when they're hopped up on their fifth or sixth caramel. Why not be there when they do?

To make Ted or Paula feel even more special, why not have two candy dishes. Make one for the common folk and pedestrian traffic as they pass by all day, and keep another one hidden away in your top drawer. When it's Totally Ted Time or Perky Paula Hour, make it a point to slide away the stinky candy and reveal the Andes or Godivas for your special guest.

EXPERT ADVICE

People love to talk about themselves, and seduction targets are no exception to this rule. So why not use this chatty fact to your advantage by discovering a hidden, or not-so-hidden, talent that your own Ted or Paula possess. For instance, maybe Perky Paula is a whiz in accounting. What could be the better "getting your foot in her cubicle" ploy than to ask her an accounting question once or twice a week, for starters.

If Totally Ted's expertise is cars, why not ask him a few "I'm hearing this funny noise on my way to work" questions and watch his eyes glaze over in sheer ecstasy as he rattles on about clean air filters and sludge-free spark plugs. Who knows, you could even get an offer to "check it out" after work.

Your engine, that is.

AFTERNOON AMBUSH

Today's corporate workforce expects a little free time come three or four o'clock, but when you've got a sexy seduction in mind, don't waste it on dishing with the girls or chatting with the guys. Invest a day or two in roaming the halls and checking in on your seductee's afternoon break habits.

For instance, does she hit the vending machine downstairs at exactly 3:32 each afternoon? Now might

Passionate Poetry

To Jane

The keen stars were twinkling,
And the fair moon rising among them,
Dear Jane.
The guitar was tinkling,
But the notes were not sweet till you sung them
Again.

As the moon's soft splendour
O'er the faint cold starlight of Heaven
Is thrown,
So your voice most tender
To the strings without soul had then given
It's own.

Though the sound overpowers,
Sing again, with your dear voice revealing
A tone
Of some world far from ours,
Where music and moonlight and feeling
Are one.

—Percy Bysshe Shelley (1792-1822)

> "He early on let her know who is the boss. He looked her right in the eye and clearly said, 'You're the boss.'"
>
> —Anonymous

be the time to race out to the bank for a roll or two of quarters! Does he head for a cup of coffee at 4:15 every day? Why not be conveniently struggling with an overflowing armful of teeter-tottering files come 4:17?

Whatever their habits, once you know about it, you're halfway to a meaningful conversation.

NEW KID
IN TOWN

There's nothing like new blood to inspire a workplace romance, and hitting on the new guy or gal is *de rigueur* for today's corporate meat market. But here's how to stand out when the rest of the crowd smells new blood and heads in for the kill.

For starters, remain aloof. At least at first. So the new-hire hottie is driving you nuts each time she asks you where the electric pencil sharpener is—again. That doesn't mean you should ask for her number right away. After all, the guys in sales have already taken that low road. To remain unique in her eyes and stand a step above the other morons, why not draw her a clever little map to the pencil sharpener from her cubicle. Make sure to depict all the other guys as apes, while maybe drawing yourself as a knight in shining armor. Make sure to depict her in an attractive light, and why not write a friendly reminder on the back to show her you really do care: "Just because you know where the sharpener is now, don't stop coming by my cubicle or life could get real—dull!" That should wow her.

The trick with workplace seduction, whether it's a new guy or your old gal pal, is to always stand out from the rest of the corporate clones. Whether it's a heart-covered tie on Valentine's Day or a Barbie lunch bag, there's nothing more sexy than confidence. Even in a cubicle.

IMPROMPTU SEDUCTION

There is nothing as daring and difficult as trying to seduce someone you've just met. From the airline stewardess high above Fresno to the cocky cashier behind the register at your favorite music store, starting from zero and ramping up to full speed ahead in a matter of minutes is as exhilarating as it is precarious. But with so little time to spare in these impromptu seductions, it helps to be prepared. Naturally, that's where we come in.

LUST AT FIRST SIGHT

Of course, impromptu seduction requires perfect timing and just the right amount of attitude and appreciation. Cockiness is one thing, but condescending is quite another. (And only one is sexy.) So, for starters, you need the ability to gauge a situation at first glance.

For instance, is the cutie in the corner booth eating alone because she's waiting for someone, or because she wants some much-needed privacy? Is the shy guy waiting on you really nervously flirtatious, or is it all an act for a bigger tip? These questions, and many others you will no doubt encounter, are all obstacles to be overcome in any impromptu seduction. Otherwise, it would be a whole lot easier and you wouldn't have to read this.

CONFIDENCE COUNTS

It helps to show confidence in these situations. For instance, few potential partners would respond positively to the following come-on: "You wouldn't be interested in going out with me sometime, would you? No, I didn't think so." Why, you never even gave them a chance.

Instead, you should feel confident that you are a desirable person with a lot to offer whoever is on the receiving end of your harmless flirtation. After all, you're not proposing marriage. Just a little shared time together to see if the two of you hit it off. Whether it be a nightcap after work or a simple cup of coffee, you need to send the message that you are worth spending time with. Your company is an opportunity, not a nuisance, and confidence can only start within. Therefore, a warning: Kids, don't try this at home, at least not until you can look in the mirror and say three times without laughing, "I'm worthy of an impromptu seduction and, by golly, I deserve it!"

PERSISTENCE POINTERS

Naturally, not every girl you hit on is going to fall swooning into your arms. Likewise, no matter what *Cosmo* says, not every guy you bat your eyelashes at is going to join you for a cup of coffee after work. However, it never hurts to ask. And ask again.

Let's say you're in the library doing a little after-hours research for work. It's a month-long project, and for the past few nights, you've noticed that the same bookish hunk sits in the same spot at the same time every night. You can't help but notice the blue eyes beneath his horn-rimmed glasses and, since you're in this for the long haul, why not make a new friend while you're at it? So, you sidle up to him with your armload full of books and whisper seductively, "Care to take a break with me?"

After looking up, startled, and blinking those baby-blues several times, he responds, "Oh, thanks, but I already have a cup of coffee." Noticing the lukewarm puddle of coffee and Styrofoam next to him, you slap your forehead on the way back to your own table. Okay, nice going. Still, maybe he's just shy. Or maybe he's just busy. That's fine, that's okay. Spend the rest of the evening hunkered down over your work and make it a point not to look his way—too often!

Now it's the next night, and there he is again! Okay, okay, calm down. He obviously couldn't be too pestered by your proposition, otherwise he could have found a new spot to dwell. Still, give him a night off and, the next night, make sure there's no paper cup next to his stack of books and move in again. Chances are, he'll relent and accompany you, if only for diversion's sake. Don't forget, this could be your one and only shot at impressing him with either: a. your modern sensibilities as you splurge for his coffee; b. your flair with a swizzle stick; and/or c. your witty banter and cleverly displayed cleavage. If not, give up for a while and wait until the last week of your research. If he's *still* there, and you *still* care, then approach him one last time. If he refuses this time, a huffy, "Your loss!" as you strut away is certainly your right and duty.

CHOICES, CHOICES

All through the ages, schoolteachers have relied on a simple trick when assigning their students homework: "For tonight's homework, class, I'm giving you a choice: You can either do all of the problems on page 48, or you can do the evens on pages 46-48. It's up to you!" Naturally, if any of the students would ever bother to compare the two assignments, they'd find the exact same number of problems. But doing one page of homework compared to two always seems like a much better deal, so which one do you think they'll choose?

So why not try this ancient schoolmarm trick as part of your impromptu seduction? For instance, if that babe behind the counter rolls her eyes at your simple request for her phone number, why not give her an alternative: Ask for her e-mail address instead. Either one gives the same result of communicating with your coquettish counter clerk. Unless she gives you the phone number for Papa John's pizza, that is.

> "The absolute yearning of one human body for another particular body and its indifference to substitutes is one of life's major mysteries."
>
> —Iris Murdoch

DATING DIARIES:
BUSTY BUKOWSKI

I've hit on, and been hit on, by enough second-rate seducers to write a book, but for now I'll settle for this quick story about one of the best impromptu seductions I've ever had the pleasure of being on the receiving end of:

Right after college I worked in a big-name bookstore selling lots of bestsellers and little else. If it wasn't Grisham or Steel, King or Koontz, few people looked at it and even fewer bought it! Still, I put in my time, read my share of free advance copies, and whiled away the hours making pleasant conversation with customers and sending in resumes to bigger and better companies.

One afternoon shift, however, a striking girl dressed in black and wearing patchouli purchased a volume of Charles Bukowski's short stories. A fan of his poetry, I commented casually on the book, but the striking girl with the good taste said nothing and simply paid for her purchase and left the store as quietly and unobtrusively as she had entered. When my shift ended an hour or two later, I clocked out and headed toward my car as usual. Along the way, the Bukowski fan cleared her throat and waved me over to her little table for two in the courtyard of a quiet bar next door to the bookstore. I greeted her pleasantly and, although I had plenty to do on my night off, I sat in the seat that she offered. Without introduction or prelude, she began reading aloud from the book she had just bought.

Mesmerized by her passionate delivery, I watched

her black lipstick move up and down over the erotic words of Bukowski's oddly crafted story. I don't remember its title, but it was about a grown man who lived alone and made love to a mannequin, which he hid in his closet.

Anyway, the story itself was a little disturbing, but the way the woman read it was mesmerizing and, I had to admit, pretty sexy. There was a quiet little Italian restaurant up the street, and after she finished the story and closed the book, I asked her to dinner immediately. She accepted, and we strolled up the street together.

Well, it turns out she was a real freak show, and did nothing during dinner but read from that crazy book. I don't even think she ate. However, I'll never forget what a great ploy that was, waving me over and reading to me like that. It didn't work out, of course, but I must admit, I've used the ploy myself over the years, and it hasn't failed me yet.

> "Beware you be not swallowed up in books! An ounce of love is worth a pound of knowledge."
> —John Wesley

YOUR SECRET ADMIRER

You don't hear much about secret admirers these days. But then, with Big Brother lurking around with eyes in the sky and hit shows like *Survivor* getting everyone excited about baring it all for anyone within camera range, you don't hear much about secrets either.

But in the sexy art of seduction, both secrets and admirers are something to be desired. Especially when they come all nicely wrapped up in the same package!

SEXY STARTERS

Let's face it, mysterious equals sexy. From blindfolds to surprise gifts, the unknown is always just a little bit more tantalizing than the known. So what do you do when a secret admirer begins showering you with unexpected affections? Go with it, of course.

Today, secret admirers have numerous tools at their disposal to remain alluring and aloof. From a long list of Web sites specifically designed to help them mask their identity, to the old standbys of delivery men doing their work, today's secret admirers have more opportunities to remain in the shadows than ever before.

Still, there's nothing like the classics, which is why your first sign that someone is interested in you will most likely be a note. Whether this note is in the form of a mysterious e-mail waiting in your inbox one morning or a sticky note on your computer monitor, mailbox, or front door, depends on the whims and caprices of your admirer.

Usually, these shy and sexy folk start small, with something pseudo-sexy like, "I've got my eye on you!" Sort of sounds like a third grade Valentine, doesn't it? But the thrill is instant and immediate: Who's got their eye on you? How does he see you? Where is she? What is he doing right now? How did she find out about you?

And the most thrilling question of all: What's next?

SPECIAL DELIVERY

After the initial secret greeting, be it electronic or sticky, there is usually a follow-up flurry of communication. More e-mails, more stickies, more construction paper cut-outs in your mailbox. Eventually, however, the thrill of these mysterious messages loses its allure and your secret admirer must do something just a little more thrilling to keep the ball in play. His next step, then, is a special delivery, most often in the form of flowers or plants. A delivery man is usually in your future, and if your secret admirer has any class at all, she will have already tipped him. If not, strike one!

So, what do you do about the flowers, house plant, or dancing teddy bear on your doorstep? Be flattered, of course. Not every modern single is willing to go to such corny lengths to impress a potential date, or mate. So take it all in stride and enjoy the attention. After all, this mysterious ride isn't quite through, yet.

VOICE MALE (OR FEMALE!)

After the notes and the flowers, your secret admirer is most likely just as excited as you are. Therefore, she will most likely make verbal contact next. Usually, to keep the allure of mystery in tact, this will often be a message, either on your voice mail at work or your answering machine at home.

This is, naturally, a little bit thrilling and a little bit scary. After all, anyone who's ever watched a single evening of Court TV knows that there's a fine line between secretly admiring and stalking! However, if you're at all normal, you've already informed everyone from your cubicle neighbors to your mom that you, yes you, have a secret admirer. This is a good thing. The more people who know, the safer you are.

For now, however, you have a message on your machine. Chances are, it will sound something like, "Hi, I don't want to tell you my name yet, I like the suspense we're building. I find you fascinating, and hopefully that will show you that I'm not a total whacko and I'm perfectly safe. I'd love to meet with you, on your terms, of course. You say when, you say where, you say how. All I'll say is HURRY! Here's my number."

Or something similarly sappy. Listen for details. For instance, if there's any hint of heavy breathing or other odd noises that sound faintly disturbing, put the kibosh on the whole thing right now. Call the number and leave a message that in no way, shape, or form can be misconstrued. However, if the voice is sexy and sounds in the right age range, not to mention sex, for you, why not give it a try.

MEETING OF THE MINDS

To meet a secret admirer, it's best to play it safe. Whatever you do, don't invite him over right away. And don't agree to go to her house first thing. Pick a public place that's mutually agreeable, like a cozy café halfway between both of your places. This way, if he seems normal and you want to hang out and chat him up, you can have a light meal in the process. However, if she seems flaky and you feel like running for the hills, you're not committed to an entire meal together.

Drive separately, and instruct your admirer to wear something noticeable. Obviously, she already knows what you look like, but you won't be able to recognize her yet. For cornballs, a carnation in his lapel might work. For hipsters, how about a temporary tattoo on her forehead? Whatever, just make sure that you can see her coming from a distance, and give yourself plenty of room to run if she's already toting a thick book of wedding invitation samples!

IN OR OUT

During your first meeting, trust your instincts. After all, with only a few notes, a bouquet or two of flowers, and one phone message, they're all you'll have to go on. Do his eyes look beady? Does she seem too clingy? Did he pull up in a work release van from the local prison? Any of the above should be warning signals, and if you're getting a hinky vibe after only a few minutes, don't bother to stick around and find out how your secret admirer found out about you, just make a firm but fair decision and nip it in the bud before your second drink.

However, if your secret admirer turns out to be that cutie from your night class or the hottie from that bookstore across from your office, why not stick around and inquire as to why they suddenly started paying so much attention. You could just be surprised!

"Never frown because you never know who might be falling in love with your smile."

—Justine Milton

FRIENDLY SEDUCTION

So, quick recap: We've learned how to seduce strangers, we've learned how to seduce coworkers, we've even learned how to seduce someone from afar. But how do you go about seducing someone you've known for years, or at least months? How do you go about seducing—a friend?

DANGER, DANGER!

Despite their "friendly" nature, friends are some of the most dangerous people to try to seduce. While you may have tons more ammunition to seduce them with, where they work, where they live, what they like, what they don't like, the consequences of getting too chummy can often be quite disastrous. After all, there's nothing more awkward than making a move on someone you've been friends with for months, possibly years.

Quite often the kissee feels betrayed. After all, were you just being his friend all that time, waiting for a vulnerable opportunity to plant one on his lips? Did you listen to her dreams and fears, her hopes and desires, all the while secretly undressing her with your eyes? And what do you say after being pushed away as your "friend" waits for an explanation: "I'm sorry."

No, the considerable price of a mistimed kiss or too-soon hug is often that of the friendship itself. Nothing is quite the same after one friend hits on another. The whole dynamic changes, and it could take years to repair the damage done by a moment's temptation or a declared desire. Few friends survive this shift in sensibilities, and so be careful when treading this most dangerous, but intriguing, ground.

COZINESS COUNTS

Still, if you *do* decide to trip lightly along this treacherous trail, the hard part of this seduction is already over: You're already friends! The shyness, the clamminess, the stammering, the blushing, should all be over and done with by now. You've seen movies together, broken bread together, and possibly even slept over at each other's homes. You have, in a word, gotten "cozy" with each other.

In other words, if you were to share coffee together down at the local Starbucks and your stir-sticks accidentally touched, and then, with a reach across to snag an extra sugar packet, per chance, your lips meet, there would at least be precedent: "Hey, we've shared a hundred cups of coffee together, my lips slipped once—and you slap me?"

The trick, of course, is not to get slapped!

INSIDE INFORMATION

Before you jump the gun and start sucking face at the coffee shop, however, have a little self control and see if it's warranted yet. The nice thing about being friends is that you know the intimate details of each other's lives. You had a great date, your friend knows about it. Your friend had a bad date, you know about it. Better yet, your friend breaks up with her boyfriend, who's a jerk, and you can be there for that world-famous "sympathy smooch."

You know: "He was a jerk anyway," you say. "He never appreciated you, not like I do . . . smooch!" This way, if you've overstepped your bounds and your friend gets back together with her on-again/off-again boyfriend, your innocent smooch will always be remembered as temporary insanity. On the other hand, if your friend has the same feelings that you do, your smooch could just turn into something a whole lot more.

It's a little like that scene in *Tootsie*, when Jessica Lange confesses to Dustin Hoffman in drag what her ideal man would say to pick her up. What better way to seduce someone than to hear her or his innermost thoughts and desires?

Then again, Dustin Hoffman got a drink tossed in his face when he actually used the line on friendly Jessica.

GATORLAND®

Swamp Trackers Camp

CAMP SCHEDULES FOR SUMMER 2001

TIMING IS KEY

To keep your face dry, and your friendship in tact, you have to be very careful when seducing a friend. While you may be at your wit's end, having waited this long, you can surely wait just a little while longer. Then again, if you've waited long enough, you might just want to set the ball rolling with a few of the following tips.

For starters, why not suggest a trip together. Sure, you're friends in your daily life, maybe you're coworkers, maybe you're neighbors, maybe you're old college roommates, but test the friendship on the road. And don't go somewhere like an alligator ranch or a Monster Truck rally. Try something pseudo-romantic, like a theater junket in the big city or perhaps even a day cruise.

If you're opting for land travel, volunteer to make reservations in advance and "mistakenly" get a room at a bed and breakfast. ("It was the only thing available, I swear!") If possible, request one bed instead of two and never, ever volunteer to sleep on the floor. After all, if your friend likes you, he obviously isn't stupid! And if he agrees to take such a trip with you, he may have an idea, maybe even a hope, that something is up. So run with it, and see where it leads.

As the trip plays out, plan outings that are you-only affairs, such as renting a boat for a sailboat ride for two, or a cozy stroll through a deserted museum, etc. Forego fast-food joints for cozy cafes or quiet bistros, and order wine, not beer. Make every available attempt to set that whole "date" vibe, and she could just end up believing it by the final night.

If she does, you'll know it. The same way you'll know if she doesn't. (Splash!)

QUIVERING QUILLS

If your romantic overtures fall on deaf ears, yet you still want to discover whether your friend wants to get more "friendly," or less, try writing him a letter as a last resort. Whether it's an agonizingly long e-mail on Sunday night before he shows up for work the next morning, or a calligraphic affair on parchment paper, pour out your heart and let your friend know exactly how you feel.

Don't be lurid or obscene, or too light or jovial; earnest and forthcoming are the cards you want on the table. Don't issue mandates such as "or else" or "never again." Instead, leave the ball in your friend's court. An open letter such as this encourages discussion, whether in your favor or not, and either way you'll at least have gotten it off your chest and out in the open.

Your friend will either shoot you down in black and white, tell you that she doesn't feel the same way, but that she'd still like to stay friends, or commiserate and throw herself into your arms! Only one of those may be desirable to you, but at least you'll have your answer, for better or worse. After all, what are friends for?

SAY WHAT?

"A woman may very well form a friendship with a man, but for this to endure, it must be assisted by a little physical antipathy."

—Friedrich Nietzsche

SEDUCING A CLASSMATE (OR NOT)

Whether you're still in school, going back to school, or your company has sent you for a little on-the-job training, there's nothing quite as testy as seducing a classmate. From "borrowing" her notes to "dropping" your books in front of him, there are as many tricks as there are tests. But in the time-honored tradition of throwing money at a problem, none of them quite compare to "dressing to impress." Which can get a little tricky.

CRYSTAL CONFUSION

You remember it quite clearly. That day you bought your very first crystal. It could have been for any number of reasons: Their supposed healing powers. Their connection to all things mystical. The mythic lore. The symbolism of Mother Earth taking years and years to create a thing of such beauty. The way they caught the light and reflected it back in a myriad of colors or directions.

Your reason, of course, was much more personal: That girl in your Psych class really dug them and you wanted her to notice you.

It was the early '90s and you were working on your twelfth official major when she walked into one of the many elective classes that would never actually go to fulfilling any of your degree requirements.

She had that darkly mysterious look, the one that told you she was probably a wild one (especially in bed), and she reeked of all things beautiful and sexy. On her neck, just above her Cure T-shirt and below her creamy maroon lipstick, was a simple leather thong at the end of which dangled a pewter dragon's claw, wrapped dramatically around a shimmering clear crystal ball.

You admired it longingly from your seat three rows back and loved the way it caught the light and played with it seductively. The way she would caress it in her black nail polish-tipped fingers and twirl the chord around endlessly, playfully. It said…something…about her. You had no idea what, but you were quite sure it was much more substantial than what the "We're #1" T-shirt leftover from your days as a high-school running back said about you.

Attempting to speak to her after yet another boring lecture on Maslow's Hierarchy of Needs, she cut you off prematurely in favor of the skinny kid with the sword tattoo on his freckly arm and the crystal balls hanging from each ear. Together they strolled to the student union, reflecting prisms of light and pealing laughter along the way.

That very day you scoured the mall for anything crystal, crystalline, or crystal-like, finally discovering that, somehow, they were suddenly everywhere. Hanging by the cash register in the record store. In the drug store next to the smiley face ties. In bookstores, coffee shops, and even the candle store.

When had all of this happened? As you strolled from vendor to vendor, trying to find just the right crystal statement that would capture your girl's attention away from tattoo-and-earring boy, you saw them on middle-aged women, older folks, peers, and even young kids. They hung, they dangled, they choked, and they clasped, all of them gleaming in the mall fluorescence like miniature, smiling faces. They seemed to be mocking you in silent unison that screamed: "Hey, loser, wake up and join the rest of the world."

And so, eventually, you plunked down your token $20 for the dangling dragon claw necklace and the matching mood ring.

"It's about time," the cashier practically sighed as she rang them up.

You wore them everywhere that weekend. "Breaking them in" so that, if your Psych crush, hippie-gypsy truly did have superior crystal powers, she wouldn't see that you'd just purchased them mere days before. The very next class period, you strutted in proudly, as if the glass, leather, and pewter hanging around your neck and clamped around your too big index finger actually did have magical powers.

You failed to notice, of course, since you weren't up on the trend back when it was cool, that, magically, the rest of the class had deposited their trendy crystals where they belonged: hanging off of their bulletin boards back in the dorm rooms next to their swim team ribbons and high school graduation tassels.

You blissfully awaited your little lady's presence in class, surprised that she, too, was suddenly crystal-free, but knowing instinctively that she was just getting them cleaned down at some New Age shop in the mall. Practically leaping down to her seat after class, you displayed your new crystals like a knight who'd just polished his armor, mistaking her laughter for flirting. When she blew you off minutes later with a sarcastic remark about your "Halloween costume," you realized that, in the world of fashion, crystals had just gone the way of poodle skirts and Izod shirts.

"Oh, well," you thought, watching her walk away with a suddenly similarly crystal free tattoo-boy, "maybe this is a sign for me to switch my major. As long as I have these crystals, how about geology?"

THOSE RANDY ROMANS

Throughout history, romance and seduction have evolved slower than equal rights and the recipe for Twinkies. Take the Romans, for instance. They were definitely party dudes and dressed the part—heck, they invented the toga and if that got too cumbersome, they just donned a fig leaf. World famous for their wine-soaked Bacchanalian festivals, the Roman orgy became so obscene and violent that they were finally banned by emperors and now can only be seen on Cinemax After Dark.

Aside from wiggling, wobbling genitalia, the Romans also perpetrated an unromantic aspect of history of treating women as mere sex objects. The Romans were heavy into prostitution. While many cultures practiced or even encouraged the act of prostitution, the Roman civilization institutionalized it. Yet despite Rome's proclivity for slaves, not all prostitutes were from the lower levels of society. There were numerous castes of prostitutes. The highest level was that of the Delicatue, women who were the kept prostitutes, or mistresses, of wealthy and prominent men in Roman society. Lower on this sex scale, not to mention the price range, were the Famosae, who were, surprisingly, the daughters and occasionally the wives of wealthy families. Next came the lowly Dorae, who walked naked and on display even when out shopping for groceries. Finally came the equivalent of today's street walkers, the Lupae, who could be found plying their trade under the fornices, or arches, of the old temples, bridges, and even the Coliseum. (It is from these women that we get the word "fornication.")

So when you think about it, seduction and romance have evolved for the better since the days when Caligula set the moral standard. And where you practice the art has moved far away from the arches of Rome. Unless you take your date to McDonald's, of course.

Passionate Poetry

To Celia

Drink to me only with thine eyes,
And I will pledge with mine;
Or leave a kiss but in the cup
And I'll not look for wine.
The thirst that from the soul doth rise
Doth ask a drink divine;
But might I of Jove's nectar sup,
I would not change for thine.

I set thee late a rosy wreath,
not so much honouring thee
As giving it a hope that there
It could not withered be;
But thou thereon didst only breathe
And sent'st it back to me;
Since when it grows, and smells, I swear
Not of itself but thee!

—Ben Johnson (1572-1637)

> "In literature as in love, we are astonished at what is chosen by others."
>
> —André Maurois

Love Is a Sickness

Love is a sickness full of woes,
All remedies refusing;
A plant that with most cutting grows,
Most barren with best using.
Why so?
More we enjoy it, more it dies;
If not enjoyed, it sighing cries,
Hey ho.
Love is a torment of the mind,
A tempest everlasting;
And Jove hath made it of a kind,
Not well, nor full nor fasting.
Why so?
More we enjoy it, more it dies;
If not enjoyed, it sighing cries,
Hey ho.

—Thomas Lodge (1558-1625)

Who Ever Felt as I?

Mother, I cannot mind my wheel;
My fingers ache, my lips are dry:
Oh! if you felt the pain I feel!
But oh, who ever felt as I?

No longer could I doubt him true;
All other men may use deceit:
He always said my eyes were blue,
And often swore my lips were sweet.

—Walter Savage Landor (1775-1864)

Passionate Poetry

The Secret

I loved thee, though I told thee not,
Right earlily and long,
Thou wert my joy in every spot,
My theme in every song.
And when I saw a stranger face
Where beauty held the claim,
I gave it like a secret grace
The being of thy name.
And all the charms of face or voice
Which I in others see
Are but the recollected choice
Of what I felt for thee.

—John Clare (1793-1864)

Song from Arcadia

My true-love hath my heart and I have his,
By just exchange one for the other given:
I hold his dear, and mine he cannot miss;
There never was a bargain better driven.
His heart in me keeps me and him in one;
My heart in him his thoughts and senses
guides:

He loves my heart, for once it was his own;
I cherish his because in me it bides.
His heart his wound received from my sight;
My heart was wounded with his wounded heart;
For as from me on him his hurt did light,
So still, methought, in me his hurt did smart:
Both equal hurt, in this change sought our bliss,
My true love hath my heart and I have his.

—Sir Philip Sidney (1554-1586)

She Walks in Beauty

She walks in beauty, like the night
Of cloudless climes and starry skies;
And all that's best of dark and bright
Meet in her aspect and her eyes:
Thus mellowed to that tender light
Which heaven to gaudy day denies.

One shade the more, one ray the less,
Had half impaired the nameless grace
Which waves in every raven tress,
Or softly lightens o'er her face;
Where thoughts serenely sweet express
How pure, how dear their dwelling place.

And on that cheek, and o'er that brow,
So soft, so calm, yet eloquent,
The smiles that win, the tints that glow,
But tell the days in goodness spent,
A mind at peace with all below,
A heart whose love is innocent!

—Lord Byron (1788-1824)

3 ROMANCE FOR ONE

Who says it takes two to tango? After all, those frozen dinners would be a whole lot bigger if the Hungry Man company thought anyone but single people were buying them. The world is full of hopeless romantics who just happen to be single, and there's no need to put your love life on hold, just because you lack a lover at the moment.

Romance is about passion, and passion shouldn't be left out of the equation just because $1 + 0 = 1$. Or a little less than one. Living life to the fullest requires treating yourself now and then, and nothing spells "treat" like r-o-m-a-n-c-e. From bodice ripping page turners to a three-hankie film for one, your heart will thank you.

And when you do get tired of dining, dancing, or drinking alone, the tips in this chapter are designed to help you add someone else to the equation, without losing your romantic self in the process.

DON JUAN: I LOVE ME!

So, what can you, a single romantic, learn from a 400-year-old master of seduction? Well, that depends on which incarnation of that legendary literary lover known as Don Juan you want to believe. Many scholars have tried to locate a person in history after whom the character of Don Juan could have been styled, but nobody who fits the mold has ever turned up, leaving us with a single fact—Don Juan is simply a fictional character.

This creation has been portrayed in so many different types of works—from plays, to poems, to operas, to Hollywood films—that his persona has been mixed and muddled to create another standard bearer for the prototypical seducer.

The first time the lusty libertine appeared was in 1630, as the lead character in Tirso de Molina's play, *El Burlador de Sevilla* (*The Trickster of Seville*). In this story, he's about as warm and fuzzy as your average porcupine. He's not very romantic, either; he just happens to be extraordinarily attractive.

Looks make up about 90 percent of his seductive arsenal. Aside from being pretty, he uses the old reliable of lying to get women into bed. A sly look and a (fake) marriage proposal help him blaze a trail into countless bedrooms. Of course, ahead of time, he orders his servant to ready his horse for a quick getaway.

This first story of the Don Juan legend was little more than a morality play. People warn him not to be such a total ass, and others swear vengeance upon him as he continues to seduce women wantonly.

Since Don Juan was kind of a one-trick pony, about the only seduction lesson to take away from the early

legend concerns the consequences of your actions, namely you could be dragged into Hell by an undead statue, which is possessed with the ghost of the father of a scorned lover. Which, by the way, became Don's fate.

For the next couple of hundred years Don's mythical tale caught on and was reproduced in several different mediums. His character was always portrayed as a scoundrel. In Mozart's opera (*Don Giovanni*), he was just as much a villain as in the original. The play by Molière (*Don Juan and the Stone Guest*), at least, gave Don Juan's multiple marriages a comical spin, but the overall message was just the same: Next stop, Hell. It wasn't until the romantic poet, Lord Byron, delved into Don Juan that the character received a personality makeover. In the early 19th century, Don became reminiscent of Casanova, with more extensive travels around the world, and more tricks up his sleeve to lure the ladies. He went so far as to seduce slaves in Greece, Sultanas in the Middle East, and even Catherine the Great.

Yes, Don was still portrayed as an amoral seducer of women, using them for his own pleasure, and tossing them aside when he was done, regardless of the damage he had done to their reputations. Ultimately he seemed headed to a hellish fate, but

Byron died before finishing.

It wasn't until Hollywood was attracted to Don Juan that he was transformed into a hero. In 1926, John Barrymore played the title character in *Don Juan*, billed as "the world's greatest lover." In the film, Don Juan did somthing that no Don Juan before him had ever done—he reformed. Hey, they couldn't have the great Barrymore pulled down to Hell by a possessed statue. Nope, in this version, Don is so smitten with a pure woman of the Renaissance that he renounces his wicked past and everyone lives happily ever after.

But that's just the beginning of the new Don Juan. Even in early versions, Don Juan was handy with a sword, and Hollywood capitalized on this element by packing the film with sword fights any time Don wasn't getting frisky with the femmes. The result: *The Adventures of Don Juan*, with the title role played by Hollywood's finest swashbuckler, Errol Flynn (who in real life was closer to the old Don Juan than his studio cared to admit). The filmmakers really romanticized things this time, making Don the victim of political set-ups and a pawn in an arranged marriage. Oh yeah, and he also manages to overthrow the evil Duke of Spain, stop all the corruption in Spain, win the love of the queen, and promise to unseat Gen. Franco later, if necessary.

Don Juan fighting for the rights of the people? It's a far cry from the original trickster who proposed marriage to every woman he met. Hollywood had another shot, this time with Johnny Depp as Don Juan in *Don Juan DeMarco*. This character returned to the original's indifference toward morality, but with a '90s twist. His capacity for love and passion was so great that he inspired those around him and brought romance back into a cynical world. Sweet, huh?

Since his introduction 400 years ago, Don Juan has become a figure as well known as Faust, Hamlet, and Richard Hatch. The lesson: Not everyone loves a lover, unless he saves Spain in the process or he looks like Johnny Depp.

passionate Poetry

The Hour Glass

Consider this small dust,
here in the glass,
By atoms moved:
Could you believe that
this the body was
Of one that loved;
And in his mistress'
flame playing like a fly,
Was turned to cinders
by her eye:
Yes; and in death,
as life unblessed,
To have it expressed,
Even ashes of lovers
find no rest.

—Benjamin Jonson
(1572-1637)

ALONE

Despite reams of research on the subject, nowhere does it actually say that romance has to occur between *two* people. Sure, it helps, but would it hold up in court? The fact is, the world is full of people who, for one reason or another, are unattached. Uninvolved. Alone. Single. Are these brave souls to live in a world without romance just because they prefer their own company to, say, that of the drunken hussy or fool on the barstool next to them last night?

So take heart. You can have romance in your life even when you're single.

TUESDAY TREATS

Who says romance necessarily means the weekend? Treat yourself to a heartfelt treat any night of the week by going out to dinner after work. On a Tuesday, even. Splurge on an appetizer or skip the house chardonnay and order something special. Flirt with the waiter or order something fattening as you enjoy the romantic surroundings of your favorite local bistro or café.

Not fond of dining out alone? Simple, zip by the store on the way home and pick up some ingredients to cook yourself a nice dinner. Pick up some flavored rice and a chicken breast to simmer up—and don't forget a small bit of your favorite dessert. Race back home, fire up your favorite aromatherapy candle and your best Luther Vandross CD and be happy that you're not on some god awful blind date somewhere!

Passionate Poetry

Heart, We Will Forget Him

Heart, we will forget him,
You and I, tonight!
You must forget the warmth he gave,
I will forget the light.
When you have done pray tell me,
Then I, my thoughts, will dim.
Haste! 'lest while you're lagging
I may remember him!

—Emily Dickinson
(1830-1886)

COZY UP TO THE CINEMA

Don't let another Sunday alone drag you down. Comb that ten-pound newspaper on your front stoop for the movie times, climb into your baggiest jeans and a favorite sweatshirt, and cruise down to the local multiplex for a good, old-fashioned double feature. Hey, it beats rearranging your sock drawer, and you'll be around real, live people to boot.

"I love Mickey Mouse more than any woman I have ever known."

—Walt Disney

Feeling wistful? Check out Hollywood's latest offerings of romantic comedies—if you dare. Or forget tinsel town's version of an affair to remember and escape with some fanciful sci-fi. Let go of your fears and chill out with a back-to-back gore fest with some horror films, or delve into a mystery with a pair of tense thrillers. Either way, splurge on the large popcorn and take advantage of those free refills. And don't skimp on the butter!

FLOWERS FOR ONE

Nothing quite says romance like a fresh bouquet of flowers. But who says they have to be delivered? The next time you're at the local grocer, why not swing by the floral section and toss in a heady mixture of carnations and baby's breath? Feeling frisky? How about a single rose for your nightstand? The smell is sure to set your heart aflutter, and nothing perks up a room like a fresh floral arrangement in your favorite vase.

IT'S JUST PAST SELF-HELP. . .

Okay, so you're allergic to flowers, a victim of dine-alone-a-phobia, and can't stand popcorn. So how do you treat yourself to a little romance, minus the "man?" Quick, grab your trench coat out of the mothballs, find your granddad's old brogan, and slip on some shades before heading down to the local bookstore to cruise the little aisle (that just happens to span half the store) called the "romance section."

Elbow your way in between the blue-haired grannies and teenage girls and discover the racy world of today's bodice rippers. Thrill to Scottish kilt-wearers, sexy single dads, and the obligatory cowboy as you plunk down your five dollars for the latest page-turner from today's hottest romance writers. See why publishers keep turning out this male-free entertainment year after year and just try to not get hooked.

After all, you don't need "man" to spell romance. Except in the pages of a book, that is.

"It is with true love as it is with ghosts; everyone talks about it, but few have seen it."

—Francois de La Rouchefoucauld

SINGLES SCENE

NEW PLACES, FRESH FACES

For the romantic, today's modern single's scene can look as barren as the upper decks of an XFL game. From smoky barrooms to online single chat rooms, the days of wine and roses have come and gone, many feel for good. Perhaps this has to do with our jaded culture. With such a high divorce rate and so many freaks and geeks running around, who can find true love today? Hollywood romances break up daily. Nobody looks like your favorite movie star. None of the guys you meet are just like good, old Dad. None of your lady friends turn out to be anything like your mother (thank God). And forget cuddling, snuggling, or squeezing. Today's wham-bam-thank-you-ma'am singles scene is all about the moment, and not about the mood.

So what's a romance deprived boy or girl to do? Why not try a new tactic and skip the singles scene altogether? After all, if no one's worth meeting there, why go?

If the bars and the clubs, the cafes and the pubs aren't doing it for you, why not try someplace new? If none of the Neanderthals in the sports bar can read the players' jerseys without help,

"Love is a fire. But whether it is going to warm your hearth or burn down your house, you can never tell."
—Joan Crawford

let alone the score, why not find your true love at a bookstore? Today's megastores feature books, tapes, CDs, DVDs, and quite often, a quiet, cozy café at which to while the night away over a decent cup of coffee and the book or magazine of your choice. Chances are, a sexy single such as yourself won't have as much time as you think for reading!

If bookstores aren't your style, try kicking up your heels at the local dance studio. We're not talking *Fame*, here, but Arthur Murray. Yes, we know the stereotype, but many a straight man has turned to the dance studio thanks to the revitalization of such sophisticated and tricky dance steps as swing, salsa, and meringue. And since you're paying good money, chances are you'll be less likely to be a wallflower and more likely to ask one of these single studs to tango.

BECOME A REGULAR

No matter your singles spot of choice, few things work the first time around. If the bookstore's holding a Sci-Fi Geekfest on your first night there, call it quits early and return next week. If the dance steps are too awkward for your two left feet one week, come back again and wear more comfortable shoes. After all, the point is to meet someone worthwhile. How are you going to know who's who if you go home with the first handsome Bookworm Bill or Dancing Daisy you meet?

Becoming a regular somewhere, aside from the local watering hole, that is, allows you to scope out the scene with a practiced eye. Not all snakes dress in leather pants and wear big, gold medallions. Some look like poster boys for the Gap. Likewise, not every freak in the world prefers stiletto heels and daring décolletage. Some look like Catholic schoolgirls, until you wind up handcuffed to their passenger seat while they take you on a tour of every adult bookstore in town.

So take your time and stay a while. Who knows, that bookish clerk or the dashing dance instructor just might turn out to be the soul mate you've been searching for.

FRIENDS

There is no greater ally in the war against dating duds than a good friend or two. Friends are there to back you up when your lame date goes down for the night or your "one" shot of tequila turns into 12!

"Love begins with a smile, grows with a kiss, and ends with a teardrop."
—Anonymous

Friends will help you keep your head when that cute guy in the bookstore asks for your e-mail address, even though he asked every other girl in the joint for theirs while you were over in the New Release section. Friends will let you know if the girl in your sights is a minx or a model citizen, and help you tell the difference when you don't have time to ask.

And when that cutie in the club breaks your heart when her boyfriend picks her up, your friends will be there to dance the polka to make you laugh. If you must be single, don't you dare be without your friends!

PICK-UP CENTRAL:
A TALE OF
TWO CLUBS

One of the most popular and long-lasting pick-up destinations for seducers and romancers alike, despite the fact that most of them aren't very seductive or romantic, are the bars of America. From local pubs to pricey bistros, singles on the prowl make such watering holes their first, and often only, stop of a weekend or even weeknight.

So even if the above description doesn't fit you, or maybe it just gave you some ideas, follow along as we explore the seedy underbelly of some of this country's favorite types of watering holes:

FEE, FI, FAUX-FINNEGAN'S:
A NOT-SO-IRISH PUB

The recent bumper crop of Irish Pubs across America is a relatively new development on the modern club scene, but don't assume that "new" necessarily means "better." After all, few of them are owned by anyone even remotely Irish. And even fewer of them resemble an authentic pub in anything more than their name.

Finnegan's Irish Pub is one such typical faux-Irish pub.

For one thing, its ridiculous location in the lobby of the local Holiday Inn couldn't get any more American. Unless, say, it teamed up with that Scottish-American icon and resided in the parking lot of the local McDonald's. For another, its sign boldly boasts every Irish stereotype known to man, from its four-leaf clover and pot of gold to its leprechaun's pipe.

All of this before you even step one foot inside of its nondescript door to hear the decidedly un-Irish rock 'n' roll music playing from four Sanyo speakers dotting the water-stained ceiling. Once inside, however, the shamrock really hits the fan.

The endless Irish clichés mix with American standbys so profusely that it's enough to make your eyes gag. For instance, who came up with the brilliant idea of putting the swimsuit-clad hottie gracing the latest Budweiser poster right next to a musty, ancient-looking golf bag? And what's with the alternating shamrock and palm tree Christmas tree lights strung around the bar? Was there a sale at Margaritaville?

Décor aside, one need look no further than the give-away beer tap toppers to register the bar's true American heritage. For no self-respecting real Irish pub would offer "Bud Ice" and "Red Dog" right next to Guinness or Harp.

Look beyond the taps, however, and you see even more evidence. Exactly when did Slim Jims and Granger's Own Pickled Pigs Feet become staples over on the Emerald Isle?

Still, you didn't come here to soak up the ambience, right? If you're like the other 99.99 percent of Yanks who pass through the doors of Finnegan's Pub at least once, you came here to scope out and, hopefully, pick up someone of the opposite sex. Well, you just might be in luck.

One pleasant side effect of faux-Irish pubs is their faux-clientele. After all, the decision to come to an Irish pub over say, a disco or a bistro, is an entirely conscious one. A statement, if you will, that goes something like this: "I'm tired of the usual bar scene. And I'm tired of the usual bar babes or bar buds. I want something different. Something new. Something exotic. But someplace where I can still speak the language. Hey, what better place than Ireland?"

Therefore, most people in Finnegan's and other faux-Irish pubs, e.g. Shamrock Sam's and O'Reilly's Tavern, are trying to add a little spice to their lives. Everyone except the die-hard regulars, that is, like the granny in the back booth who keeps lighting her candle and blowing it back out.

Naturally, to succeed in a place like Finnegan's, you need an attitude. Imagine that you must be the exotic stranger the little hottie in the corner has come to meet. Or that you are the spice that hunk on the barstool longs for. Hey, and if you can throw in a fake Irish accent, you'll be right at home.

It doesn't hurt that many Irish pubs, for some strange reason known only to their proprietors, are located in hotel lobbies. Naturally, this makes the opportunity for one-night stands a no-brainer, considering a good 75 percent of the bar's patrons need only to stumble up a few flights of stairs and make sure their room key still works to fall into bed.

Whether they're alone or not is up to you.

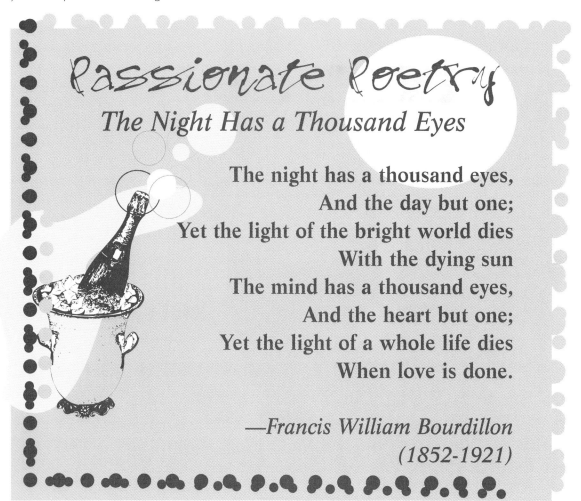

passionate poetry
The Night Has a Thousand Eyes

The night has a thousand eyes,
And the day but one;
Yet the light of the bright world dies
With the dying sun
The mind has a thousand eyes,
And the heart but one;
Yet the light of a whole life dies
When love is done.

—*Francis William Bourdillon*
(1852-1921)

WOOING WOES

While dating at the workplace has become a rite of passage of sorts as overworked and underloved hipsters seek out romance anywhere they can, this occupational option comes with its fair share of workplace wooing woes.

DAISY FLUKES

It's your fault for losing all of that weight. You should have known better. Having been a size 10 since the early '80s, you've bought all of your clothes accordingly and developed the usual favorites and non-favorites. But that was before your new promotion.

Who knew that accepting all of that extra responsibility would be so hard? So time-consuming? So calorie expending? And who knew they'd go ahead and hire that hunky new Rick guy to replace you? And who knew he'd need so much help acclimating to your old job that you'd have to spend even more time at the workplace helping him, in close cubicle quarters, no less?

And who knew the resulting excitement, nervousness, adjusting, and overtime would lead to a gradual deceleration of your usual eating habits. And who knew it would happen so gradually, so slowly, so totally, that you'd wake up one morning to find that all of your old pants were just too damned big?

And who could have timed it any worse? On the one Memorial Day of your life when you actually had…a date! And not just any date, but a date with, of all people, that hunky Rick from work who finally, on one of those long work nights together, had asked you to a family picnic that was the highlight of his social calendar.

And how, when it was such an important event to him, your first date and first meet and greet with his extended family of overachievers and fashion plates, were you to show up looking like some junior high kid in baggy drawers and your nice "date" panties half hanging out over the top? You've been through the front of your closet, the back of your closet, even your back-up box of old clothes in the garage. All to no avail. Everything hung down to your knees and exposed everything you wanted to conceal. You even tried a last-ditch effort to find an open clothing store, but everyone was out enjoying the beautiful weather, not to mention the national holiday.

"If I were a girl, I'd despair. The supply of good women far exceeds that of the men who deserve them."
—Robert Graves

This was a definite "shorts" moment, only…you had no shorts. Then, in desperation, you remembered the bag of "rags" above your washer and dryer and attacked it mercilessly, finally revealing at the very bottom a pair of well-preserved, wrinkle-free, nicely folded denim shorts.

Unfortunately, these shorts were of the Daisy Duke variety. A little too short, with the frilly, lacy, border at the hem. Fortunately, due to your unexpected, unplanned weight loss plan, they fit perfectly, making you feel like the little college girl who'd bought them in the vain attempt to keep up with American fashion, though you really thought they looked ridiculous at the time and most certainly do now.

Still, the picnic hour is approaching and, just after you'd slipped them on beneath a rugged, oversized flag T-shirt that would hopefully take the attention away from your hopelessly outdated "undercut" shorts, you hear Rick's knock at your door.

You stay within a mere inch of his personal space until you get to the car, and then complain of a "chill" (despite the summer weather) and cover yourself up to your knees with your already baggy shirt all the way to the picnic.

Rick, seemingly unaware of your denim underwear, talks blissfully of how successful he's become at work, thanks to your expert tutelage. You admire his strong hands on the steering wheel, his nice taste in watches, his full head of hair, his deep voice and straight teeth and hope above hope that you can pull this day off without ruining the definite spark you feel inside the car. (Which could, come to think of it, be caused by the lack of fabric on your lower buttocks and the leather of his passenger seat.)

The picnic is in full swing by the time you get there and, walking across a sun-swept lawn alive with sailing Frisbees and the aroma of grilling hot dogs, you momentarily forget your lack of undergarments and eagerly shake hands with Rick's parents. Unfortunately, they have all the time in the world to take notice of your exposed flesh, and both of them eye you coolly despite Rick's glowing review of how you've helped him acclimate to work.

As the picnic proceeds, no matter how hard you try and stretch your T-shirt into a nightgown, glaring stares follow you everywhere you go. The only one not staring, it turns out, is Rick. His blissful smile, his warm hand in yours, his chivalrous offer to bring you back a plate as you gratefully find a picnic table bench with which to cover your now well-aired buttocks, all attest that he's still enamored with you. Until, that is, Rick introduces you to his "boyfriend" during a lull at the picnic behind the row of port-a-potties lined up out back.

"Wow," the boyfriend, Serge, announces in between playful giggles with his lover. "Thank you so much for the performance. I mean, those Daisy Dukes were the final straw. I'll look like a dream compared to you. Rick's family will have to accept me now."

Rick thanks you too.

Humiliated, you smile and congratulate the happy couple, glad to be of help. Meanwhile, you spend the rest of the picnic sipping warm Kool-Aid loaded with rum and quietly plotting the best way to get Rick fired from your old job.

Finally, sweet success! The bars, the bookstores, the clubs of your choice have finally yielded up a pearl among the oysters and you, yes you, have a date! Congrats! Now, don't blow it by taking your future lover to some generic eatery just because you've been programmed by the media and your older brother to think that's what a first date is.

Instead, why not break the mold and impress your date by doing something unusual or, better yet, unexpected!

JUST MARRIED

If you can swing it, and chances are if you keep your ears open you can, try to get invited to a wedding for your first date. Not only is the food free, aside from that last-minute wedding gift that is, but the entertainment is usually good, and oh yeah, there's quite often a live band!

Romance is bound to be catching when you watch the vows being exchanged and the lucky couple dance the night away, and there's nothing sexier than a little vicarious living. Besides, when the evening's over, you don't have to spend the rest of your life looking at each other.

Unless you want to, that is.

Passionate Poetry

To the Virgins, Make Much of Time

Gather ye rosebuds while ye may,
Old time is still a-flying,
And this same flower that smiles today,
To-morrow will be dying.

The glorious lamp of heaven, the sun,
The higher he's a-getting,
The sooner will his race be run,
And nearer he's to setting.

That age is best which is the first,
When youth and blood are warmer;
But being spent, the worse and worst
Times still succeed the former.

Then be not coy, but use your time,
And while ye may, go marry;
For having lost just once your prime,
You may for ever tarry.

—Robert Herrick
(1591-1674)

PICNIC PERKS

Since food is one of the expected requirements of a first date, just like sweaty palms and indigestion, why not warn your date to dress casually and surprise her with a lavish picnic, courtesy of the local gourmet store or deli. A nice bottle of wine (don't forget the corkscrew) and a few well-sealed containers of pate or roasted chicken, followed by something sweet like chocolate covered pretzels or individual cheesecakes, are sure to go down as smoothly as the comfy blanket beneath you.

"Anyone can be passionate, but it takes real lovers to be silly."

—Rose Franken

If you can't find a park that's open after dark, why not try the picnic area at your apartment complex or maybe even the patch of wooded lawn in your office park. Anywhere is fine as long as it's private, secluded, and, most of all, safe. Make sure the weather is permitting and don't forget the essentials, such as candles for mood lighting and just the right Luther Vandross CD on your battery-powered boom box, and you're bound to make a good first impression.

Passionate Poetry

MEETING AT NIGHT

The grey sea and the long black land;
And the yellow half-moon large and low;
And the startled little waves that leap
In fiery ringlets from their sleep,
As I gain the cove with pushing prow,
And quench its speed i' the slushy sand.
Then a mile of warm sea-scented beach;
Three fields to cross till a farm appears;
A tap at the pane, the quick sharp scratch

Take Two and Call Me Every Morning!

I wasn't even supposed to be there. I was graduating from college and the gang at my second job, a local restaurant in town, wanted to throw me a congratulatory party.

"We'll meet you at the Raw Bar," they shouted on my way out the door with a tip-apron full of extra singles from an impromptu collection they'd taken up for me. "Don't be late!"

Of course, with my college-boy sense of direction, I went to the Raw Bar on the south side of town even as they all sped directly for the north one. Now, still nursing my lukewarm first beer of the night, I had finally gotten a bartender at the other raw bar to summon the most sober of the group to the bar phone. Needless to say, the party had been a roaring success, and none of them were in any condition to come and meet me.

I sat back down on my warm bar stool and finished my beer. "Oh, well," I thought to myself, rising to leave, "at least I won't have a hangover tomorrow."

Just then a teacher from the school where I had just completed my student internship walked through the door with a friend of hers. Embarrassed to be caught in a dingy bar all alone, I quickly turned to the bartender and ordered another beer.

Meanwhile the long-legged beauty I lusted after day in and day out strode effortlessly to a table for two and joined her friend for a pitcher and some steamed shrimp. I watched balefully from behind the expert camouflage of my 300-pound biker/barstool neighbor as her delicate hands alternately lifted her frothy beer and peeled a still steaming shrimp.

How different she seemed from the consummate teacher who often wrote me "helpful" little notes after witnessing yet another disastrous attempt on my part to take my unruly 5th grade class through the halls quietly.

"If you divided your line in half," she wrote in elegant script, "they'd be much easier to control. Sincerely, Ms. Ricardo." I'd saved every note and devoured them as religiously as I did my college advisor's half-hearted evaluations.

And now she was here, live and in person. My teaching degree, and thus my stressful internship, was over now. There would be no more little notes from "Ms. Ricardo." No more expert advice in the teacher's lounge while I secretly vibed her with sexy e.s.p. and suggestive rapid eye movements. But it didn't matter anyway. My flirtations had gone unreturned and already the other bachelors at the bar were making plans to swoop in on the two unescorted beauties and their half-eaten shrimp.

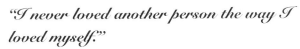

"I never loved another person the way I loved myself."

— *Mae West*

I slid my half-empty beer and a hefty tip across the bar and left without a word. The humidity in the warm, Florida night air reminded me of the dull headache forming in the back of my weary head, and I drove my battered Corolla to the brightly lit gas station across the street. Inside I grabbed a diet cola and a single packet of Tylenol and returned to my car.

Across the street lay the salty weathered raw bar and all of its lifesaver and fish net glory. I sipped at my

PASSIONATE POETRY

Jenny Kissed Me

Jenny kissed me when we met,
Jumping from the chair she sat in;
Time, you thief, who love to get
Sweets into your list, put that in:
Say I'm weary, say I'm sad,
Say that health and wealth have missed me,
Say I'm growing old, but add,
Jenny kissed me.

—Leigh Hunt (1784-1841)

soda greedily and felt my tension lighten and my headache disappear. Stowing the bright yellow packet in my pocket, I sat in my idling car and wondered why I hadn't stayed. Why hadn't I at least tried to make pleasant conversation and get to know her away from school? I'd never see her again anyway. What did I have to lose?

"Two souls with but a single thought,
Two hearts that beat as one."
—Fredrich Halm

Finishing my soda, I returned to my old parking space and strode back into the raw bar confidently. All right, but at least I walked back in! I ordered a pitcher of light beer (I was guessing) and with trembling hands brought it and a clean glass over to Ms. Ricardo's table.

She seemed surprised to see me and my heart fluttered as she rose to greet me. Or so I thought.

"Thanks for the offer," she replied as I hefted the sweaty pitcher of beer. "But…maybe you and Cheryl can enjoy it. I was just leaving. I've got this nasty headache." Sure, it could have been a line, but, she was rubbing her temples rather strongly.

Just then the crisp, yellow

packet in my jean pocket called out to me and I snatched it up, ripped it open and deposited two extra-strength Tylenol into her warm, soft hand.

Her eyes lit up and she swallowed them with a fresh glass of beer.

"Gee," she said with a smile she'd been afraid to reveal on school grounds, "Suddenly I feel a whole lot better!"

I've often looked back on that night in amazement. So many things seemed to "align" in just the right order. What if I'd gone to the "right" raw bar? What if I'd never gotten that aspirin? What if I'd gone home instead of coming back? What if she'd left before I got back? What if she preferred . . . Advil?

Oh, well. I guess I have plenty of time to find the answer to my questions. We've been married for five years. You'd think, by now, I'd have found the courage to ask them.

4
ROMANCE FOR TWO

Whether you're living together or just dating, married for two weeks or going through the blissful stages of hot, furniture-wrecking, jungle love, romance for two is far different from single romance. No more singles bars or happy hours, no more hooking up with strangers or waking up in strange places.

You are together, and only the two of you can do anything to change that. Accordingly, the many peculiar practices of single romance no longer apply. You are in a whole new ballgame now, one with different rules, different players, and a different playing field. Maybe you're living together, or taking turns sleeping over at each other's place. Maybe you're working together, or commuting together to work in the city.

Either way, you are seeing more of each other than ever before, and to keep that a good thing rather than a tired rerun you'd rather skip, you might just want to check out the following tips for staying romantic, even when you see each other every day.

ROMEO & JULIET:
HAPPILY
NEVER AFTER

Who can forget Shakespeare's star-crossed lovers and their hormone-filled romp through England's literary landscape? From daggers and swordplay to poison and chubby monks, this one had it all. There's not a puppy-loving teenager alive who can't relate to the themes in this passionate tale of love found and love lost, betrayal and revenge, romance and brutality.

But it's not merely bookish nerds who take this oft-told story to heart. Hollywood has had its hand in sharing this tumultuous tale with millions of movie fans throughout the years. It started in the silent era, carried over into talkies, and got hip with Franco Zefferelli's version in the 1960s, not to mention *West Side Story*. After that came remake after remake, starring everyone from Leonardo DiCaprio to Gwyneth Paltrow.

Romeo and Juliet are seen as romantic ideals of passion and pain. Meet a great girl? "She's better than Juliet!" Met a real dude dud? "Well, he's no Romeo." The phrase "Just like Romeo and Juliet" is used when blissful romance intrudes on a couple's life, no matter how briefly.

But let's put aside the fairy tale romance and examine what life might have been like had Romeo and Juliet somehow avoided enough

trailer-trash dramatics to pique the interest of Jerry Springer—not to mention knives and poison—and lived happily ever after.

For starters, few affairs that begin as passionately as Romeo and Juliet's ever end up anywhere but divorce court. After all, how long could they keep up that intensity? The sleepless nights, that cold air out on the balcony, the climbing and the running and the hiding

and the necking. After a while, wouldn't they have wanted a quiet night in for a change? A Blockbuster night?

And if they fluently coined poetic term after term for a rose or the moon, how well do you think they would have fared in the new releases aisle?

"Adam Sandler? Notteth on your life!"

"Jasmine Bleeth? Never, dare I say, never!"

"*Fletch*? A pox upon your house, fair maiden, and a curse upon your bosom!"

"*The Hooters Girls Go To Summer Camp*? Again? May your codpiece shrivel and dry up before the cock crows!"

Date night aside, let's say Romeo and Juliet shacked up together. Lord knows the Capulets and the Montagues wouldn't allow it, but say the rebellious lovers moved to Seattle and started up a racy lingerie dot-com, heavy on the tights, that required them to live together to cut down on their overhead.

> **Give her *two* red roses,
> each with a note.
> The first note says,
> "For the woman I love"
> and the second,
> "For my best friend."
> —Anonymous**

Could you imagine breakfast in the star-crossed lover's breakfast nook:

"Did notteth your dear nurse teach you any cooking skills whatsoever? Oh, that I had shacked up with her kind soul instead."

"It's been six years, kind sir, and not a finger have you lifteth to help me around this dump you call an abode."

And how about shopping night:

"Spaghetti? Again? Is that all you know how to

cook? I'd rather sup on the apothecary's concoctions than your limp noodles yet again."

"Quarrel with me in the dairy aisle again, dear sir, and I'll unhand you of your sword and run it straight through your gullet. It's spaghetti or Lean Cuisine, take your pick!"

And don't forget Valentine's Day:

"Shall I compare thee to a summer's day, a drive-in movie, a brand new DVD, ah, forget it. Redeemeth this coupon for one car wash."

No, for these two powder kegs to survive as lovers past the third act, a long-distance relationship would be the only possibility.

After all, Romeo has always been depicted as a pretty boy, both in words and film, and as Juliet aged, she would no doubt become resentful as the years waged war with her face, and left pretty boy's unscathed. Not to mention, there's not much need for swordplay and tights these days, so what would the man of the family do?

No, some love is meant to burn out, not fade away. Romeo and Juliet's love was, no doubt, the textbook definition of this popular saying. For those of us looking for long-lasting love, we would do better to read Dr. Ruth than Shakespeare!

SEXY STEPs

No matter how long the two of you have been together, or hope to be together, chances are you will hit a snag in the romantic road one day soon. Whether it's your first fight (okay, first fight in public) or your first week without sex (okay, first week without sex in public), it doesn't take long for the blushing rose of your puppy love to fade into the gray haze of a committed relationship.

Still, just because you are in daily contact or can't afford to go out to dinner each night like you used to, there's no reason to let the passion die just because you've run out of neon condoms!

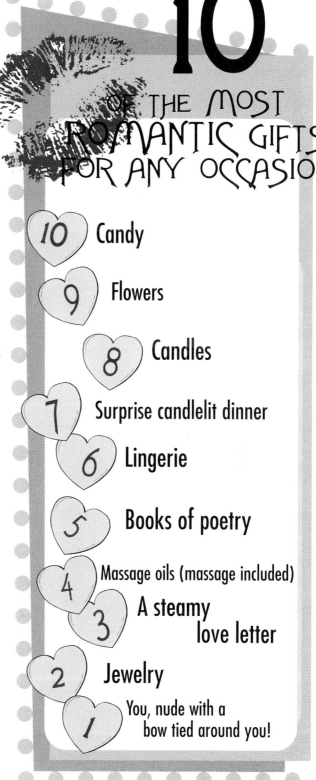

10 of THE MOST ROMANTIC GIFTS FOR ANY OCCASION

10 Candy

9 Flowers

8 Candles

7 Surprise candlelit dinner

6 Lingerie

5 Books of poetry

4 Massage oils (massage included)

3 A steamy love letter

2 Jewelry

1 You, nude with a bow tied around you!

OIL THIS

Stop for a second, and try to remember the last time you had a really good massage. Heck, try to remember the last time you had *any* kind of massage, good or bad. While you've got your thinking cap on, now try to recall the last time you gave a massage, any kind of massage, to anyone.

Hmm, still thinking? Well, you're not alone. Unless you got a gift certificate to a professional masseuse for your birthday, chances are you haven't had a good massage in years. That's because this long lost art is slowly fading from the courtship rituals of a culture that wants everything in a hurry. Sadly, this motto carries over into the bedroom. For when the modern version of foreplay is "Wow, you look hot tonight," there's not much room for a long-lasting, deep-tissue massage before the rubbers come out and the heat is on.

But if your love life is suffering from those living-together blues, why not invest in an inexpensive bottle of scented lotion and per chance a scented candle or two and turn bedtime into some fun downtime. Sometimes, the mere intimacy of strong hands on bare flesh is enough to satisfy those weeknights where intimacy is more important than Must See TV.

SLUMBER PARTY

Okay, so maybe you tried the massage thing and all it does is turn into a cocoa buttered glop in the bedroom. But all you want is a little more intimacy and a lot less routine. Why not start a tradition that turns one night of the week into the grown-up version of a slumber party?

For starters, if you're not living together, invite your lover over to spend the night. If you do sleep together, try sleeping in the guestroom for a change of scenery or going to bed an hour or two early instead of watching Letterman and Conan—just don't go to sleep too early. To make the bedroom more romantic, try dim lighting or using candles instead of the lamps. Forego mood music and read aloud to your lover from a book of romantic

poetry. Even try playing a game on the bed, and the winner can be awarded a sultry surprise.

To make slumber party night even more special, invest in matching PJs or boxers, and invite a snuggly teddy bear to join your little family—or the other kind of teddy works well, too. Make popcorn or break into the SnackWell's cookies for a special treat that brings the kid out in both of you, and chances are you'll be doing lots more laughing than if you had tuned into those late-night talk shows.

"If it is your time, love will track you down like a cruise missile."

—Lynda Barry

"The first duty of love is to listen."

—Paul Tillich

OH, THE GAMES PEOPLE PLAY

The bedroom is not the only sexy place in the house, however. When you invest in your favorite childhood games, any room can turn into a passionate place. Forget the frozen dinners, forget the boob tube, forget that handy copy of *Kama Sutra* he thought would be romantic. Instead, why not take a trip to the local mega mart and spend $20 on an arm full of classic board games: Candyland, Operation, Battleship. Or go to the software section and look for your favorite Playstation game. You name it, your retro evening will turn into a weekly tradition in no time. Grab some take-out on the way and make sure to have plenty of kiddy snacks on hand for later, such as jawbreakers, Now & Laters, or Twizzlers.

Roll the dice, pick the cards, and move those game pieces around the board to turn any night into game night. After all, who can get bored playing Chutes and Ladders? Especially if you're naked.

Love's philosophy

The fountains mingle with the river,
And the rivers with the ocean,
The winds of Heaven mix for ever
With a sweet emotion;
Nothing in the world is single:
All things by a law divine
In one spirit meet and mingle.
Why not I with thine?

See the mountains kiss high Heaven
And the waves clasp one another;
No sister flower would be forgiven
If it disdained its brother;
And the sunlight clasps the earth
And the moonbeams kiss the sea;
What is all this sweet work worth
If thou kiss not me?

— Percy Bysshe Shelley (1792-1822)

COZY COOKOUT

Pick a sedentary weeknight and skip the take-out food or frozen entrée. (What is that thing?). Swing by the grocery store on the way to her place or fire up the grill at his place and cook out instead. The fire won't be the only thing burning up as you share a bottle of wine or crack open a six-pack and let the chicken sizzle as the stress of another workday melts away.

Crank the Bob Marley or UB40 in the living room and leave the patio door open as you fire up that citronella candle and take turns swatting mosquitoes off of each other's necks. There's nothing like food, any kind of food, cooked on the open grill, and since there's nothing to do but wait until those (chicken) breasts are hot, that leaves you plenty of time to rediscover a little of that lost romance in your life.

Dance barefoot on the deck or sit on each other's lap as the sun sets on a beautiful evening together. Just don't have so much fun that dinner burns. Then again, let it burn! There's always take-out.

I love you!

TO MY DEAR AND LOVING HUSBAND

NOW THAT
TAKES THE CAKE!

Forget what Richard Simmons says, we don't have enough cakes in our life. Sure, there's the occasional birthday and that Yule log from Aunt Margaret once a year. And, every once in a while, a sumptuous dessert at a restaurant. But don't wait for a special occasion to sweeten up your love life with a special cake just for two.

No matter where you live, today's ultra-competitive grocery store chains almost all have built-in bakeries that specialize in specialty cakes. From birthdays to anniversaries, from soccer championships to graduations, these bustling bakeries are well-equipped to turn your diminutive dessert into rousing romance.

Order your cake in advance, and be sure to have the cake decorator write something cute, funny, or sexy on top. Personalize it with your names and a heart-shape or two, and be sure to get your lover's favorite to make it even more tempting.

No matter what you have for dinner, when you unveil your sweet surprise, you're bound to make an impression that counts. Don't forget the milk!

If ever two were one, then surely we.
If ever man were lov'd by wife, then thee.
If ever wife was happy in a man,
Compare with me, ye women, if you can.
I prize thy love more than whole Mines of gold
Or all the riches that the East doth hold.
My love is such that Rivers cannot quench,
Nor ought but love from thee give recompense.
Thy love is such I can no way repay.
The heavens reward thee manifold, I pray.
Then while we live, in love let's so persevere.
That when we live no more, we may live ever.

—Anne Bradstreet (1612-1672)

COUPLE ROMANCE:

It's official: You are a couple! Well, not just you, of course. You and your lover, your baby, your sweetums, your hotcake, are a couple. And as such, you have certain realities to face. After all, your days of swinging singles spots are over. You certainly need to put your Little Black Book on the shelf. And you might want to get a P. O. Box for that subscription to *Sexy Swedish Strippers* while you're at it!

You've gone from buying her dinner, to going Dutch, to possibly even splitting that grocery bill right down the middle. Heck, you may have even learned her ATM PIN code by now! You're thinking in terms of "we," rather than "me." You're even wearing clean underwear for a change!

Whether you're living together, commuting to each other's abodes each weeknight and all weekend, or having one of those long-distance romances, we've got some helpful tips to keep you "coupling," even after you become a couple.

COHABITATION NATION

With modern America's apartment com-plex mind-set, more doting couples are shacking up than ever before. Since so many of us wait until we're hitched to buy a home, what else are we supposed to do in the meantime? But splitting the rent isn't the only reason to invite your lover into your living space. After all, you *do* want to see them, night and day, day

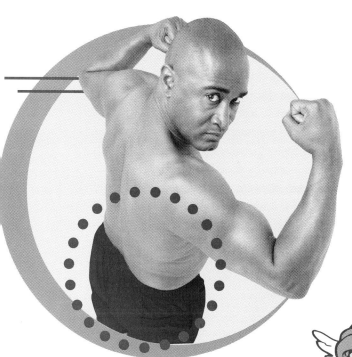

So why not embrace this fact and make the most out of it? Cozy up on the couch in front of a roaring fire. Splurge on scented candles and flowers once a week. Learn how to cook—together! After all, you're living together because you want to! (Just remember this when that bath mat you just stepped onto after a luxurious shower turns out to be his size-XL pair of underwear—yesterday's underwear!)

"Love is the same as like except you feel sexier."

—Judith Viorst

and night, don't you? *Don't* you? You do want to share half of your closet space, half of the shelves in your medicine cabinet, and slide over your six-pack shelf for her chilly bottles of Chardonnay, right?

And even if you don't, you are now! Still, many loving couples rush into the act of living together without thinking of the consequences. Who pays the phone bill? Who takes out the trash? Hey, who used all the hot water? After all, you're not just roommates, you're also lovers. Which puts quite a dramatic spin on things.

For with a roommate, you could do certain things that aren't quite appropriate for your new live-in love. Such as, say, order pizza seven nights a week. Or leave the dishes in the sink, the dishwasher, or perhaps even the oven, until Sunday evening. Or watch the Sci-Fi Channel non-stop all Friday with a bag of Oreos on your lap and a carton of milk right next to the remote. Or even sing the entire version of "American Pie" at the top of your lungs in the shower at 6 a.m., even if you only know the chorus.

Now you have a lover's feelings to consider. You're not just sharing your space with someone, you're sharing your life. Opening yourself up, becoming vulnerable, and letting them into all the nooks and crannies no one has ever seen before!

SONNET XLIII

How do I love thee? Let me count the ways.
I love thee to the depth and breadth and height
my soul can reach, when feeling out of sight
For the ends of Being and ideal Grace.
I love thee to the level of every day's
Most quiet need, by sun and candlelight.
I love thee freely, as men strive for Right;
I love thee purely, as they turn from Praise.
I love thee with the passion put to use
In my old griefs, and with my childhood's faith.
I love thee with a love I seemed to lose
With my lost saints,—I love thee with the breath,
Smiles, tears, of all my life!—and, if God choose,
I shall but love thee better after death.

—Elizabeth Barrett Browning (1806-1861)

The nice thing about going back and forth between each other's abodes is the inherent slumber party effect that vibes around your whole sleepover deal. She's still getting used to where to find a coffee mug, and he's still trying to figure out where you keep the extra toilet paper. Or perhaps your schedule only allows you to spend weekends together.

Even better! Use the week apart to plan something special, each and every weekend! Whether it's a musical concert or a rainy day in bed, make your time together as special as possible with little cards, special gifts, and hidden notes on his pillow or in her stack of towels.

LONG DISTANCE LOVE

In the long annals of romance, the long distance love has always had its own, special place. While the time together may be ecstasy, the time apart is often torturous, and few couples can last in this type of relationship for long periods of time. But whether it's work or the lack of it that separates you, there's no reason to doom yourself to long spells of misery and despair.

The phone becomes a vital instrument in this type of coupledom, so make better use of it by leaving him romantic messages on his voice mail. Few couples can afford the extra large phone bills that accompany this type of affair, so make the best use of your time on (the phone) line by skipping the

I love you .... and miss you... and love you....

COZY COMMUTING

Okay, maybe you're not living together—yet. Perhaps you're sharing space at each other's place instead. Well, that's fine. No reason you can't be just as romantic just because you don't see each other every day. In fact, in some ways, you can be even more romantic!

After all, you still have some down time in which to do romantic things. If he's coming over after work, get there first and welcome him "home" with some romantic music and candlelight. If she's coming over for the entire weekend, stock up on fresh toothpaste, soap, cheesy teddy bear hand towels, and maybe even a matching sleep shirt!

bitching about your boss or traffic. Instead, cut right to the important things in life and, of course, all that lovey dovey stuff.

Invest in a box of cheap greeting cards and a roll of stamps and spend your lunch hour composing cheesy love poems or long missives about how much you miss her. Mail one every other day and hope she returns the favor! Send care packages for the upcoming weekend, consisting of phone cards or 48 hours worth of romantic reading! Dash off cute eGreeting cards and let them pile up on his hard-drive at work for a nice surprise come Monday morning.

No matter what you do to celebrate both your time together and your time apart, there's no reason to fall into that depressing old saying: "Out of sight, out of mind!"

"Absence diminishes small loves and increases great ones, as the wind blows out the candle and blows up the bonfire."
—Francois de La Rouchefoucauld

CULTURE SHACK (UP!)

Romance can easily fall to the wayside when couples live together and, more importantly, shop together. From his Frosted Flakes to her Special K, more fights erupt in the crowded aisles of grocery stores than all the boxing rings in Atlantic City.

HOODED VS. CREW

When it comes to sweats, you are strictly a Fruit-of-the-Loom, generic, in-and-out type of guy. You know there are millions of brands out there, from Polo to Hilfiger to Old Navy to J. Crew, but you simply don't care. Your lifelong motto has been and always will be: "It's a sweatshirt, for Pete's sake!"

Every winter, for as long as you've been financially independent (or, at least, since your mom refused to keep shopping for you), you've swung by one of the Marts (K- or Wal-, it doesn't really matter) and done your sweat shopping for the season.

For $5.99 a pop, unless you time it right and they're having a "2 for $10" sale, you grab a gray top and gray pants, and a blue top and red pants. With this simple purchase, and not much more than a $20 bill, you've just acquired not just two "sweatsuits," but an entire range of combinations, including but not limited to, gray top/red pants, blue top/gray pants, etc. The only variation in your routine is what size you buy them in. In those rare years when you've actually used that gym membership you plunk down $500 every January 1, you grab your sweats in size Large to emphasize your temporarily

5. Easy access to the nearby monastery.
4. Two words: Breaking & Entering.
3. Easier to cut in on homeless guys' soup line.
2. That tattoo of Alf you got on your forehead during your last drunken shore leave.
1. It might be a while before the "My Boss Sucks" you shaved into your hair at that wacky office party grows out.

firm pecs, abs, and thighs. Other years, when your workaholic job and that nightly order of take-out General Tso's Chicken has precedence, you grab the sweats in XL for the ever-popular "baggy look."

Other than that variable, however, you've been fairly constant in your sweat shopping for more than eight years now. Until, that is, you informed your current girlfriend, a design major over at the local Fashion Institute, that you "needed a few pairs of sweats" and would be back forthwith.

"Great," she'd said enthusiastically, jumping up and grabbing her purse. "I'll come with."

"Fine," you think but don't say. "You can wait in the car and then we'll have brunch somewhere with all the money I'll save."

Unfortunately, as you pull into the local cheapo mart parking lot, she has a violent reaction much like that of young Damien when his parents tried to drag him into church one fine Sunday morning in that horror movie *The Omen*.

"This is a joke, right," she snaps bitterly when her head quits revolving around her neck. "You're not actually going in there, are you?"

"Yeah," you snort, finding a parking space. "They're just sweats, for Pete's sake."

"What moron told you that?" she shrieks from over the Styrofoam top of her to-go coffee. "Buying sweats is just as important as buying jeans or a sports coat these days. Don't you know that?"

"No," you laugh, assuming that this normally reasonable and sane young woman is the one who's joking. "Now, let's go."

"Look, honey," she says, although the way she pronounces that last word makes it sound anything but sweet. "You simply cannot purchase anything you put on your body inside of a store ending in -MART. Except, perhaps, for deodorant or soap. Now, the mall should be open by now. Let's go to a real store."

Groaning and silently wondering how much is left on your credit card, you succumb to her wishes and leave your inexpensive, comforting Cheap-Mart behind as it slowly dwindles in the rearview mirror.

At the mall, your fashion maven girlfriend sternly instructs you on the finer points of sweatsuit purchasing. Only, she doesn't call them that, she keeps saying "active apparel" until you finally ask what that means and she speaks slowly, loudly, as if she were a kindergarten teacher: "Sweat suits!"

She points out the finer, minute differences in "attitude" between hooded with zipper (for tough-guy wannabes) and hooded without zipper (the real thing.) You ask her how she knows such things and she looks at you as if you'd just asked her if there was a three-pound booger hanging from your nose, complete with no answer whatsoever.

She points out the advantages of a V-neck collar over a crew neck, and says she can spot a difference in future income potential just by which one a man decides to wear. She instructs you on the finer art of choosing materials, poly cotton blends vs. the real thing, fluff vs. pill, etc. She illuminates at least seven shades of gray you never even knew existed, including nightshade, thunderstorm, flannel, and winter cloud. She even takes you to one store where, much like purchasing jeans or slacks, the sweats no longer come in S, M, L or XL, but with waist sizes and inseam measurements: 36 x 32, 34 x 30, etc.

Of course, none of these finer points come cheaply. You notice quickly that nightshade costs more than flannel, thunderstorm less than winter cloud, but none of them are even close to your good old $5.99. Hooded with zipper is more than hooded without, and the unacceptable (to your girlfriend anyway) poly blend is much cheaper than the real thing.

Passionate Poetry

A Red, Red Rose

O my luve's like a red, red rose.
That's newly sprung in June;
O my luve's like a melodie
That's sweetly play'd in tune.
As fair art thou, my bonnie lass,
So deep in luve am I;
And I will love thee still, my Dear,
Till a'the seas gang dry.
Till a' the seas gang dry, my Dear,
And the rocks melt wi' the sun:
I will luve thee still, my Dear,
While the sands o'life shall run.
And fare thee weel my only Luve!
And fare thee weel a while!
And I will come again, my Luve,
Tho' it were ten thousand mile!

—Robert Burns (1759-1796)

What used to take ten minutes stretches well into the afternoon, and finally you just hold up your hands and submit: "Fine, great, whatever. You decide and here's my credit card."

She complies willingly and you come home with four bags, each from a separate store, and each containing "active wear" you know that you'll never wear, actively or otherwise. At least, not after you break up with fashion queen, who you silently give yourself two more weeks with, just so she doesn't think you're breaking up with her over the sweats. When, in fact, you most definitely are.

For now, of course, you reach back into the deepest recesses of your closet and somehow find, wedged in between the Christmas decorations and your collection of Bill Cosby sweaters, your gray, red, and blue sweats from the previous year.

Although you won't be able to wear them for the next two weeks, you sigh contentedly, knowing, at least, that they're back there somewhere and wondering if you'll be able to return the "active wear" you've just purchased after 14 long, grueling days.

ROMANTIC DATES

When you're romancing for two, the term "date" takes on an entirely new meaning. Gone are those pleasant jitters that accompany you on the way to pick her up. Gone are the heady days when a simple touch of your hand could send his pulse racing. Naturally, your dates often go from wild and crazy to safe and normal. Which isn't exactly a bad thing, you just want to make sure that you're still being as romantic as possible, even after, in the words of blues legend B. B. King, "the thrill is gone."

To achieve this feat is neither far-reaching or impossible. All it takes is a little originality, a little time, and a little effort. Oh, and lots and lots of fun!

CHANGE YOUR TUNE

Nothing livens up a date like a little live music. And whether you live in Pittsburgh or right next door to the Philharmonic, it's easier than you think to take in a little live music most any night of the week.

If you know your baby grooves to reggae, why drag her to the symphony? Instead, scope out the local ska clubs and sample a few on their reggae nights. If he's into country, hit the line dancing lineup and you just might find a new favorite. When you do hit on a club that makes you both feel comfortable and boasts a talented local band or two, make it a point to check it out once or twice a month to spice up those otherwise dull date nights. The local talent will appreciate a few new fans, and your lover might just regain a little of that lost twinkle in his eye.

EXOTIC CUISINE

Chances are, if you and your lover are like most couples, you tend to hit the same, tired, chain restaurants come date night. And even if they're not chains, if the wait staff greets you with a personalized version of "You again!" it might be time for a change of scenery.

Sampling the foreign cuisines of any city, big or small, is an undertaking just perfect for restless couples who have gotten a little bit tired of the boring and mundane, whether in their restaurants of choice, or even in themselves. To spice up your eating life, and thus your love life come date night, why not let your fingers do the walking through your local restaurant guide and try something new for a change. Indian, Thai, German, Greek, they all offer a wide range of tastes and textures for a palette just waiting to be impressed.

And as you and your lover explore the different foods and smells and decorations of all those different cultures, you just might find that you rediscover romance along the way!

COOKING IN COOKING CLASS!

Who says you have to let someone else do all the work when you go out on a date? After all, if you want something done right, as they say, do it yourself! A cooking class could just be the perfect chance for you and your lover to put the burner on broil!

First, take a trip to the local library, community college, or high school and check out the schedule of cooking classes. Chances are, you might have to go through a little red tape, not to mention a few bills, to enroll yourselves, but the tradeoff is fun and frolic instead of food and a bill, and what's not a good investment about that?

Once you're officially students, put everything you've got into date night in the kitchen, and explore the full potential your new class has to offer. Make friends with your stove partners or chat up the teacher

for the sexiest recipes on file. Laugh, smile, and have a blast as you bake, broil, poach, and grill, and when class is over, don't stop there.

Hit the bookstore on your way home and scour the remainder racks for the best cookbooks a few bucks can buy. Whether it's stir-fry or strudel, cakes or chicken, you can continue the fun back home as you try a new recipe each week. We give this one an A+!

Passionate Poetry

September

We sit late, watching the dark
slowly unfold:
No clock counts this.
When kisses are repeated and the
arms hold
There is no telling where time is.

It is midsummer: the leaves hang
big and still:
Behind the eye a star,
Under the silk of the wrist a sea, tell
Time is nowhere.

We stand; leaves have not timed the
summer.
No clock now needs
Tell we have only what we
remember:
Minutes uproaring with our heads

Like an unfortunate King's and his
Queen's
When the senseless mob rules;
And quietly the trees casting their
crowns
Into the pools.

— Ted Hughes (1930-1998)

CHANGE IS GOOD

As couples grow old together, whether by days, weeks, months, or years, it is hard to resist falling into that time-honored trap known as a "rut." First date night goes, then going out to dinner goes, then dressing up for each other goes, then the perfumes and colognes go, then, for the most part, the hot monkey love goes. While few couples admit it, most couples fall into this trap much easier, and much quicker, than they prefer.

To avoid this trap, couples must be ever-vigilant against the laziness and sloth that creeps into long-term relationships. And whether it be a new restaurant on a new night, a new outfit or a new cologne, change is good. Even changing your hairstyle . . .

Passionate Poetry

Sweet, Can I Sing?

Sweet, can I sing you the song of your kisses?
How soft is this one, how subtle this is,
How fluttering swift as a bird's kiss that is,
As a bird that taps at a leafy lattice;
How this one clings and how that uncloses
From bud to flowers in the way of roses;
And this through laughter and that through
*   weeping*
Swims to the brim where Love lies sleeping;
And this in a point I snatch, and capture
That in the ecstasy of rapture,
When the odorous red-rose petals part
That my lips may find their way to the heart
Of the rose of the world, your lips, my rose.
But no song knows
The way of my heart to the heart of my rose.

—Arthur Symons (1865-1945)

"Love is a much nicer place to be in than an automobile accident, a tight girdle, a higher tax bracket, or a holding pattern over Philadelphia."

-Judith Viorst

HAIR CAESAR

You've been begging your boyfriend for three months now to do something, anything, with his hair. You can't remember how many times you've told him the "Opie" look is out, yet still he refuses to change.

Every month, when it's time for him to get it cut, he says the same exact thing. "You know, honey, I think you're right. Maybe Frank and I will do something different with my hair for a change."

Frank, of course, is your boyfriend's 87-year old barber, whose one sole concession to modern hairdressing was the time he threw away the bowl he used to turn over on people's heads for his favorite, "Little Lord Fauntleroy" look.

Frank has a pair or two of scissors lying around, but ever since his arthritis got so bad, he's started using nothing more than one of those electric clippers, giving your boyfriend's head a decidedly one-dimensional (not to mention unflattering) look.

One month, when you'd withheld sex for several

days, and he was ready to do just about anything to get back in your good graces (not to mention bed), you convinced him to skip Frank's "just this once" and join the rest of the 21st century.

Dragging him into your salon for "the works," you read three entire copies of *Vogue* while Hans, your favorite hairdresser and Broadway musical fan, worked your boyfriend over like a lump of clay on a potter's wheel. Shampoo and baby powder, thinning shears and clippers, cologne and mousse all conspired to make your formerly boring boyfriend a magical babe magnet. It was all you could do to keep Hans from beating you to the punch and asking him out to the local playhouse for a rousing evening.

Showing his brand new, thoroughly modern, utterly cute new haircut off at your favorite restaurant that night, you noted with pride your boyfriend's newfound sense of confidence and charm. He practically beamed underneath those straight and hanging bangs, which set his delicate forehead off like a diamond under a jeweler's light.

One of those cheesy, roving photographers captured the two of you in a tableside embrace and, for once, you splurged and bought the keychain, no longer embarrassed to be dating Opie, but instead boasting a George Clooney-esque clone instead.

After a night of ceaseless, Caesar-inspired passion worthy of Caligula himself, you dozed later than usual, only to find your new beautiful beau gone without a trace. A note next to the coffee machine mentioned something about needing orange juice, but when you reached into the fridge for the creamer, you noticed a full one-half gallon standing sentinel, cool and frosty.

An hour later, butchered and battered by good old Frank's nearsighted shampoo shenanigans, your handsome Caesar entered your apartment looking more like a nicked Napoleon. Sighing, you clutched your restaurant keychain as proof of your one, hot night of attractive accompaniment and gave up. After all, you had to admit your boyfriend's enduring faithfulness (even to a barber) was a good sign.

Besides, how long could it be before Frank (God rest his soul) went to the big barbershop in the sky, anyway?

Beautiful Dreamer

Beautiful dreamer, wake unto me,
Starlight and dewdrops are waiting for thee;
Sounds of the rude world heard in the day,
Lull'd by the moonlight have all pass'd
away!

Beautiful dreamer, queen of my song,
List while I woo thee with soft melody;
Gone are the cares of life's busy throng,--
Beautiful dreamer, awake unto me!

Beautiful dreamer, out on the sea
Mermaids are chaunting the wild lorelie;
Over the streamlet vapors are borne,
Waiting to fade at the bright coming morn.

Beautiful dreamer, beam on my heart,
E'en as the morn on the streamlet and sea;
Then will all clouds of sorrow depart,--
Beautiful dreamer, awake unto me!

—Stephen Foster (1826-1864)

"Love is like the measles. The older you get it, the worse the attack."

—Mary Roberts Rhinehart

IN LUXURY'S LAP

So, you want to be a millionaire? You want to marry a millionaire? Same difference. As long as the seven figure checks keep rolling in, does it really matter if they're yours or your spouse's? (Just make sure you get a cut in the prenuptial agreement.)

Even if a cool mill or two is not in your future, who among the vast landscape of humanity hasn't at some point dreamed of spending thousands, tens of thousands, or even hundreds of thousands of dollars on life's finest luxuries for the one you love?

We'll show you how to be romantic while holding yourself to a budget a little later, but, for now, it's time to go for the gusto. These are options for those in the top one percent of the income bracket, when they want to treat their spouses to something special, or if they want to impress the latest leading lady on the Hollywood scene.

Yes, it's still the thought that counts more than the price tag, and often times the small things are the ones you truly end up treasuring for a lifetime. But that single long stem rose he got you for your one-week anniversary that you've been storing in the freezer may not be looking very romantic after you've been married for four years, and those homemade birthday cards you have displayed on the mantle from each year of your blissful relationship bring you dangerously close to earning the title of "el cheapo."

Rest easy, though, there's always that chance (even if it's more likely you'll get struck by lightning) that you'll win the lottery after the jackpot has rolled around to $80 million, and you will need to know what to do with your newfound riches.

AIN'T IT GRAND (OR TWO)?

Start off simply. You may want to go with a nice fragrance, for him and her. For her, there's Jean Patou's Limited Edition Joy for $730 per ounce. For him, try out Clive Christian's No.1 for $1,820 per ounce.

If you'd rather take her out for a nice night on the town, the best thing to do (beforehand) is to buy her a stunning outfit to wear, the kind that will make both of you look good. A good outfit would be a Burgundy Suede Dress by Versace ($2,500), Blahnik ring lizard pumps ($850), and an antique silver opera bag ($1,000). Not a bad ensemble, eh?

If you're looking for more "around the house" type romantic gifts, try a classic music box. A hand crafted Reuge music box crafted from burl vavona (a type of wood most people probably haven't even heard of) is a great gift at $3,800. You could also try a higher class of home decoration by splurging on a Faberge Egg. The "Gold Crown" model, with its golden crown, will show him he's the king of your world for a mere $5,000.

Better than that (and an all around more pleasant way to express your love) is a gift of a crystal statue. Perhaps an "Our Love" sculpture from Steuben. It's a solid block of crystal with an engraving of two swans whose curved necks combine to form a heart. It's a great way to tell her you love her for $8,000.

Does he bring sunshine into your home and into your life? Here's a great way to show him that. The lyrics of "You Are My Sunshine" have been genuinely hand-written and signed by its writer, Jimmie Davis (who was also the governor of Louisiana not once, but twice). Because of his death in November 2000, this one is great for collectors as well. On the finest acid-free archival paper, it goes for $25,000. Go on, tell him how he brightens your day!

ISLAND HOPPING

Would you rather spend your millions on vacations than hard merchandise? Take your lover on a trip! Of course, there's the "typical" trip to the Riviera, but those beaches can get crowded, and Europeans still haven't caught on that most people don't look very good in Speedos. The bare breast thing they have down pat.

But there comes a time in everyone's life when you just have to leave crowded beaches, lines to the bathroom, and tacky tourist shops (even in the Riviera) behind. When that time comes, look into getting hold of your own private island. It's the absolute ultimate in luxury, and there is no better way to assure some time alone with the one person you love most. Your own sandy beaches all to yourself, acre upon acre of land to do whatever you want. All it takes is money.

There's actually quite an assortment out there. If the Mediterranean is more your taste, there's plenty to go around. If you like it cold, get some land off the Scandinavian Coasts or near Western Canada. Islands off Australia and New Zealand are available for the super-rich hardcore surfer. You can camp near Africa or South America if you like a more tropical feel, and, of course, there are plenty of islands in the Caribbean for the best in relaxation. If you prefer freshwater, there are even islands in the great lakes and some of the great rivers of the United States.

How much does all this cost? Actually, not as much as you might think. Islands are available from just $85,000. Of course, that's a measly 1-acre spot off the coast of Sweden. A 98-acre island in Lake Huron, though, goes up to $395,000.

Do you like the Canary Islands so much you'd like to buy one? Be prepared to shell out cash in excess of $2,000,000. Yes, having your own island gets pricey, up to as much as $7,500,000 for a spot off the Italian coast, or $25,000,000 for your own place in the Bahamas. It may sound like a lot of money, but it's nothing compared to the prestige of saying you own an island and the fact that you can take your lover there and traipse all over the island naked without worry of authorities or hostile natives.

JUMPING JEWELRY!

One of the easiest ways to go out into the shopping world and spend a fortune before you even notice the digits in your bank account balance shrinking is to go out on a spending spree for silver, gold, platinum, diamonds, and pearls.

We're not talking the cheap stuff, either. We're talking about gems such as a platinum diamond line necklace with eighty-five diamonds strung all the way around from Tiffany's that runs a modest $120,000. Remember, though, a lady of elegance never loads herself with all of her fine jewelry in one night out. It's far better to have one or two stunning pieces (matching pieces, if two) that will give you a good sparkle, but not so much to make yourself so bright that everyone shrieks in terror and has to don their sunglasses to block the glare coming from your earrings, necklaces, bracelets, rings, tiara, anklets, and belly-chain.

If you want to start (relatively) small, you can go for something simple like a fern leaf-shaped diamond brooch for a paltry $7,250. It will add a little sparkle to her dress without overshadowing her smile.

Perhaps she'd rather have a nice bracelet? Well, there's a nice Platinum Bracelet from the Etoile collection for just $12,750. Or, you can go with a Diamond Hexagonal Link Bracelet, a flashier piece for $24,000. To go nicely with that would be the ring from Tiffany's diamond petal collection for $15,000.

Is her neck looking a little bare? Not too showy would be an 18-inch necklace strung with cultured pearls for about $11,000. More on the hip side would be a choker from the Vannerie collection, which has 853 round brilliant diamonds—a steal at $42,000. If you truly wish to adorn your neck in extravagance, the clear choice is a platinum necklace with a huge Colombian emerald surrounded by diamonds from the Ashford collection for a whopping $145,000.

On the guy's side, perhaps his old Timex wristwatch is looking a little beat up? It's time to upgrade to that old status symbol of the elite super-rich, the Rolex. Sure, Rolex has some lower priced (again, relatively) models, but to really make an impression, go with the President Platinum for $37,000 or, even better, a Platinum diamond bezel model for about $75,000.

Guys, listen carefully. If she's going to get you a watch like that, it may be time to pop the question. Even though they may not admit it, women compete fiercely in the "I have the biggest diamond ring" game. In that department, many jewelers will help you put together the perfect engagement ring for the love of your life.

First of all, don't go with anything less than platinum for the ring and mounting. It's more precious than mere gold. As far as the diamond goes, you can go for a cute smaller carat weight for less, but just ask your girlfriend, size matters. Besides, you can get quality along with it—a good ring of platinum with a quality stone of say, 10 carats will only run you $305,000 or so. But can you even put a price tag on love and romance? Yep—$305,000.

A GIRL'S BEST FRIEND

Okay, if you're going to drop that much, or anywhere near that much, cash on an engagement ring (even if it's imaginary cash on an imaginary ring for an imaginary fiancé), you owe it to yourself to learn at least the basics about shopping for a diamond. You may have heard something about the four Cs to look for, but it's worth the investment of time to learn what they stand for, so you can avoid being a cheap, clueless, and careless consumer.

Starting off with the very basics, you may want to know what, exactly, a diamond is. Why are they so expensive? Is it because they're supposed to symbolize love? Or do they symbolize love because they're so expensive? Is there a global conspiracy between women and diamond miners?

Simply put, a diamond is crystallized carbon in a pure (or nearly pure) form. Because carbon is one of the strongest elements found on the Earth, diamonds are the hardest transparent substance on the planet (that's why they can cut glass). Diamonds are so strong that they're actually used in some cutting tools and abrasives. The final quality that makes diamonds so special is their ability to reflect light. Due to their crystalline structure, diamonds have a distinctive ability to collect light within itself and shine it outward with a stronger and more concentrated brilliance. Hence, the "sparkle."

Back to those four Cs. Since we're playing with an unlimited budget here, they're the most important things to consider when purchasing the diamond. They stand for cut, clarity, color, and carat. All of these factors are individually important in determining the quality of a diamond, and they all combine to determine the value of every unique gem.

If you're hearing terms like "brilliance" and "fire," what's being talked about is the diamond's cut. These luxurious and dramatic sounding words refer to how much and how brightly the stone sparkles. The degree of sparkle, sorry—the amount of fire flowing from a diamond is largely determined by its cut.

Cut is graded in terms of being ideal, very good, good, fair and poor. It sounds simple enough, but we're sorry to say that this is the easiest scale of diamond quality to remember. It also loses some of its simplicity when you find out that a typical round diamond has anywhere up to 58 facets that need to be aligned in precise geometric relation to one another—all on a surface that's usually smaller than your pinky-fingernail. Sounds like a job requirement for diamond cutters should be tiny fingers to make all those cuts.

On an ideal cut diamond, any light that enters the stone from the top is bounced through its sides and reflected back up through the top portion with all the bezels, called the crown. The more accurately the light is directed by the cut of the gem, the more brilliance a stone has, the more it sparkles to the eye, and the more valuable that diamond will be.

Next, we come to clarity. It's rare to come across a diamond that has no flaws, though not so rare that you can't find a few at any given jewelry store. Hmm, maybe the diamond industry just likes us to think they're rare so they can push up the price.

Regardless of any conspiracy theories, flaws in a diamond can come both internally and externally. External flaws are mostly scratches resulting from wear and tear or errors in the cutting process. More important to the quality and value of a diamond are internal flaws, called inclusions.

For the most part, inclusions come in three forms: Dark spots, clouds, and fractures (or feathers). Dark spots are just that—spots of carbon inside a diamond that are nearly black. Clouds are minute inclusions that can't be clearly seen, but degrade the transparency of the stone. Fractures are the most common of inclusions. They are breaks and fractures within the chemical structure of the stone. Unfortunately, it seems, not all diamonds are created equally.

The grading scale of diamond clarity is as follows. FL (flawless) is the top grade a diamond can receive. A diamond is named flawless if no inclusions can be seen under a 10-power jeweler's magnifying glass. Next on the scale is IF (internally flawless). A diamond of this classification may show some slight superficial damage to the exterior, but its internal structure is not broken in any way.

Down from there is VVS_1-VVS_2 (very very slight inclusions, with sub-grades of 1 and 2). To the naked eye, these diamonds appear to be flawless. Even with a jeweler's magnifying glass inclusions of this grade are difficult to detect. Then, there's VS_1-VS_2 (very slight inclusions, also graded in severity between 1 and 2). Again, these cannot be seen with the eye alone, and are still difficult to catch with magnification, but these flaws are slightly larger than the previous category.

The next grade is SI_1-SI_3 (slight inclusions, this time going from 1-3). In this class, the flaws begin to become visible by the human eye without magnification, but only if you really really squint hard under good lighting conditions. Until you get to the sub-3 class, that is. Inclusions of that size can be seen rather easily.

Last (and least) on the diamond grading scale is I_1-I_3 (imperfect). These flaws are seen with the naked eye without trouble. I_1 stones are still pleasing to the eye, but when you get down to I_3, you're talking about the Quasimodo of diamonds.

The third C that should be on your mind now (if it isn't Confusion, Consternation, or C-ya later!) is for color. "What?" you may be asking, "I thought diamonds were supposed to be colorless!" Well, the absolute top grade of diamond is. After the part about clarity, though, you should know that few diamonds are perfect enough to be of the highest quality. Most diamonds have a natural shading of yellow in them.

As color should be an easy scale to grade, the diamond industry had to throw a little complication in there, grading color by both groups and letter grades. Don't worry, though, it's still fairly manageable. The categories are colorless, near colorless, faint yellow, very light yellow, and light yellow.

These are pretty self-explanatory, but then you get into the letter grades. As of now, the best grade a diamond can receive is a D. (Don't you wish that had been true in school?) D through F (unlike the school system, they include the E) are the colorless category. From there, the more yellow you get, the further down the alphabet you go. G through I are near colorless, J through M are faint yellow, N through R are classified as very light yellow, and S through Z are light yellow.

For the most part, the further down you go, the lower in value you get. The twist comes in when you get to X through Z. These shades are just about as rare as colorless stones, and their color is seen to be more pleasant a shade of yellow. Fancy yellow diamonds, as they are called, compete in value with their colorless counterparts. Until someone finds an A, that is.

There's also a brown color group, but trust us, you don't want to give a lady a brown engagement ring!

The final C in the wonderful world of diamonds stands for carat. This is the simplest, yet most complex aspect of a diamond. The simple part is that it only measures the weight (and therefore size) of a diamond. The complexity comes in when you ask that age-old question, "does size really matter?"

To some, size is indeed the most important aspect of a diamond. They don't care how pristine a stone may, or may not, be as long as they have the biggest rock on their finger.

In terms of value, however, size only matters if the other factors fall into place as well. The better the cut, clarity, and color of a diamond, the higher its price-per-carat. Therefore, a 1.11 carat diamond with a very good cut, a color grade of H, and a clarity of I_1 is less valuable than a .9 carat stone with an ideal cut, color grade of G, and a clarity of SI_1. One other aspect to look for is shape. This may not have much effect on a stone's value, but some may say that a round cut diamond, being the most popular style, will yield the highest resale value (in case he pisses you off and you decide to pawn the thing). Other shapes are marquise (the top kinda looks like a football turned sideways), pear (your standard teardrop shape), oval (egg-shaped), heart (this one should be obvious), princess, radiant, and emerald. These last three are all rectangular shapes with different styles of beveling on the crown.

Armed with all this knowledge, go out there and seek an ideal cut, flawless, colorless diamond of the highest carat weight you can find! Hey, money is no object when it comes to love (and fantasy).

5

ROMANCE FOREVER

Whether you're married, going steady, common law housemates, or simply hopeless romantics, it takes a lot more than joint bank accounts and flowers on your anniversary to keep the sparks flying long term. Commitment is one thing, passion is another. But to have both, now that's romance!

But what do you do when date night equals the new Adam Sandler flick and a pizza; or Valentine's Day means stale chocolates and flimsy flowers; and foreplay means turning off the TV?

Not to worry. The following pages contain everything you need to know about keeping romance alive, even after the thrill has chilled a little. From spicing up your weeknights to romantic weekends, from passionate poetry to saucy snacks, you'll be eating out of each other's hands in no time.

ROMANCE & SEDUCTION
HOW TO
KEEP IT UP

Believe it or not, romance and seduction are relatively new concepts—for human beings anyway. Wild animals have always performed elaborate courtship rituals involving colorful plumage, "romantic" hoots that sound like squeaky brakes, and pheromone-filled nocturnal emissions with that special *eau de skunk* fragrance. Humans, however, have proved themselves to be nowhere near as inventive or sensitive as their four-legged friends.

People for centuries have searched for ways to keep love alive. Take the ancient world, for instance. Modesty was almost unheard of and nakedness was as common as the plague. Genitalia, far from being considered obscene, were instead displayed prominently. In Egypt, sun worshippers of both sexes donned expensive oils and little else, except for an occasional transparent linen for the ladies and a beaded skirt for the gents.

But when it comes to seduction and romance, men and women can take a different tack. The Phoenicians clearly were a male dominated culture. The name for their chief God, Asshur, was derived from the same word they used for

penis. To top it off, so to speak, they practiced the pretty unromantic custom of having their young women impale themselves on the stone phallus of Asshur prior to their wedding night.

Today, there's still a gap. Do women want a strong man who can cry? Do men want a throwback who waits for them to open the door, or an independent person who stands as an equal. Or maybe you don't want to think about it.

Passionate Poetry

One Day I Wrote Her Name Upon the Strand

One day I wrote her name upon the strand,
But came the waves and washed it away:
Again I wrote it with a second hand,
But came the tide, and made my pains his prey.
"Vain Man," said she, "thou do'st in vain assay,
A mortal thing so to immortalize,
For I myself shall like to this decay,
And eek my name be wiped out likewise."
"Not so," quoth I, "let baser things devise
To die in dust, but you shall live by fame:
My verse your virtues rare shall eternise,
And in the heavens write your glorious name,
Where, whenas death shall all the world subdue,
Our love shall live, and later life renew."

—*Edmund Spenser (1552-1599)*

WAYS TO KEEP GOING

For centuries people have continued to make incredible efforts to stay attractive to their mates. In medieval times, women shaved their eyebrows and plucked out their lashes, a practice still alive in the back streets of Los Angeles. For the gents, the fashion was dominated by fanciful codpieces (otherwise known as "cods"), which often enhanced their owner's attributes.

Sixteenth-century women used wooden corsets to achieve an unnaturally narrow waist and a wide hip line, while the men of this period preferred padded doublets and those always-sexy, tight-fitting hose. The tailors of the 17th century finally lowered the neckline for women, while the men trotted around in silk and lace and yelled, "Oh, behave!"

Seduction secrets of the women of the 1800s included high-waisted dresses worn with little underneath and wetted with lavender water to make them hug their bodies. (When's *that* one coming back in style?) Men, on the other hand, wore tight pantaloons, knee breeches, and make-up. By the 19th century, of course, the more traditional roles of women in dresses and men in suits ruled the everyday, punctuated by flappers of the '20s and the mini-skirts of the '60s.

Nothing comes closer to saying romance and seduction than the fanciful folds of modern fashion.

From silk boxer shorts to stiletto heels, clothes are the human being's answer to ornate plumage and the mating dance. (Minus the stinky pheromones!)

Women, of course, have a leg or two up on men in this desirous department. Their arsenal of seductive wear spans the gamut from expensive perfume to even pricier evening gowns, with everything from negligee to necklaces. Want to turn him on after a ball game some boring Tuesday night? A flashy red number from the bottom of your lingerie drawer and a pair of black heels send a crystal clear message. Dining out for Valentine's Night? Show up wearing the same number under your evening coat and see how quickly he cancels your reservations! See how easy that is?

Guys, on the other hand, have a lot less to work with. Snug jeans are a turn-on, but too snug and your lady friend will have you the butt of snide comments at tomorrow morning's coffee break. An unbuttoned shirt may mean either, "Run your fingers across my chest" or "Do you know how to sew?" Other than that, the question usually comes down to "boxers or briefs?" and "clean or dirty?"

THE **BOOB** TUBE

There is no mistaking that one of the biggest factors in introducing seduction into modern society has been the advent of television, more specifically the introduction of paid advertising. The battle cry of modern programming, from newscasts to pitchmen, is that "sex sells." Kissing in the rain. Feeding each other overripe fruit. Painting your boyfriend's nails. A man with a baby in his arms. A woman stranded with a flat tire, waiting for a prince to show up in his late model Saturn. All of these and more constitute the American media's idea of romance and seduction.

THE I.C. PERSEPHONE CORSETS

"JESSICA"   "CESSELA"   "MINUSKA"

TOP 10 WAYS TO KILL THE MOOD!

1. Leaving the bathroom door open after heavy usage.

2. Forgetting to brush your teeth for a few weeks.

3. Having C-SPAN cranked up in the background.

4. Referring to all his body parts by their clinical names.

5. Cameras flashing everywhere!

6. Inviting her into your tub of fried chicken grease.

7. Playing a John Tesh CD.

8. Trying to mimic everything you see on the Adult Channel.

9. Constantly asking if every new position makes you look fat.

10. The sudden realization that he resembles George W. Bush!

Many Americans, of course, buy into it.

Want to get a hot date, like the beauty in our commercial? Here, just drink this diet cola. What, can't you hear those slurping sounds? No? Then eat this chocolate bar. See how it slides suggestively between the model's collagen lips?

Like a lot of other things, TV has given romance and seduction a bad rap. After all, it's more than just candy and soda that makes your lover respond.

Much, much more.

LIVE-IN LOVE

If you've ever done it for any amount of time at all, living together isn't always the beach party it's cracked up to be. Yes, it sounded great, at first. Sure, it looks great on all those lovey dovey commercials where the stud in the boxer shorts and the hottie in the halter top eye each other seductively in the tiny bathroom while he shaves and she watches. And, yes, even those kinky Uncle Ben's commercials have been known to steam up a few TV screens by showing that couple getting aroused by the cooking rice.

But in real life, he's probably been wearing those boxer shorts so long they can stand up by themselves, and if she steps on his toes one more time in their cramped bathroom, he's likely to use that razor in his hand for more than just shaving. Ah, the joys of live-in love. But just like everything else we've discussed, you don't have to follow the same path as everybody else. Here's how to love living together.

HOBBY HOUNDS

You don't hear much about hobbies these days. In fact, the last time you admitted to having one was probably on your very first resume way back when. After all, with twelve hour workdays and weekends spent trying to forget all that overtime, who can indulge in the luxury of a hobby? But don't overlook this simple yet effective tool for adding a spark to your love life.

Who cares if you can't sew, paint, or even paint-by-numbers. Making your lover something, especially when it's for your shared home, is about as romantic as it gets. Few crafts, even in this hurried modern world, are quick and painless, and your lover will appreciate the time and effort put into her gift, no matter what it looks like when it's done.

But why make it one-sided? Spend a Sunday at the crafts store and pick a project that takes two to complete. If crafts aren't your things, join the throngs and head down to Home Depot for a project that will make your live-in loft more livable. Either way, you'll be doing something constructive, and you'll be doing it together, and isn't that what really counts?

BACK TO SCHOOL

No one says you have to stay at home just because you live together. Why not branch out and check into the local college or adult program and take advantage of the nightly programs offered. From computer classes that could help your career to healthy cooking classes that could help your cholesterol, you're bound to find something that piques your interest.

Whether it's just for fun or an investment in your future, and maybe even your future together, you'll soon start looking forward to your weekly or twice weekly visits "back to school." Plan a weekly dinner around your class and spend time before or after class cozying up in the library "studying."

Furthermore, these hidden venues are a great place to feel like kids again as you sit next to each other and pass goofy notes back and forth while you should be paying attention! And hey, now if you want to do your homework together, there won't be any grownups snooping around with bowls of pretzels right when you're doing a few twists of your own!

SLUMBER UPGRADE

So you walk into the local department store to buy your boyfriend something new to sleep in. You're tired of his baggy boxers, ratty underwear, and pizza-stained Budweiser T-shirt and have suddenly decided it's time for a change.

Besides, your mother is coming to stay with you for the weekend and, now that she's finally gotten over the fact that you're both "living in sin," you don't want her to think your sweet, sensitive life partner is a total slob in addition to being a total sinner.

Of course, it's been a while since you've actually bought anything for him to sleep in, let alone yourself, and it takes some time adjusting to the newfangled aisles in the scattered men's department.

First you have to wade through the sweatsuits, which only *look* like something comfortable to sleep in, and the boxer shorts, which could actually be something to sleep in, if they weren't weighed down with all of those buttons, patches, designs, labels, seams, and pockets.

"For a male and female to live continuously together is, biologically speaking, an extremely unnatural condition."
—Robert Briffault

Passionate Poetry

Love and Sleep

Lying asleep between the strokes of night
I saw my love lean over my sad bed,
Pale as the duskiest lily's leaf or head,
Smooth-skinned and dark, with bare throat made to bite,
Too wan for blushing and too warm for white,
But perfect-coloured without white or red.
And her lips opened amorously, and said--
I wist not what, saving one word--Delight.
And all her face was honey to my mouth,
And all her body pasture to mine eyes;
The long lithe arms and hotter hands than fire
The quivering flanks, hair smelling of the south,
The bright light feet, the splendid supple thighs
And glittering eyelids of my soul's desire.

—Charles Algernon Swinburne (1837-1909)

Finally, you arrive at an aisle which is directly located under a hip, with-it banner proclaiming, "Sleepwear," which you had already passed by several times before because the clothes underneath looked like something you might wear on a hiking trip to the Rockies instead.

There are coordinated sets of sweat suit gray rimmed with hunter green and navy blue. Long pants with drawstrings, a pocket on the side, a button fly and everything else one would *never* need in bed including pleated front panels, an extra button and cuffs at the hem.

A nearby display rack contains matching flip-flops, striped socks, a backpack and even a baseball cap emblazoned with the trendy logo, "Night Cap."

Does your boyfriend actually need a side pocket…in bed? What's it for, after all? His Swiss army knife in case a serial killer creeps in the bedroom window? Sleeping pills? Bubble gum? A paperback book to guard against insomnia? Beer nuts to guard against withdrawal in between baseball and football seasons? Or did some crack marketing exec. assume that all modern couples bring condoms with them everywhere they go these days? Even on a boring old Tuesday night? Or has the kid genius never heard of a nightstand, where most self-respecting sinners keep their prophylactics, vibrators, and porn mags? What about all the fancy piping and matching stripes, plaids, and patterns? Even if you *did* buy him such elaborately executed sleepwear, you'd never actually let him sleep in them. They were much too good for that. They would hang neatly in the closet, protected by hangers and plastic, awaiting such special occasions as Valentine's night, hospital visits and your one-year anniversary. Not to mention any and all natural disasters

TOP 5
Signs Your Slumber Party's A Bust

 5 — "Lights out" really means, "Lights out."

 4 — There's way too much "slumber" and not enough "party."

 3 — "Spin the Bottle" replaced by "Spin the Bible."

 2 — "Get your cookies" really means "Get your cookies."

 1 — Members of the opposite sex must sleep in separate rooms.

"Never go to bed angry. Stay up and fight."

—*Phyllis Diller*

that forced you out of your apartment to stand on the sidewalk weeping and moaning with the ill-dressed and completely uncoordinated sleepwear-clad neighbors.

A teenage salesgirl in work clothes less dressy than the "sleepwear" you're currently considering not buying titters at your serious request for a pair of simple pajamas with manly prints such as duck decoys or golf clubs. Naturally, she has to call for her manager when you threaten to write a letter of complaint to the CEO of the company.

The manager, hardly older than the salesgirl, offers you 20% off of said sleepwear, which brings them down from "out of the question" expensive to "only just ridiculously" unaffordable. However, he reminds you, "After all…didn't you say your mother was coming over? With our unique line of coordinated, yet comfortable, sleepwear, your mom could stay much longer than a weekend. Why, with sleepwear like ours, she could visit for weeks on end and still never catch your—boyfriend—wearing anything unacceptable."

You consider his point carefully before buying all three shades of gray, hunter green bordered sleepwear, as well as the hat, flip-flops, and backpack. Who knows, maybe the bickering when the credit card bill comes in will take his mind off the fact that your mother's weekend trip just got extended—indefinitely!

"Laugh and the world laughs with you. Snore and you sleep alone."

—Anthony Burgess

PASSIONATE POETRY

My Love's A Match

My Love's a match in beauty
For every flower that blows,
Her little ear's a lilly,
Her velvet cheek a rose;
Her locks are gilly gowans
Hang golden to her knee.
If I were King of Ireland,
My Queen she'd surely be.

Her eyes are fond forget-me-nots,
And no such snow is seen
Upon the heaving hawthorn bush
As crests her bodice green.
The thrushes when she's talking
Sit listening on the tree.
If I were King of Ireland,
My Queen she'd surely be.

—Alfred P. Graves (1846–1931)

PECULIAR PROPOSALS

One way to give your lover a romantic high hat that will last for a long time is to take the giant leap and propose marriage—assuming you're both ready for it. Popping the question releases a flood of romantic feelings. So what's a good way to do it?

DATING DIARIES

One Day, Her (Dimestore) Prince Did Come...

My girlfriend, Robin, had worked on a cruise ship before becoming an elementary school teacher. She had often told me about the lonely nights at sea when the poolside steel drum band would play a calypso version of "Someday My Prince Will Come," just to remind her that things would one day get better.

When it came time to propose, I remembered this story and was grateful that our one-year anniversary was approaching, just in time for Halloween Eve. That meant there were plenty of costumes to choose from in the department stores.

When I finally had as many prince-oriented items as I could cull from the picked-over Halloween aisles, I put my covert plan into motion. Robin's principal gave me permission to sneak into her room during the last half-hour of the day and propose in front of her class. It was her first year of teaching, and as such, her first class was very special to her. I knew she would want them to be a part of this (hopefully) auspicious occasion.

As I was working at a junior high school right up the street at the time, I next asked my own principal if I could skip that week's faculty meeting for "personal reasons." She agreed, but soon caught wind of just how personal those reasons were. By the time I had changed from my shirt and tie into my complete princely regalia, right down to baggy green leggings, purple satin slippers, a bright red Dracula cape and a jeweled plastic crown, she had reconvened the faculty meeting. It was now being held in the parking lot...right beside my car!

> "A good marriage is at least 80 percent good luck in finding the right person at the right time. The rest is trust."
>
> —Nanette Newman

After my facial blush no longer matched the exact color of my cape, I hastily sped away from the other teachers' good-natured jeers and drove up the street to my girlfriend's school. The buses were already there, and of course the concerned bus drivers wondered why a tights-wearing, crown-capped, cape-flowing young man with four eyes and a goatee was sneaking up to one of the portables carrying a gray felt box.

I wasn't the only one sneaking that day, however. Just as my principal had "leaked" news of my proposal to my faculty, so had Robin's. Middle-aged heads, chalkboard-dusted sweaters, and numerous pairs of beady eyeglasses poked out from behind the numerous trees dotting my girlfriend's elementary school lawn. I have no idea who was watching these teachers' classes, but half of the school's faculty was hiding out behind those trees like something out of a bad Tarzan movie.

There were so many of them that their twitters at my hodge-podge prince costume nearly drowned out the sounds of my approach at the back of my

girlfriend's portable classroom. They were so loud, in fact, that I had to knock three times just to get her attention. When I did, I almost died from embarrassment at her, and the rest of her class', hilarious outburst at the sight of one unexpected, and sweaty, dime store prince at the back door.

Somehow Robin regained her composure and allowed me into her classroom; thirty very confused, excited and nervous 4th graders crowded around us as I bent on one knee in front of the chalkboard and proposed to my girlfriend of almost exactly one year. Meanwhile, her nervousness and shock before answering allowed plenty of time for the school librarian to enter the room with a video camera to record the entire scene for posterity. Not to mention the next day's televised morning announcements!

"Miss Ward," I croaked, forgetting the stately, prince-worthy speech I'd spent the entire night before composing, "Will you…marry me?"

"Yes," she finally gasped. "But…why did you come on the day when I'm wearing a FAT outfit?"

(Hint to all future proposers: Check with parents, sisters, roommates, etc., to see if the proposee's outfit is suitable for numerous pictures, videotapes, and possible nightly news appearances.)

Laughter and celebration then ruled the day, and a few of the more confused children leapt outside the door just as the final bell rang and announced to the entire school, "Miss Ward just got married!"

And, eight months later, she did.

But that's another story.

"Long engagements give people the opportunity of finding out each other's character before marriage, which is never advisable."

—Oscar Wilde

ENGAGE IN THIS

PASSIONATE POETRY

Well, it's game night again and, along with the rest of the cheering girlfriends sitting in the rickety stands, smelling of bubble gum and mosquito repellent, you settle in for yet another four-hour softball game. And, while you certainly admire your boyfriend's snug uniform pants and bulging cup, you do wish he'd quit that sophomoric habit he'd picked up of late: shaving numbers, letters and words into the back of his head.

Although you realize he's not the only one on the computer company's softball team to partake in such sophomoric shenanigans, he is the most outspoken. On his head anyway.

For while the rest of the team simply slices a simple #1 shape, or possibly his initials or jersey number, your man goes it one step further. At first, you thought it was

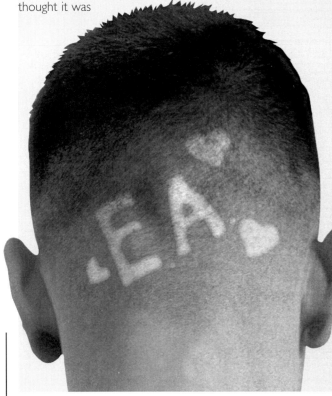

To a Husband

This is to the crown and blessing of my life,

The much loved husband of a happy wife;

To him whose constant passion found the art

To win a stubborn and ungrateful heart,

And to the world by tenderest proof discovers

They err, who say that husbands can't be lovers.

With such return of passion, as is due,

Daphnis I love, Daphnis my thoughts pursue;

Daphnis, my hopes and joys are bounded all in you.

Even I, for Daphnis' and my promise's sake,

What I in woman censure, undertake.

But this from love, not vanity proceeds;

You know who writes, and I who 'tis that reads

  Judge not my passion by my want of skill:

  Many love well, though they express it ill;

And I your censure could with pleasure bear,

Would you but soon return, and speak it here.

—Anne Finch (1620-1720)

5 Ways to Get Your Boyfriend to Quit Shaving words into his head.

5 Tell him it'd be much more "unique" if he shaved them into his pubic hair.

4 Shave in "666" while he's sleeping.

3 Tell him your last boyfriend had a much bigger "razor."

2 Tell him it draws attention to his bald spot.

1 Shave "goodbye" into yours.

"Many a young lady does not realize just how strong her love for a young man is until he fails to pass the approval test with her parents."

—Anonymous

beneath his cap. Another time he shaved your ATM password back there. Your favorite, however, was the time he'd shaved the shape of a heart smack dab in the center of his skull.

Call you sentimental, but that one really made you his favorite "athletic supporter."

Since then, however, as your second softball season of your otherwise blissful relationship stretched into its final innings, you have grown tired of the weekly ritual. He'd run out of original shapes, sayings, slogans, initials, combinations of numbers, geometrical patterns, and now each week he obsessed over some new thing to carve back there to win your approval and admiration.

You've told him, emphatically, that you couldn't care less if he ever shaved another single word back there. (Hint, hint.) But he'd replied that it was the least he could do to show his appreciation for your undying support.

Of course, he could have shown his appreciation in several other, more concrete ways, such as a dinner after the game or silver and gold, but you'd left it at that. He'd seemed so earnest.

Now, however, as your man's team comes up for its final bat of its

cute when, in honor of the first game you attended nearly a year ago, he had his favorite barber shave your initials onto the back of his head, which he revealed during the second inning by lifting up his cap while he stood in the batter's box.

"Aaahs" and "Ooohs" from the faithful girlfriends surrounding you drowned out the infield chatter, not to mention the announcer's booth. From then, as the season progressed, he'd continued to show his appreciation for your attendance in other "scalp writings" as well. One week he "wrote" your birth-date final game of the season, you're simply relieved that the shavings will be done and over for another few months.

Cringing, you hear his name called up next to bat and steel yourself for the inevitable unveiling that always occurs at this precise moment each game. Expecting yet another flower, heart, or phallic pattern to creep up amidst his ever-thinning buzz cut, you are baffled instead by a series of letters, followed cryptically by a question: WYMM?

A buzz electrifies the gabbing girlfriends seated next to you, as you quickly try to decipher the message as a group:

"Wild Young Mad Man?"

"Huh?"

"With Y'all M & M?"

"Does he want you to go buy him some M & M's, dear, or does he mean that rapper, Eminem?"

"Wild Year Moo Moo?"

"Is that some kind of sexual inside joke, honey?"

"Where Your Mom Mashes?"

"Is he commenting on your mashed potatoes, sweetie?"

Finally, the combination of letters sparks some distant, long-forgotten memory inside of your romantic head. Visions of veils and trains, bouquets and candles fill your head as, despite yourself, you rush the field like an overeager fan after an NCAA victory.

"Yes, yes, YES!" you scream as he drops his bat and, from deep inside his bulging cup, produces a fuzzy, gray, warm ring box.

"Will you marry me?" he asks officially, revealing the cryptic order of his shaved head for the clueless fans still buzzing in the bleachers.

Your tears are his answer, even as your wily feminine mind composes the first line of your handwritten vows: "Do you solemnly swear to love me, obey me, and never shave your stupid head again?"

MARITAL MUSINGS

Who says there's no romance once you get married? After all, you just have to work at it a little harder, and find things romantic that others might not. Here's how:

THEIR "TRASHY" SECRET

It was one of those stupid fights a couple has after five years of mostly blissful marriage. Ron had just come home from another long day at work. Of course, as appropriate for a modern married couple, Ron's wife, Tracy, had only gotten home a couple of minutes before, after her long day at work.

"Hey, babe," Ron said cheerily, dropping his keys and wallet off on the wicker table in the foyer.

"Don't you 'hey, babe' me," Tracy grunted over a load of laundry she'd just started.

Puzzled, Ron looked at his wife for a minute, just before the fireworks started, it turns out. She was still in her fashionable work outfit, tailored slacks, silk blouse, crested blazer. Her hair was pulled back and stray wisps from the long day spilled over

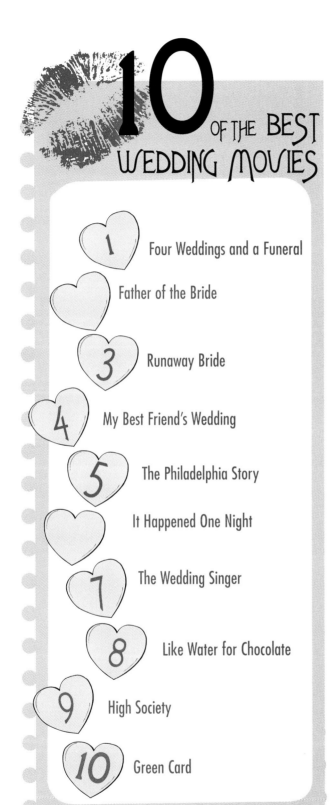

10 OF THE BEST WEDDING MOVIES

1. Four Weddings and a Funeral

Father of the Bride

3. Runaway Bride

4. My Best Friend's Wedding

5. The Philadelphia Story

It Happened One Night

7. The Wedding Singer

8. Like Water for Chocolate

9. High Society

10. Green Card

her beautiful face. Even after five years, catching her in moments like this one still took his breath away. If she only knew how—

"Don't you stand there in front of me with that 'innocent dreamer' look of yours, either," Tracy said, advancing on Ron with a handful of colorful plastic. "Would you mind explaining...these?!?" she finished with a flourish, opening her clenched fist to reveal several candy bar wrappers, no doubt left behind in the load of khaki work pants of Ron's that she was slipping into the washing machine.

He smiled for a minute, hoping his still-boyish charm might soften her concern.

"That's it?" she asked instead, slamming the candy wrappers down next to his wallet and keys. "You're just going to stand there and smile while your arteries clog by the minute?"

The upscale marketing research company Ron worked for had recently offered blood tests to all of its employees. When his results came in, Ron and Tracy were both surprised to see his cholesterol levels so high. Since then, she'd been urging him to eat better.

Snickers and Baby Ruths were definitely not on her list.

"Fine," she said, deserting her load of laundry and grabbing her purse and keys off the wicker table instead. "If you don't want to be around to enjoy our twilight years together, then I don't know why you ever married me in the first place."

Embarrassment at getting caught, frustration from a long day at work, and the "mother hen" tones of her afternoon "scolding" suddenly combined to raise the hackles on Ron's neck.

"Me either," he spat pettily, just before she slammed the door in his face.

Minutes later, of course, Ron felt the first twinge of post-flare-up guilt and quickly finished her load of laundry and began tidying up the house to make himself feel better.

Noticing a bulging trash bag in the middle of the kitchen floor, Ron caught his wife's not-so-subtle hint and headed out the front door for the quick trek to the apartment complex Dumpster.

On the way past the deserted tennis courts, a faulty seam in the dollar store trash bag stretched to its limit and split right in two. Cursing himself for making such a cheap purchase, Ron began stuffing the scattered coffee grounds and banana peels back into the remaining half of the bag.

Ron stopped when he noticed the glaring labels of products they'd never bought before and that looked completely unfamiliar. Fat-free cheese slice wrappers

"Marriage is like the army. Everybody complains, but you'd be surprised at how many re-enlist."

—Anonymous

hastily re-wrapped around regular, oily slices of cheese.

Low-fat sour cream containers still mostly full. Healthy Choice cereal boxes full of regular Raisin Bran and Apple Jacks. A coffee can claiming it contained "Half the caffeine of regular brands" still full of rich smelling, regular coffee. Lite lunch meat and dessert wrappers. Low-fat potato chip bags bearing regular, greasy Ruffles!

No wonder things had been tasting differently lately! Tracy had been switching healthy products out with Ron's usual, fattening ones! But when did she find

Passionate Poetry
Marriage of the True Minds

Let me not to the marriage of true minds
Admit impediments. Love is not love
Which alters when it alteration finds,
Or bends with the remover to remove;
O, no! it is an ever-fixed mark,
That looks on tempests and is never shaken;
It is the star to every wandering bark,
Whose worth's unknown, although his height be taken.
Love's not Time's fool, though rosy lips and cheeks
Within his bending sickle's compass come;
Love alters not with his brief hours and weeks,
But bears it out even to the edge of doom.
    If this be error, and upon me prov'd,
    I never writ, nor no man ever lov'd.

—William Shakespeare (1564-1616)

the time? In between their hectic schedules and long workdays, Ron could only imagine her getting up half an hour early each morning and stealthily replacing his usual chocolate chip cookies with dietetic ones by moonlight. The socks on her always-cold feet padding around the darkened kitchen floor while he slept two rooms away snoring peacefully, none the wiser.

Maybe she really did want him around for the rest of her life, after all.

Gathering up the devious garbage, Ron made two trips and dumped all of her "evidence." Then he washed his hands, grabbed his wallet and keys, and drove to the one place he knew he'd find her: The deserted movie theater near their apartment complex.

Once a week Tracy called from her office and asked Ron if he wanted to see a twilight movie with her after work. And once a week he declined, claiming some fictional last-minute meeting or looming deadline. The fact was Ron liked his movies at night, where crowds swelled, laughter roared, popcorn flowed and everyone had a good time.

Those cheapy twilight shows were for little kids and old folks.

Ron parked next to Tracy's car in the empty parking lot and bought a ticket to the first chick-flick he saw. Out of habit, he headed straight for the concession stand.

Balancing a diet soda, licorice, and a bag of popcorn, Ron found Tracy in the third theater he tried, watching exactly the kind of blaring action-adventure movie she never let him rent in the video store!

Creeping up behind her, Ron sat down with a flourish. She looked startled to see him, but not just because he'd snuck up on her.

"What are you doing here?" she smiled, their fight quickly forgotten. "You never come to the movies with me after work."

"I missed you," Ron said honestly, not telling her about the garbage discovery. "I'm sorry I blew up at you. I'm just—"

"We're both tired," she finished for him, reading his mind. "And you shouldn't be such a sneak and—I shouldn't be such a nag."

Ron held her face in his hands in that darkened theater and corrected her: "No—you should."

She smiled warmly until she saw the bag of popcorn resting gently on his handrail. "Honey," he explained, "I didn't get any butter on it. And look, it says these Twizzlers are 'low fat.'"

She looked surprised, if not exactly happy. "Well," she grunted, holding his hand as yet another car chase played out across the giant screen in front of them, "that's a start, I guess."

Not really, he mentally corrected her. It was more like a new beginning . . .

(RE-) DISCOVERING DATE NIGHT

"Date night" is a term that has become part of our popular culture as more and more long-term couples rediscover the art of "dating." After all, a date used to be something you did with a seductive stranger. You know, a cocktail or two at the bar while you wait, some harmless flirtation until you're led to your table for a little food and a whole lot of footsie. Couples didn't date, they "did" dinner or dined in.

Not anymore, however. Today's cozy couples find that "date night" can be as refreshing as ever, and twice as much fun now that they know each other so well. To rediscover date night for yourself, just heed the following tips. Your "date" will be glad you did!

WEEKEND WARRIORS

Many cozy couples avoid going out on the weekend because that's when the "kids" are all out, crowding the best restaurants, filling up the movie theaters, and generally throwing a monkey wrench into their otherwise passionate plans. But don't let crowds of teenage puppy lovers get you down. Instead, why not avoid the chain eateries and movie theaters and try something different for a change.

Passionate Poetry

She Dwelt Among the Untrodden Ways

She dwelt among the untrodden ways
Beside the springs of Dove,
A maid whom there were none to praise
And very few to love:
A violet by a mossy stone
Half hidden from the eye!
Fair as a star—when only one
Is shining in the sky.
She lived unknown, and few could know
When Lucy ceased to be;
But she is in her grave, and, oh,
The difference to me!

—William Wordsworth (1770-1850)

Let your fingers do the walking through the yellow pages and find the address of a restaurant you've never tried before. Then call it up and get directions, and even make reservations if necessary. Okay, you may arrive at a hole-in-the-wall, but at least you'll be together to watch out for flies in each other's soup!

If you do enjoy a Friday night flick, why not skip that big blockbuster's first weekend and see something that's been out a while instead. The crowds will be smaller and you could just get an entire row to yourself!

If dinner and a movie aren't your thing, check out local attractions such as planetariums, local theaters, or concerts. These struggling operations could probably use a few new customers, and you can enjoy a relatively uncrowded and romantic atmosphere while doing a good deed at the same time!

"Life is the flower for which love is the honey."
—Victor Hugo

20 MOST ROMANTIC SONGS OF ALL TIME

1.) "I Swear"
All for One
2.) "I Do (Cherish You)"
98 Degrees
3.) "Always"
Bon Jovi
4.) "My Heart Will Go On"
Celine Dion
5.) "You Were Meant for Me"
Jewel
6.) "Every Breath You Take"
Police
7.) "Truly, Madly, Deeply"
Savage Garden
8.) "Faithfully"
Journey
9.) "Open Arms"
Journey
10.) "Greatest Love of All"
Whitney Houston
11.) "Tonight I Celebrate My Love"
Roberta Flack & Peabo Bryson
12.) "Endless Love"
Lionel Richie & Diana Ross
13.) "Can't Take My Eyes Off You"
Lauryn Hill
14.) "Lost In Your Eyes"
Debbie Gibson
15.) "Everything I Do, I Do It for You"
Bryan Adams
16.) "Amazing"
Lonestar
17.) "Have I Told You Lately"
Rod Stewart
18.) "Stay"
Lisa Loeb
19.) "The Power of Love"
Celine Dion
20.) "Breathe"
Faith Hill

HOT FOR A HOUSE OR: A
REAL (ESTATE)
COMMITMENT

Frank and Marie walked through the house, carefully eyeing the features the real estate agent described in exhaustive detail.

"These stone urns at the corner of the pool are a feature unique to houses of this period," she said, then paused for effect. "The *finer* homes in this area will have these. It's part of the Spanish Mediterranean revival design that was popular during the 1920s. And of course this is one of the most historic and *beloved* areas in all of Madisonville."

Frank was having a flashback to the film *American Beauty*. He was beginning to understand why Kevin Spacey's character, who was married to a real estate saleswoman, was always stoned. But Marie was absolutely starry eyed. She wasn't listening so much as absorbing the descriptions through every pore.

How they landed here, looking at a house where a year ago they couldn't even afford to maintain the lawn, seemed more like a movie than reality.

They both worked at a dot-com that had limped along until it was purchased by a much hotter dot-com. This one came with money, customers, and stock options. Frank and Marie didn't know what a stock option was, but they both knew how to do their jobs. A graphic designer, Marie laid out page after page of Web links, and Frank made sure they worked. The "hits" kept on coming to the segment they worked on, "'50s R&B Songs," and they received not only their regular paychecks, but a notice that their options had started to kick in.

Marie—lanky, soft spoken, and striving for an Uma Thurman look—finally asked the question: "What do we do with these?"

They lived together and pooled their money, and while Frank knew almost as little as she did about stocks, he decided to take charge. He called his Dad, who was an executive with a Fortune 500 company. Frank, who sported a shaved head and was still growing (though his zits were finally going away), tried to sound all business.

"Hey, dad, we're getting something called stock options. So, like, what are they?"

"How many?" his father asked, wondering whether there were enough of them to affect his son's financial future.

"Uh, I don't know," he responded between sips of Yoo Hoo Plus.

"Well, usually there's some document that records how many you have," his dad explained, "when they can be exercised, and what price."

"I'll call you back."

They had stuffed the option statements in the kitchen drawer with their paycheck stubs, matches, rubber bands, pens that didn't work, a screw driver, and a ball of twine they had used to wrap a package two years earlier. Frank dumped the drawer out on the floor, and he and Marie tried to sort out the options from the junk. Frank found a coupon for 75¢ off a package of Nips. "Wow, this is worth something," he said.

Soon they stacked up the options and looked at the dates, the amounts, and the price.

"Uh. Let's see," Marie said. "We have 45,000 shares that can be purchased any time after next month for $3 to $5 per share. What does that mean?"

Back on the phone, Frank explained their situation to his Dad, who was ready with a calculator and a copy of The Wall Street Journal stock pages.

"Let's figure what we have here," he said in his best parental tone. "Mormusic dot-com's symbol is MORM. Looks like you're doing great. The stock is selling at $67.50. How many shares do you say you have?"

"Uh, 45,000."

There was a long pause as his father calculated the number. "How many did you say?"

"Uh, 45,000."

"If you cash in those options next month, you'd have roughly $2,857,500. Are you sure that's right?"

"I don't know, we've just been throwing that stuff in the drawer."

Frank double checked to be sure he was right, said the number over to himself "two point eight million dollars" and hung up before his dad could give him investment advice.

Frank was stunned. He looked at Maria and his Nips coupon and knew his life was going to change.

"Hey, Marie, we might want to look for a bigger apartment or something."

But when Marie found out the dollar total, she immediately brought out all the real estate information she had been hoarding for months.

"How about a house?" she stammered, and the next thing he knew he was walking through mansions that seemed more fit for royalty than a computer programmer and a Web page designer, but, then again, maybe they were the new royalty.

Now, instead of staying late at work, they were out by five to look at another house. Their agent was one their friend Sam at work had suggested. He said she wouldn't "diss" them because they were so young. "Her son is working for buyafish.com over on Magoo Street," Sam said. "So she knows what we do, sort of."

The list of properties was endless: Frank Lloyd Wright knockoffs, Stanford White knockoffs, Greek revival, Spanish Mission revival, all

sturdy and lavish with rolling green lawns. They reeked of the kind of money Frank never thought he'd have at this age.

Out of character for Marie, she was persistent in pursing the real estate she had secretly dreamed of. She rubbed the banisters and fondled the frescoes with a sensuousness he only wished she had for him.

As the month wore on, Frank contacted a stockbroker his father recommended so he could do something called "exercise" the options. (They needed a work out?) Anyway, the broker seemed knowledgeable, and Frank wanted this over with. The broker droned on about how they needed to set aside so much for taxes and how to avoid short-term capital gains, and other jargon Frank knew nothing about. Finally, Frank simply said, "Marie wants a house, and so we need enough for that."

"How much for the house?"

"Uh, I don't know. Like $1 million."

"We can handle that," said the broker.

Whatever, Frank thought.

As the option deadline approached, Frank grew more and more nervous. He'd never owned a house.

He barely owned the Honda with 145,000 miles on it. Now he was moving into some place where you could get lost. But he never said a word to Marie.

Toward the end of the month, there were rumors swirling around the office about a big contract that had fallen through. And while Frank had never before watched any of those shows on TV about money (except *Who Wants to be a Millionaire?*), he now was glued to the late reruns of *Dollar Talk* and *Stock Sense*. It was about 11:30 one night when he saw a face he recognized. It was the company founder, a guy not much older than Frank, with droopy eyes and a calming voice. Frank heard him say that while the stock price was falling, the company was still as solid as ever, though profits were years away. He mentioned something about "stickiness" and turning more to "B2B," but there was a little graph charting the stock, and it looked like it was in a straight nosedive.

By the time the option date hit, the stock was selling for $1, which made the options Frank and Marie held worthless. The real estate lady stopped calling, and Marie put her decorating books and pencil drawings back in the closet.

"I guess we can renew the lease on this place for another year," Frank said one night as they sat at home with nothing to do. "We liked it here fine until we saw those other places."

Marie just sighed.

Frank felt in his pocket for his Nips coupon. At least that was something he could count on.

6

ROMANTIC DESTINATIONS

What could be more romantic than a trip, right? Well, there are trips and there are trips. After all, it's a little hard to be romantic in the Motel 6 up the road from your house. Or is it?

If home is where you hang your hat, romance is likewise something you bring along inside of you, wherever you go. From the beaches of Maui to the art fair up the road, any destination is as romantic as you make it.

To help you on this romantic journey, we've gathered a collection of romantic destinations that range from exotic to the everyday. But no matter how far you travel or how little you spend, this compilation of romantic destinations would be worthless without a little, or a lot, of good old-fashioned TLC—or one of the other cable channels.

SIRENS & MERMAIDS:
GOING OUR WAY?

So, you think Frank Sinatra and Elvis were the first to use crafty crooning to drive members of the opposite sex nuts? Try again. Long before Ol' Blue Eyes was playing gangster in Las Vegas and Elvis somehow made fringed white leather pants macho, there were some groups of women who sang seductive songs to lure potential lovers.

They were mythical creatures known as sirens and mermaids. Half animals and half women, they were one hundred percent seductresses, and they were damn good at what they did. Hey, would you expect the daughters of gods and muses to be slackers?

Like many timeless legends, the details vary from story to story. The most well known sirens, those of Greek mythology, had the legs of birds and the upper bodies and heads (or sometimes just the heads) of women, sometimes with wings, sometimes without; you may have seen some of these chicks' descendants around closing time at your local tavern.

They were supposed to have been very beautiful (from the waist up, at least), but even more seductive was the music they made. One legend has it that the three Siren Sisters succeeded in seducing one of the gods. They made an error in judgment, though, and went after one of the married gods. Naturally, the wife became wrathful and took vengeance—big time. She had the Sirens banished to an isolated island off the coast of Italy.

They lived out their lonely existence, alienated from associating with humans, but one god was merciful. Poseidon, the God of the Sea, took pity on them and blessed their heavenly voices, so that they could sing from the shores and lure sailors to their island. Has a seaman ever passed up an opportunity to visit with three lonely beautiful women? Okay, they had

PASSIONATE POETRY

Love Song

My love, we will go, we will go, I and you,
And away in the woods we will scatter the dew;
And the salmon behold, and the ousel too,
My love, we will hear, I and you, we will hear,
The calling afar of the doe and the deer.
And the bird in the branches will cry for us clear,
And the cuckoo unseen in his festival mood;
And death, oh my fair one, will never come near
In the bosom afar of the fragrant wood.

—William Butler Yeats (1865–1939)

to look past the bird-legs, but most sailors have seen much worse than that.

In a twist to make a soap opera writer salivate, the god's wife who had originally banished the girls heard of Poseidon's adventure, and acted. She didn't exactly want to go head-to-head against Poseidon, who was one of the most dominant deities, so she diverted her fury back to the Sirens themselves. She cursed them, making their passion for pleasure far beyond that of the mere mortals they were going to attract to them, and altering their emotions so much that they felt the need to slaughter all the men they loved.

Sure it sounds bad, but the classical writers claimed that those who perished by the Sirens died while in the height of sexual arousal. So effective were their seductions, the men not only willingly died for their love, but were happy to do so. (Note to the networks: The TV rights are still available!)

So insatiable was the Sirens' thirst for men and so irresistible their indulgent overtures, only two ships ever sailed safely past their Island. Jason and his rambunctious bunch of buddies known as the Argonauts survived with the help of Orpheus, who drowned out the Sirens' sounds with his own singing.

The only man ever to hear the Sirens' song and live was Odysseus. Before setting sail, he was warned by a sorceress of the danger he faced. Heeding the warning, Odysseus had his entire crew stuff wax into their ears, and had himself tied to the ship's mast, without the wax, so he could hear the song without having the ability to steer them off course, and so he could let his men know when they were safe to remove the wax.

From there, the legend goes in all kinds of different directions. Some say the Sirens were forced by fate to jump into the ocean and drown themselves once someone resisted their sensuous song. Some say that the Sirens lived on the Isle of Lesbos, and they eventually got sick of waiting for men to pass by, and so began lesbianism.

One of the most popular claims is that when they jumped into the sea, they learned how to breathe underwater, grew fishtails, and became mermaids, spawning a whole new race of creatures. (Actually, there are those who speculate that the

transformation from Sirens to mermaids came about by an error in translation, since the Latin words for "wing" and "fin" are strikingly similar.)

Regardless of how it happened, from the Sirens came mermaids. Originally, they played much the same part as well. The legend is that mermaids were often seen resting on rocks near beaches. Usually, they would be depicted as holding a hand mirror while brushing their hair and singing a lovely tune.

Either way, a mermaid's purpose was to lure the seamen with the beauty of her looks or her song, then pull her unsuspecting victims under the waves. Some say the mermaids hoarded the bodies of their victims, other say they brought them to an enchanted city under the sea. Either way, the poor old salt ended up dead. Even more gruesome is the idea that mermaids used the bodies of their victims as offerings to the sharks in exchange for safe passage through their waters.

With all the legends, myths, and stories of sirens and mermaids, the idea of a mermaid has come to encompass both creatures, and they have become ingrained in our folklore. The tales are varied, but Hollywood has convinced people to think of the mermaid as being gentle and seductive creatures rather than tempting murderesses. Just look at Daryl Hannah in *Splash*, or Ariel in Disney's animated version of *The Little Mermaid*.

BED & BREAKFAST & YOU

To start our little tour of romantic destinations, why look any farther than your own backyard? After all, the rise in popularity of those quaint and cozy bed and breakfasts have most likely brought one, two, or maybe even more to your very own neighborhood. So don't overlook the obvious and give these friendly folks a call when the time has come to take your romance on the road.

GET RID OF THE GADGETS

Any weekend or mid-week getaway should be hassle free, and that includes *not* bringing along the assorted and sundry techno gadgets required for today's modern workaday world. The beepers and cell phones, Palm Pilots and laptops should definitely remain at home, no matter how long you're going away or how far you travel.

Simply booking a romantic weekend at a gorgeous bed and breakfast and even opting for the "ultra-romantic" Hugh Hefner package doesn't mean you can get away with carting in your briefcase full of weekend work. Take a break and show your lover proper respect by turning all of your attention on him or her. After all, how romantic is a bubbling bubble bath if you're afraid your laptop might take a bath too?

SKIP THE SCHEDULES

Another thing to leave behind on your romantic getaway is your day planner. Whether it's electronic or old-fashioned, the planner's well-oiled schedule and a romantic getaway don't mix. After all, there's a reason most bed and breakfasts look like old Victorian gingerbread houses or antique doll houses: You're supposed to be going back in time. Traveling to a distant world where traffic was less congested, phone lines less busy, and couples lavished each other with passion and romance.

Laziness is included in the price of admission, and lounging is definitely encouraged. Whether it's sleeping extra, extra late and luxuriating at a late brunch in bed or simply rocking on the front porch with the other hopeless romantics, skip the sightseeing and gaze into each other's eyes. You'll never know what you might discover.

RESERVATIONS REQUIRED

Don't get lazy about your travel plans just because you're traveling less than 20 miles. Chances are, on any given weekend, or even any given weeknight, you and your lover are not alone in your hopelessly romantic notions. Bed and breakfasts are often overflowing with loving couples just itching for a cozy weekend away from the hustle and bustle of their daily lives, even if they're only a few blocks from their office buildings.

So do your research and plan ahead. Check out the Internet, scour the yellow pages, or better yet, show up in person and survey your bed and breakfast options before making a reservation. For starters, if you don't like the looks of a place, don't go there. Many a dilapidated hotel has started calling itself a "bed and breakfast" just to trade on the classier establishment's better reputation. After all, a bed and breakfast should take you away from the normal,

everyday blasé hotel room experience. So if it looks like a regular hotel, no matter what it calls itself, keep moving.

Also, don't book yourself into one of those commune-type bed and breakfasts that doesn't offer room service, doesn't have a lot of privacy, and insists on bringing all of its guests together for "mandatory" ice cream socials and nightly Trivial Pursuit marathons. What's romantic about all that? Room service should always be an option, and better yet, insist on it when you finally do make a reservation.

Also inquire as to the number of rooms, the number of other guests, the availability of food and other treats after hours.

SPECIAL PACKAGES, SPECIAL WEEKEND

To make the most of your bed and breakfast experience, make sure to seek out those bed and breakfasts that cater to loving couples with special packages such as the "wild wooing weekender" or "the

second honeymoon." These deluxe packages may cost a little more, but the romance quotient goes up exponentially with the additional price.

Such packages boast perks that include fresh roses on your dresser, chilled champagne, and chocolate-covered strawberries upon arrival, private romantic dinners in your room, and other such amenities ranging from in-room Jacuzzis to complimentary his-and-her bathrobes.

If you'd rather spare the expense and do some of the work on your own, however, why not "borrow" from the bed and breakfast flyer and whip up a special package of your own. For instance, tuck fresh flowers and bath oils in your overnight bag. Purchase matching sleepwear especially for the occasion, or buy those miniature bottles of your lover's favorite after-dinner drink for a nightcap. Any or all of these little touches

will be sure to light your lover's fire, and you won't have to burn a fist full of bills to get it started.

MISSING MEALS

No matter if you spend the entire weekend inside your room, don't go skipping meals. It's not good for your metabolism and won't slice your bill in half come check out time, either. They're not called bed and breakfasts for nothing. Meals, and not just in the morning, are often included in the room price.

Even if you're not hungry at your regular old mealtimes, get them to go or have them delivered anyway. After all, you never know when the hunger will strike, and having a tray of scones or muffins around after an evening love-in could just come in handy.

TOP 5 SIGNS You're at a BAD Bed and Breakfast

5 Your personal wake up call (from the warden himself).

4 Tea and scones for breakfast? Nope. Tootsie rolls and Jolt? Sure thing.

3 The rates seem cheaper 'cause they're by the hour!

2 That yellow stuff in the heart shaped tub ain't champagne.

1 Your complimentary Mace and Stun Gun welcome basket.

SECOND HONEYMOON (WHETHER YOU'RE MARRIED OR NOT)

You don't hear a lot about second honeymoons these days, perhaps because few of your friends are married, or maybe just because nobody takes them, married or not. After all, second honeymoons get a bad rap. Single people or couples who aren't wed feel they can't go on them, and even married folks figure they have to wait until they're retired and have the down time.

But nothing could be further from the truth. Travel agents and hotel desk clerks don't care if you're single, engaged, married, or divorced. They're just happy to have your business. And if you're looking for a great way to celebrate your love for each

other, and take a hopelessly romantic trip in the process, a second honeymoon provides a great reason to get out of town.

CAUSE to CELEBRATE

As the name implies, second honeymoons are cause for celebration. Traditionally, they are a wonderful opportunity for older married couples to renew and reinvigorate their undying love for each other with a long, romantic getaway full of room service and hanky panky. But where's the rule book that says you have to

"Honolulu, it's got everything. Sand for the children, sun for the wife, sharks for the wife's mother."

—Ken Dodd

be married to enjoy the benefits of rediscovering your love for one another?

Instead, why not give yourself a reason to celebrate?

Perhaps you've been together for two years without a single breakup, affair, fistfight, or broken dish! Yippee! Perhaps you've made it through your first year of cohabitation without becoming a codefendant in a conspiracy to commit murder trial. Yes! Maybe you've just spent the last three months in blissful love and need a break from the rat race. Yowza!

Either way, you deserve a trip down to the local travel agent, or even an online one, to find yourself a quick little getaway to somewhere romantic. Whether it's a tropical resort or mountain chalet, an oceanfront condo or a hotel penthouse downtown, the location is up to you. As are the reasons for going.

CAREFREE KIT

No matter where you go, make sure to bring the romance along when you pack an extra bag full of treats for you and your loved one. From scented candles to passionate potpourri, from sexy sleepwear to erotic love toys, make sure to bring this special kit along as your carry-on. After all, you don't want your love luggage to end up in Boise while your shoes and underwear come along for the ride.

If you're not comfortable packing, why not splurge and call ahead to the hotel and have them do the work for you. Clever concierges can usually find anything for anybody, and it's likely they've heard this type of request before. Perhaps the hotel even has a special package your travel agent didn't know about, or you

MOST ROMANTIC DESTINATIONS

Paris

Tahiti

Hawaii

Florence, Italy

Acapulco

Niagara Falls

Las Vegas

Rio de Janeiro

Venice

Rome

Tijuana

Canadian Rockies

Bahamas

Florida Keys

Martha's Vineyard

can create one. Either way, don't rely on the simple accoutrements of your hotel, lodge, or resort to be romantic. Pack a seductive suitcase, just in case.

UPGRADE FOR LOVE

Despite your budget, think of your "second honeymoon" as something special. After all, if it was just another weekend away, you'd be calling it a "weekend away." For this trip, you might want to haggle with the desk clerk, travel agent, or customer service representative and get the best room, package, or accommodations you can afford.

If it's $75 more for an oceanfront view, as opposed to a parking lot view, splurge. If the hotel with the fancy name and the monogrammed towels is $100 more a night than the chain establishment right next door, it might be worth the fancy soaps and complimentary

happy hour that budget buster affords you.

Check out the amenities while you're at it. If you and your lover equate a poolside cocktail or afternoon snack with romance, don't settle for a place with a

"A little girl at the wedding afterwards asked her mother why the bride changed her mind. 'What do you mean?' responded her mother. 'Well, she went down the aisle with one man, and came back with another.'"

—Anonymous

Coke machine and grab-your-own towels. Splurge for the place with the poolside bar and grill and let the daiquiris and potato skins come to you! If you're health nuts, check out a spa. Lazybones? Go for the deluxe room with open-air patio and killer view.

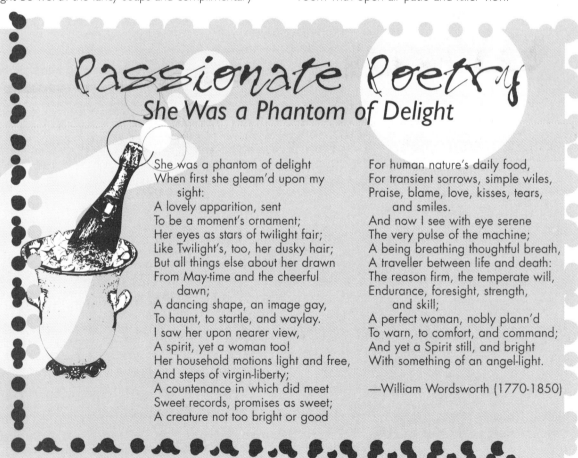

Passionate Poetry
She Was a Phantom of Delight

She was a phantom of delight
When first she gleam'd upon my
    sight:
A lovely apparition, sent
To be a moment's ornament;
Her eyes as stars of twilight fair;
Like Twilight's, too, her dusky hair;
But all things else about her drawn
From May-time and the cheerful
    dawn;
A dancing shape, an image gay,
To haunt, to startle, and waylay.
I saw her upon nearer view,
A spirit, yet a woman too!
Her household motions light and free,
And steps of virgin-liberty;
A countenance in which did meet
Sweet records, promises as sweet;
A creature not too bright or good

For human nature's daily food,
For transient sorrows, simple wiles,
Praise, blame, love, kisses, tears,
    and smiles.
And now I see with eye serene
The very pulse of the machine;
A being breathing thoughtful breath,
A traveller between life and death:
The reason firm, the temperate will,
Endurance, foresight, strength,
    and skill;
A perfect woman, nobly plann'd
To warn, to comfort, and command;
And yet a Spirit still, and bright
With something of an angel-light.

—William Wordsworth (1770-1850)

The choice is yours, but wistfully gazing out at the parking lot and wishing you were staying in the hotel across the street isn't exactly romantic, is it?

PLAN AHEAD

Since you're not even married yet, there's no sense in rushing your "second honeymoon." Planning, and especially booking, ahead allows you the chance to take advantage of a beautiful resort's slowest season, and best prices! Bug your travel agent to find out when the best time to travel to your destination of

choice falls on the calendar, and plan accordingly. Don't have a travel agent? Get one!

Not only will planning ahead get you great deals on places you might not have been able to afford otherwise, but it will give you something to look forward to while you're waiting for your time of departure. Buy a calendar and have fun marking off the days. Throw a party for two at the end of each month that goes by and build up the anticipation by shopping for special clothes or even a new set of luggage to mark the occasion.

Sure, your whole trip may only last one long weekend, but if you celebrate a little bit each month along the way, you'll be busy building up the excitement until you're almost ready to pop!

And what's more romantic than that?

ROMANTIC TRIPS

No matter what special occasion you're celebrating or how long you and your lover have been together, there's nothing like a nice, romantic trip to show each other just how much you care. From exotic resorts to sleepy sleepovers, the choice is all yours. To help you plan the perfect passionate pilgrimage, however, why not check out the different kinds of trips available.

OVER THERE!

Nothing quite says romance like a tempting trip abroad. And whether it's passionate Paris or libertine London, careful planning and the proper budget can make any trip over there a lot easier than you think. Hooking up with a

reputable travel agent is the first step, being honest is the second.

"We love because it's the only true adventure."

—Nikki Giovanni

You don't want to pretend to have more money than you do, and all travel agents understand that making their clients poor isn't the best way to reel in repeat customers. With enough lead time and a reasonable budget, most travel agents can work wonders these days. You may have to hook up with a package tour to make your dreams of roaming the Greek islands or wandering from Irish pub to Irish pub a reality, but being together will make all of the other trivialities worth it.

If you don't trust travel agents, the Internet is teeming with international Web sites all catering to the consumer with package deals that scream out both economy and romance. Be sure to read the fine print, however, and even if you don't want to avail yourself of a travel agent, try asking a local travel agent if they've ever heard of the tour operator or Web site. If they have, they'll tell you, and if they haven't, that's not necessarily a bad thing. Just be sure to cover your bases and tread carefully, and you should be all right.

After all, there's absolutely nothing romantic about getting ripped off in a foreign country.

COZY CRUISE

Nothing says "I love you" like you and your beloved sprawled by the pool, as you sip mushy fruit drink concoctions and watch the Atlantic Ocean slip by while your cruise ship sails along at a steady clip. Forget airplanes and rent-a-cars, hotel rooms and bumpy roads. Forget land altogether. Check out the unexpected pleasures of a cruising cruise ship, and enjoy ravishing romance while on the wide open seas.

From lavish buffets to "cozy" rooms just perfect for cozy couples, today's opulent cruise liners have

Passionate Poetry

There Be None of Beauty's Daughters

There be none of Beauty's daughters
With a magic like Thee;
And like music on the waters
Is thy sweet voice to me:
When, as if its sound were causing
The charméd ocean's pausing,
The waves lie still and gleaming,
And the lull'd winds seem dreaming;
And the midnight moon is weaving
Her bright chain o'er the deep,
Whose breast is gently heaving
As an infant's asleep;
So the spirit bows before thee
To listen and adore thee;
With a full but soft emotion,
Like the swell of Summer's ocean.

—Lord Byron (1788-1824)

everything you could ever dream of, and more. Rock climb for breakfast and lounge by the pool for lunch, in between meal after meal spent gazing adoringly into your lover's eyes as the stresses of your workaday world melt into the ocean far, far below.

Or lock yourself in your room and have the steward slide your six meals a day under the door! Who cares? It's your money, your cruise, and you'll need a lot of energy for your indoor itinerary!

ROMANTIC
RESORT

For today's techno-savvy traveler, the world is your oyster, which is especially good for lovers. Hop on the Internet and check out romantic resorts around the globe, all with the click of a mouse and a wandering eye. Take virtual tours of remote islands or tropical paradises without ever leaving your own home, and enjoy this virtual tour with your lover to make things twice as fun.

"Ooh" and "aah" over sandy beaches and towering palm trees, colorful bedspreads and expansive verandas overlooking lush waterfalls and crystal clear bodies of water. Thrill to tempting packages that take care of everything, from the flight to the room to the afternoon tea!

Don't feel like traveling too far? Check out the local talent and search for romantic resorts in your own backyard. You might be surprised at what your own city, county, or state has to offer when you explore the local locales either online or off. A mountain retreat, an oceanfront resort, a secluded hideout, or a romantic bed and breakfast might just be the tempting trip you're looking for, and when you can drive there in your own car, that's all the more money you can spend on loving luxuries once you arrive.

PASSIONATE PACKAGES

Take the hassle out of passionate planning with a perfect package. Nowadays travel agents recognize that their customers are not lazy, they're just pressed for time. Hence the need for a trip! So in the effort to keep those customers happy, they happily deal with clients who make their life easier by offering all-in-one packages that make their guests at home by doing all the work.

Check out all-inclusive packages at resorts like Sandals and Temptation, where everything from food and drinks to midnight snacks is included in the price of admission. Forget traveler's and wallet belts, leave your money at home and settle up before you even set foot on the plane.

There's nothing sexier than not worrying about money on a romantic getaway, and these places make it easy by providing your every need, all under the easy umbrella of "it's included!" The bill may shock you, but paying it off over time is just one of the many advantages of checking out these all-inclusive adventures.

ROMANCE
AROUND THE CORNER

Don't confuse a romantic trip with a retro check balance, however. It doesn't take an intercontinental plane ride or French to English dictionary to equate with romance, although it certainly helps. But even the most expensive, exotic, and extravagant trip can become a desirous dud if the romantic intentions aren't earnest. And if you've got the latter covered, anywhere you go is likely to be romance central.

So why not skip the travel agent and the savings account withdrawal, and find romance somewhere closer to home. While you're at it, why not look right around the corner?

SCENIC SETTINGS

No matter where you live, chances are your local chamber of commerce has found *something* to brag about in those handy brochures they give away to visiting businessmen and other dignitaries! Whether it's pristine beaches or rocky mountain tops, lush botanical gardens or historic battlefields, check out your town's information center or library to uncover secrets about your very own hometown. Then go visit them.

Perhaps there's a cheesy roadside attraction you've ignored not far from you and right off the Interstate. Use it as an excuse to go visit and book a room at the local chain hotel in honor of your visit. Once your cultural excursion is over, relax by the pool or sample all the treats at the local eateries as you revel in

"Music makes one feel so romantic, at least it always gets on one's nerves, which is the same thing nowadays."

—Oscar Wilde

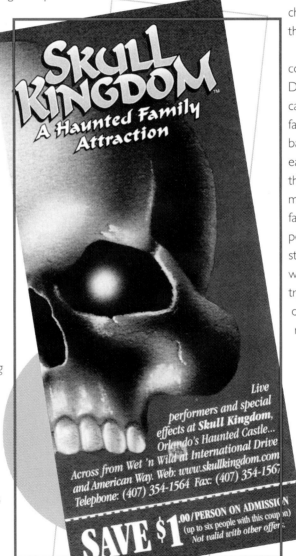

Live performers and special effects at *Skull Kingdom*, Orlando's Haunted Castle... Across from Wet 'n Wild at International Drive and American Way. Web: www.skullkingdom.com Telephone: (407) 354-1564 Fax: (407) 354-1567

SAVE $1.00/PERSON ON ADMISSION (up to six people with this coupon) Not valid with other offer.

hometown cheesiness and the chance to get away from the humdrum of home.

Maybe there's a big concert a few towns away. Don't grumble that you can't go because it's too far to go and then drive back. Book a hotel room early and stay long after the rock group or musician is gone. Pop your favorite CD by the performer in your car stereo and make it a weekend to remember by trying to sneak backstage or pretending to be music reporters.

No matter what your backyard has to offer, you'll never see it if you don't go looking, and there's nothing more romantic than adding a little adventure into your life. Even if it's nothing more adventurous than checking out The World's Biggest Ball of Yarn.

NO MORE
WINDOW SHOPPING

Perhaps there's a downtown hotel you and your lover visit, if only to grab a drink in the fancy bar downstairs. Perhaps there's an exit full of chain hotels, movie theaters, and souvenir stands you drive by wistfully every day on the way home from work. Perhaps you see a billboard for a local resort that looks way beyond your means. Quit dreaming, and start doing! There's nothing more romantic than a plan put into action, and your first step is to call that downtown hotel, take a detour through that highway exit, and dial the number on that scenic billboard!

Chances are, these places aren't as expensive, exotic, or as out-of-reach as you think. And if they are, ask for a local resident's special. If you get laughed at, ask for the resort or hotel's "off season." You could just get lucky. As for that highway exit to nowhere, however, why not drive off one Friday evening after work and find a place to stay for the weekend. Or just pick your lover up from work on a Thursday and make Friday a personal day to extend your long weekend.

Be spontaneous, and just pull off anyway. Didn't pack any clothes? Check out the local outlet stores or Mart for some cheesy duds none of your friends will ever see anyway. Use the giveaway shampoo and soap liberally and splurge on toothpaste and brushes in the gift shop. Throw caution to the wind and surprise your love, and yourself, with a trip out of nowhere that ends up taking you somewhere you've never been before.

And who knows where *that* could lead?

How to Say "I Love You!"

Ich liebe Dich (German)
Je t'aime (French)
Sarang Ham-nida (Korean)
Jeg elsker dig (Danish)
Wo ai ni (Mandarin)
Ngo oi ney (Cantonese)
Ik hou van jou (Dutch)
Sukiyo (Japanese)
Bahibak (Lebanese)
Ya tyebya lyublyu (Russian)
Eu te amo (Portuguese)

Ti amo/Ti voglio bene (Italian)
S'agapo (Greek)
Ina sonki (Hausa—Nigeria)
Yo te amo/te quiero (Spanish)
Kocham cie (Polish)
Seni seviyorum (Turkish)
Aloha au ia'oe (Hawaiian)
Myliu tave (Lithuanian)
Mahal kita (Tagalog)
Lubim ta (Slovak)
I ovelay ouyay (pig latin)

LOCALS ONLY

Forget the open road and the reservations. Maybe you just need some down time to explore a few locals only establishments you've never ventured into before.

"Love is the only game that is not called on account of darkness."

—M. Hirschfield

How about that funky coffee shop in the beatnik district? How about that musty museum you've been driving by for years? Maybe there's a new play at the local theater. Or a talent show at the local high school. Chances are, you won't have to go far to find something new and fun to do if you just fill the gas tank, pack a bag, and start exploring your own hometown.

When you get tired of cruising around, find a reasonably priced hotel or motel and check in for the weekend. Splurge on a paperback romance in the gift shop and take turns reading the dirty parts to each other in bed. Go skinny-dipping at 2 a.m. or close the lobby bar down singing karaoke or watching some sport you've never bothered with before. Bully the kids in the game room and play the best games for as long as you like and study the brochures in the hotel lobby for something new to do when you get sick of laying out by the pool or sleeping in.

You never know, your town just could take on a whole new meaning when you see it through the eyes of a tourist. Who knows? You could go home a lot happier than when you left!

PARTY TIME
SHORT TRIPS TO SOMEWHERE (WEIRD)

Although they don't occur as often as happy hour and aren't quite as regular as last call, parties can be passionate places to seduce, or be seduced by, sexy strangers. The happening music, the tasty snacks, the open bar, the cozy furniture, all combine to set the scene for rambunctious romance.

But beware, party people aren't always what they seem.

MIAMI TWICE

At first you weren't too excited about the upcoming Halloween costume party. Number one, you're not exactly the "costume" type. Number two, you'd have preferred to sit at home alone eating those six bags of candy you'd purchased. (Despite the fact that you haven't had a trick or treater knock on your hi-rise condominium door in the four years you've lived there.)

However, your manager from work was throwing it and, ever since you'd sent the wrong floppy disk to the local Kinko's and had close to a thousand copies of the wrong promotional material reproduced, you figured you could use the brownie points. And then some!

For a costume, of course, you'd done what any self-respecting grown woman would do in the same situation. Meaning you'd worn your most comfortable terry cloth robe and gone the easy route as Janet Leigh from *Psycho*. Sure, it didn't win you many points for originality, but at least you got to be comfortable and it didn't cost a dime.

Your manager was duly impressed and, to show you that there were still no hard feelings for the Kinko's calamity, introduced you to a "close, personal friend" of hers, currently dressed as Don Johnson from *Miami Vice*. Sure, the look was corny but, wasn't that the whole point of a costume party?

Besides, your terry cloth robe had taken all of three minutes to think up, find, and throw on. At least this guy had taken the time to sort through his attic and hunt his ten-year old outfit down in honor of the occasion. And hey, he obviously hadn't let himself go. If he could still fit into a 1980s fashion fad, he was obviously into keeping himself fit.

Besides, he was wicked cute and definitely had the look complete, down to the charcoal stubble beard and neon pink T-shirt inside the white cotton suit. Why, he'd even skipped the socks, leaving an inch of tanned ankle showing above his breezy alligator loafers. His hair was delightfully feathered and, unless the Miami police department had started issuing *underwear* holsters, he seemed glad to meet you too!

You spent hours discussing your favorite episodes and, in honor of the show's setting, drinking numerous daiquiris. Too numerous, it seems. As the last night of October slowly melted into the first morning of November, you found yourselves back at your place indulging in a few "vices" of your own.

When you sent him off the next morning, looking just as fresh as Don Johnson in his clothes from the night before, you promised to meet at a popular downtown bar that coming Friday to see if the sparks were still there.

And, when you both showed up at the local hot spot a week later, it was evident that they still were. What wasn't evident, however, was why he was still

dressed like Don Johnson. Again?

Sure, the shirt underneath the white jacket was turquoise instead of pink this time, but…Halloween was long over and the fact that people were giggling behind his back and the bartender kept calling him "Crockett" wasn't exactly a turn-on.

Could it be that he was just insecure and didn't want to risk turning you off (too late) since you'd seemed to like him in it so much the first time? Or maybe it was his "lucky" suit and he was wearing it again to show you that you were a source of great fortune in his life. Maybe his house had caught on fire that morning and, since he hadn't had a chance to climb back up into the attic and put his *Miami Vice* suit away until next Halloween, it was still sitting on his chair and was thus the first thing he'd grabbed.

At least, you hoped so. His answer, when you finally worked up the cocktail-inspired courage to ask him about it, was much more disturbing.

"This is my look," he explained as the dreams you'd quietly built around the two of you spending a sweltering and humid eternity together crumbled around you like a snow cone in South Beach. "All my suits look like this. The chicks really dig it."

There was more to his speech, of course, but you'd quickly tuned him out. You realized, all of a sudden, that your crafty manager had finally paid you back for that thousand-dollar Kinko's mistake.

In spades.

7
SEVEN

EVERYDAY ROMANCE

Keeping romance alive is the kind of challenge that baffles men and frustrates women. Let's say it's Tuesday afternoon around 2:30. It's no holiday, no special occasion, no birthday or anniversary, or even occasion for a little afternoon delight. How do you make that moment romantic? Perhaps it's a well-timed phone call after a lover's annual physical or a quick e-mail to say "I love you" in between business meetings.

Unfortunately, as committed couples grow more complacent about living together or celebrating yet another anniversary together, it gets harder and harder to make the effort to be romantic. We've all seen those couples who sit down next to us in restaurants, order dinner, eat it in quiet desperation, and leave without ever having said a kind word to each other, much less the waiter.

To avoid that kind of couple complacency, enjoy the following chapter and learn how to meet the challenge of putting more romance into every single day.

EVERYDAY ROMANCE

Halloween has plenty of treats for the diehard romantic and mistletoe's a no-brainer. But what happens when your love life is in dire need of a boost, yet the calendar says that the next declared holiday isn't for three months? (Unless you consider National Earwax Day a *very* special occasion, that is.)

Don't fret. In this age of animated e-mail greeting cards, 24-hour flower delivery, and special-interest groups creating their own holidays,

Hallmark be damned, there's bound to be an occasion worth celebrating right around the corner. Here are some tips to make romance possible any day of the year.

CREATE YOUR OWN HOLIDAY

Why do greeting card companies get to decide when you can send flowers, give sappy cards, and feed your lover high-caloric treats? Go them one better when you take out a sheet or two of scratch paper and create your very own holiday—from scratch. But where to start? Look to your lover for inspiration, of course.

Perhaps your four-month anniversary is in the offing. Maybe tomorrow is exactly one hundred days until his birthday. Or it could be that she just came back from the dentist with a clean bill of dental health? Who cares about the occasion, it's the celebration that matters.

Use your computer or pick up some poster board (you still remember where it is from your junior high school days, don't you?) and create a sign or banner for

Happy 15th Day without a Cigarette!

your brand new holiday: "Happy Fifteenth Day without a Cigarette!" Fold some construction paper in half and design a fancy greeting on the front, followed by some sentimental or romantic words inside: "Your breath has never smelled better!" or "No one misses old skunk breath!" Wrap an inexpensive but thoughtful gift, such as a chocolate cigar or those bubble gum cigarettes, and whip up or order dinner to mark the auspicious occasion.

DON'T FORGET THE LITTLE GUYS

St. Patrick's Day and the Fourth of July aren't the only holidays on the calendar these days. What about the "little" holidays? To find out what they are, subscribe to one of those free e-mail holiday reminders out there (you can't miss 'em) or do an Internet search for "holidays" to discover one of the many sites that track down a holiday for (almost) every day of the year. Check out something fun or funky to celebrate in the coming week, such as The Day Tissue Was Invented.

Buy a blank card and write a lovingly clever message inside, such as, "If you ever left me they'd have to invent the world's biggest tissue," and present it with a themed gift, such as something sexy wrapped in tissue or a corkscrew sticking out of her favorite bottle of wine.

Forget mistletoe and heart-shaped boxes of chocolate. Any holiday can be sexy with a little thoughtfulness. Even National Wear-a-Fig-Leaf Week! (Also see "A Year of Holidays," page 171.)

If you ever left me they'd have to invent the world's biggest tissue.

HAPPY HOLIDAYS

January 25th is Opposite Day

February 25th is Chocolate Covered Peanuts Day

March 6th is Dentist's Day

April 10th is Golfer's Day

May 12th is Limerick Day

June 4th is Old Maid's Day

July 14th is National Nude Day

August 18th is Bad Poetry Day

September 27th is Ask A Stupid Question Day

October 12th is International Moment of Frustration Scream Day

November 18th is Occult Day

December 26th is National Whiner's Day

HAPPY TUESDAY!

It's a well-known fact that Mondays suck, Wednesday is hump day, Thursday is Must See TV, TGIF starts the weekend, a quiet rock band named The Bay City Rollers taught us all that S-A-T-U-R-D-A-Y NIGHT spells Saturday night, and Sunday is for cuddling up with Starbucks and a big, fat newspaper under the covers. But what about poor old Tuesday?

After all, Monday is ancient history by the time Tuesday night rolls around, and the rest of the week is all downhill. Why not celebrate? As an extra bonus, unlike Easter or Groundhog Day, Tuesday happens every week! Why not create a new tradition by making every Tuesday just a little more memorable.

It doesn't have to involve numerous shots of peach schnapps at some all-night bar, naked sky surfing, or even dinner at a fancy restaurant. Instead, why not offer to pick up your lover and drive him to work on Tuesday morning. Even if it's out of your way, it's worth getting up a little early one day a week for the payoff after quitting time. After work, see an early movie and luxuriate by spreading (or making) out in a mostly empty theater. Become regulars at a cozy little bistro halfway between your apartments or right around the corner from home, if you're lucky enough to be cohabitating.

Or just pick up a different type of take-out food on the way home from work each Tuesday night; there must be more to Eskimo cuisine than Eskimo pies. Enjoy it over candlelight and with special music. (Are those whales singing?) Don't wait for Friday to show your lover that she can light up any night of the week—even Tuesday.

SURPRISE!

If committing yourself to doing something special every Tuesday is a little too burdensome (lazybones), then why not sneak up on your lover and surprise her when she least expects

IF THOU MUST LOVE ME

If thou must love me, let it be for nought

Except for love's sake only. Do not say

"I love her for her smile...her look...her way

Of speaking gently...for a trick of thought

That falls in well with mine, and certes brought

A sense of pleasant ease on such a day"—

For these things in themselves, Beloved, may

Be changed, or change for thee—and love,
*   so wrought,*

May be unwrought so. Neither love me for

Thine own dear pity's wiping my cheeks dry,

A creature might forget to weep who bore

Thy comfort long, and lose thy love thereby.

But love me for love's sake, that evermore

Thou may'st love on, through love's eternity.

—Elizabeth Barrett Browning
(1806-1861)

it. (Warning: This does not mean a loud "gotcha" as she walks down the dark corridor to your apartment or steps into the shower and you perform your near-perfect Norman Bates imitation.) Otherwise, morning, noon, or night, every day is a wonderful opportunity to find romance in unexpected places.

For instance, why wait until after work to bring romance into your life? Be the early bird and sneak out of the house one morning for a surprise breakfast in bed. Sure, it may just be no more than sugar-laced pastries and caffeine-loaded liquids, but what better way to face the day than with the idea that someone thought of you from the moment the day began.

If your average Sunday involves rearranging the battery drawer or your boxer shorts, set the alarm and head out for a day at the park or her favorite spa. Call

"You can't buy love, but you can pay heavily for it."
—Henny Youngman

in sick for each other one Monday morning (hey, you can miss one day a year) and spend it in bed. Or simply stay up late one Thursday night watching the hilariously un-scary stuff on the Sci-Fi channel and feeding each other popcorn.

No matter what you do, your lover will appreciate your thoughtfulness, as well as the surprise. Who knows, she might just up and surprise you tomorrow. Or the next day. Or, better yet, when you least expect it!

ROMANCE ON A BUDGET

There's no law that says romance has to equal maxed out credit cards, another loan from your parents, or an empty wallet after the romantic evening is done. While it never hurts to splurge on your lover from time to time, with everything from chilled champagne to a romantic weekend, even that would get rather unromantic if you did it every night. (Okay, maybe not, but just for argument's sake, stick with us here!)

Despite what today's high-powered, not to mention high-paid, advertising execs might tell you, romance comes from the heart, not the bank account. So don't let your love life go stale just because you're a little short on bread!

FRISKY FREEBIES!

In case you haven't noticed, there is a revolution going on inside your computer. The Internet has given rise to a frugal community of cheapskates and bargain hunters, all logged on and surfing their way to free

PASSIONATE POETRY

The Rose in the Deeps of His Heart

All things uncomely and broken,
All things worn – out and old,
The cry of a child by the roadway,
The creak of a lumbering cart,
The heavy steps of the ploughman,
Splashing the wintry mould,
Are wronging your image that blossoms
A rose in the deeps of my heart.
The wrong of unshapely things
Is a wrong too great to be told;
I hunger to build them anew
And sit on a green knoll apart,
With the earth and the sky and the water,
Remade, like a casket of gold
For my dreams of your image that blossoms
A rose in the deeps of my heart.

—William Butler Yeats (1865–1939)

bride, order the free CD, and turn its delivery date into a sexy night for you and your lover.

Maybe your favorite candy company gives away free samples to every new visitor. Log on, for free, and order your lover's favorite style of sweet. When it arrives, leave it on her pillow for a sweet goodnight.

Perfume and makeup samples abound in cyberspace, why not order several and save them up to make a simple travel tote for your next weekend getaway. A free book of poetry from a publisher makes a great gift for her nightstand.

No matter what the freebie, your lover's sure to be surprised at your thoughtfulness.

A ROSE BY ANY OTHER PRICE TAG

Roses are hands-down the favorite symbol of modern romantics, but few can afford to splurge on these luxurious items on a regular basis. Well, who says

goods and services at a hundred different sites offering giveaways, contests, and more.

Simply type "free stuff" into your favorite search engine and sit back. Within seconds you'll get back close to a zillion hits, all directing you to "free" sites that specialize in directing you to stuff that won't cost you a cent. Most of these sites specialize in free books, CDs, coffee, or chocolate samples, calendars, cards, stickers, etc. Sound like kid stuff? Sure it is, but what's wrong with treating your lover's inner child?

Perhaps a new singles site is offering a free smooth jazz CD to every new member who signs up—for FREE. Though the last thing on your mind, at the moment, is connecting with some Russian mail-order

you need an entire dozen to turn your lover on? After all, a single rose can mean a whole lot more if you take advantage of it.

For instance, there's nothing sexier than getting a special surprise upon climbing into bed at night. (And, no, we don't mean your *Penthouse* collection stacked under the comforter.) A single rose on your lover's pillow is a great way to say "I love you," without asking immediately after, "Can I borrow a few bucks?" And if you can't wait until bedtime, hide your rose in the lettuce crisper and ask your lover to reach inside the next time you're making a dinner salad or breakfast omelet.

Need a few other places to hide that single rose? How about between the pages of her favorite romance novel? Underneath the remote control? Just sticking out of her purse? If she's taking a bath, sprinkle them on top of the running water for a splashy surprise.

Who knew you could do so much with a single rose? Why, you'll never have to buy a whole dozen again!

FLOWER FRENZY!

Also consider that there are plenty of other types of flowers out there, just waiting to be plucked up by anyone willing to take the time to be a little more creative when building a bouquet. Besides, nothing can make a romance wilt like a lack of ingenuity, so show her that she inspires you to dream up new ideas.

If you really want to blow her socks off (and ideally a few other pieces of clothing as well), take the time to put together a bunch of flowers that actually have a meaning. As you explain what each flower in the vase means and why you picked that type especially for her, she'll be panting with every word. Or napping. Whatever.

Ladies, don't be afraid to jump into the game as well. Flowers may not be the most macho gift to give your beau,

With love

Passionate Poetry

SONNET 18

Shall I compare thee to a summer's day?
Thou art more lovely and more temperate:
Rough winds do shake the darling buds of May,
And summer's lease hath all too short a date:
Sometime too hot the eye of heaven shines,
And often is his gold complexion dimmed;
And every fair from fair sometime declines,
By chance, or nature's changing course untrimmed;
But thy eternal summer shall not fade,
Nor lose possession of that fair thou owest,
Nor shall death brag thou wanderest in his shade,
When in eternal lines to time thou growest;
So long as men can breathe, or eyes can see,
So long lives this, and this gives life to thee.

—*William Shakespeare*
(1564-1616)

but the only reason all his guy friends would mock the flowers squeezed between the empty beer bottles and dirty dishes is that they're jealous nobody sends them any. Besides, it may help encourage him to get in touch with his sensitive side, which seems as visible as the dark side of the moon.

> "We come to love not by finding a perfect person, but by learning to see an imperfect person perfectly."
> —Anonymous

The whole idea of each flower having a meaning—a kind of botanical secret code—stems from the city of Constantinople (that's Istanbul today). The Brits and French picked up on it and pretty soon there was a whole array of flower talk.

LOVE'S LABOR

To express your love with a flower may seem simple at first, but there are countless nuances. Maybe work has been hectic lately and you've been a little "distant" as the playoffs reach the final stages. Make sure she knows that her investment of love will have returns by bringing her a bouquet of ambrosia, the flowers that mean "your love is reciprocated." If your love, for whatever reason (and it's none of our business,) has to be kept on the sly, send some cape jasmine or a mimosa bloom, both of which represent secret, concealed love.

When you're in an ultra-romantic mood, the kind where you just sit and stare at her for long periods of time, pondering how lucky you are (until the Prozac wears off), sweep her off her feet with forget-me-nots, zinnias, bluebells, and daisies, all of which represent true and everlasting love and affection. And if you really want to give your lover an ego boost, give him a tulip, which means he is the perfect lover (hey, lie a little).

BOUQUET BEAUTY

If she's been avoiding mirrors lately, or if he's been grimacing at his growing gut, a calla lily will tell her you find her or him beautiful (especially if someone dropped about 10 pounds). Or try a hibiscus, which represents delicate beauty, or jasmine, which stands for grace and elegance. Then there are always orchids, the flowers of magnificence—uh, maybe not if there's a weight issue.

A blue camellia will tell her she's the flame of your heart, and if accompanied by a fleur de lis, which indicates burning, you've got—heartburn. Forsythia flower buds will tell him you're seething with anticipation, or simply say "come to me" with stephanotis (a kind of vine with a waxy white flower).

On the sappier side of desire, there's the primrose for the "I can't live without you" vibe, or the pink camellia that tells your man you're longing for him. Perfect for anyone in a long-distance relationship are red carnations, which mean you are aching to see her. Give chrysanthemums to show you appreciate her loveliness and cheerfulness, or a white carnation to tell her how sweet and lovely she is. Pansies are known to spread a message of merriment. Use them as you wish.

MIXED MESSAGES

There are some flowers, however, that have meanings that you might not want to send (or, then again, maybe you do). Begonias mean "beware." Geraniums signify stupidity and folly, so try to avoid those unless you've been busted for leaving the toilet seat up too often. If you want your guy to stay with you, avoid lavender heather, which means solitude, or even worse, cyclamen plants, which is another way of saying "good-bye."

If you feel you need to get even more creative with your floral arrangement, or if you just want to impress your lady by going for the most obscure flower you can find, here's a list of a few other flowers and their meanings.

Aster	Dainty love
Azalea	Chinese symbol for womanhood
Baby's Breath	A pure heart
Bachelor's Button	Hopeful love
Cactus	Endurance
Camellia	Good luck (for a man)
Carnation	Fascination
Carnation (pink)	I'll never forget you
Crocus	Happiness
Dahlia	Elegance and dignity
Fern	Magic
Freesia	Trust and friendship
Gardenia	You are lovely, or secret love
Gladiolus	Generosity, or natural grace
Gloxinia	Love at first sight
Golden Rod	Success
Hyacinth	Sorrow

Hydrangea	Thanks for understanding
Ivy	Fidelity in marriage
Jonquil	Sympathy
Lily (Day)	Chinese symbol of motherhood
Lily (Eucharis)	Charming maidens
Lily (Tiger)	Prosperity
Longi Lily	Modest and pure

Radical ROSES

If you just can't resist the power of roses, there are ways to get creative with them, as well. They come in more colors than red, and even combining them can send some wonderful messages.

Red Rose – Love and passion

Pink Rose – Perfect happiness, or grace and gentility

Deep Pink Rose – Thank you

Light Pink Rose – Admiration

Yellow Rose – Friendship

White Rose – Innocence and purity

Peach Rose – Enthusiastic desire

White and Red Rose together – Unity

Long Stemmed Rose – I will always remember you

Short Stemmed Rose – You're my sweetheart

Assorted Colored Roses – You mean everything to me

Lily of the Valley	Return of happiness
Magnolia	Nobility or dignity
Marigold	Grief
Monkshood	An enemy is near
Moss	Charity
Myrtle (Wax)	Discipline
Myrtle	Love
Narcissus	Stay as sweet as you are
Oleander	Beauty and grace
Orange Blossom	Your loveliness equals your purity
Orchid (Cattleaya)	Maturity
Palm Leaves	Victory and success
Pine	Hope and pity
Poinsettia	Be of good cheer
Primrose (Evening)	Young love
Snapdragon	Presumption
Stock	You'll always be beautiful to me
Sweet Pea	Thank you for a lovely time
Sweet William	Smile for me
Tulip (Red)	Declaration of love
Tulip (Yellow)	There is sunshine in your smile
Tulip (Variegated)	You have beautiful eyes
Verbena	May you get your wish
Veronica	Fidelity
Viscaria	Dance with me
Violet	Faithfulness and virtue, or modesty
Violet (Blue)	I'll always be true
Violet (White)	Let's take a chance on happiness
Wallflower	Fidelity through adversity
Wisteria	Welcome
Water Lily	Purity of heart
Xeranthemum	Eternity and immortality
Yarrow	Healing
Zinnia (Mixed)	Thinking of an absent friend
Zinnia (Scarlet)	Constancy
Zinnia (White)	Goodness
Zinnia (Yellow)	Daily remembrance

THE WAY TO A MAN'S HEART...

Okay, ladies. You're not off the hook, here. Romance is a coed activity, after all. So if a rose isn't exactly what your man is looking for, why not tempt your man with something you know he'll love: Food! After all, there's more to a man's taste buds than steak and potatoes. You can still tempt your lover with a few budget-conscious tips.

Say your man's a sports fan of the highest order, despite your weekly opposition to the sports bars and all-day football marathons. Succumb once in a while to his jock side by combing the candy aisle at the local grocery or drug store. If it's baseball season, why not pick him up a bag of that chewing tobacco gum the kids

are so fond of. Or perhaps even some baseball cards, complete with gum. For football, grab a bag of chocolate footballs and pork rinds (pig skin, get it?) and set them in front of him during halftime. Ring-Dings make great imaginary hockey pucks, and if those nauseating cheese puffs don't look like mini-basketballs, what does?

Your munching man will thank you, even if his waistline won't!

IT'S THE LITTLE THINGS THAT COUNT

Maybe it's dawning on you that the little things can help keep the romance in your life (as long as they are occasionally interspersed with some of the big things). So in the endless quest to put just a little bit more romance back into every single day, it's often the little things that count—like, cutting off a little hair!

GREAT CLIPS!

In the dream, you are always Ross from *Friends*. Not Joey, the cool one. Not even Chandler, the funny one. Not even Tom Selleck or Giovanni Ribisi. Just Ross, the goofy one. But, more important, the one who got to sleep with Rachel. You guess it's better this way, even though, in the dream, much like on the show, all Ross and Rachel ever do is fight anyway.

One night, deep into the dream, you fondle Rachel's famous hair, the one that's been splashed across every magazine cover for the last six months. Kinda long, kinda short. Kinda feathery, kinda straight. Kinda wispy, kinda hard to describe. Definitely…hot!

When you wake up, sweaty and scared, you find the bed sheets tangled firmly in your grip. The next morning, at breakfast, your girlfriend gives you the cold shoulder.

"What's wrong, honey?" you ask innocently over juice and junk food (it's your turn to cook). "Nothing at all," she snorts. "Except that my boyfriend's been moaning and groaning in his sleep lately and calling out a…name. A name that most certainly isn't *mine*!"

You beg her to tell you the name, paranoid that your secret crush on Rachel has finally been exposed. Instead, as punishment, she refuses to crack, although she

downs her burnt popcorn anyway.

This goes on for a week. Lustful longings in your sleep, uttered cries, gasps, shouts, and a name that is driving your girlfriend, not to mention you, crazy. You just can't help it. Every night, as Ross, you are in yet another scenario with your TV girlfriend. Ross and Rachel on that couch in the coffee shop. Ross and Rachel strolling hand in hand through Central Park, or Perk, take your pick. Ross and Rachel shopping for pasta.

It's not entirely your fault. You don't even like the show *that* much, and certainly never started watching it religiously until your girlfriend moved in and turned every Thursday evening into an "event" rather than just another weeknight.

Finally, she announces that, since her current "look" obviously isn't doing anything for you, she's decided to

Seventeen Magazine

get a complete makeover, starting with her hair.

"Oh, wow," you think naively, "She's gonna come home tonight with that Rachel cut and won't we be in business then. That'll put those stupid dreams of mine to rest. Goodbye Ross, Hello Rachel, live, in person, and up close."

That evening, feeling guilty over your stupid, childish dreams and wanting to prove to your girl- friend that she is really the girl of your dreams after all, you make her favorite dinner and set a romantic table. The candles are lit, her favorite CD's are spinning on the stereo, the flowers are fresh and the pasta is steaming.

When she walks in the door, just in time for your crescent rolls to emerge fresh from the oven, it is all you can do to keep the cookie sheet from spilling to the floor.

"Ta da," she says proudly, sporting a new look that is less like Rachel and more like "Chemo," as in, therapy. "How do you like it?"

Closely shorn and thickly gelled, her short, short, *short* hair is neither pixie-ish nor feminine. Like a tomboy (with an attitude) from the playground, she looks overdressed in her entirely ladylike work wear.

"What's the matter?' she asks. "I thought you'd like it."

"L-l-like it," you stammer, remembering that this night is supposed to be all about apology. "I love it!"

"You better," she says, sitting down to eat. "Now, would you like to explain to me why you've been calling out Ross' name in your sleep all week. Or do I have to get a sex change as well?"

Passionate Poetry
Love's Omnipresence

Were I as base as is the lowly plain,
And you, my Love, as high as heaven above,
Yet should the thoughts of me your humble swain
Ascend to heaven, in honour of my Love.
Were I as high as heaven above the plain,
And you, my Love, as humble and as low
As are the deepest bottoms of the main,
Whereso'er you were, with you my love should go.
Were you the earth, dear Love, and I the skies,
My love should shine on you like to the sun,
And look upon you with ten thousand eyes
Till heaven wax'd blind, and till the world were done.
Whereso'er I am, below, or else above you,
Whereso'er you are, my heart shall truly love you.

—Samuel Daniel (1562-1619)

SPICING UP ROMANCE

Nothing sucks the romance out of a relationship quite like the ravages of time. And we're not talking wrinkles or love handles here, either. Lovers, like white-hot flames, often burn out before the long night of their

> **"If variety is the spice of life, marriage is the big can of leftover Spam."**
> —Johnny Carson

relationship is through, and today's lovers are even less patient than ever. Heck, it's common to hear couples who have only been together a few months say things like, "It's just not like it used to be."

Duh! After all, it used to be puppy love, young love, fun love, hot, monkey, jungle love. The sex was better, his breath was better, the dates were better, her hair looked better, and you didn't know quite so much about his toe jam or her drinking problem.

Routines also suck the life out of passion, seduction, and

romance, and it's inevitable that long-term lovers eventually settle into a pattern of TV during the week, date night on Saturday, a day apart on Sunday, and sex once or twice there in between. Date night equals dinner at the same old restaurant, complete with her milk pills, and his unbuttoning his belt just after dessert. You've met his crazy uncle and he's fallen under the spell of your pretty sister and the usual petty arguments over who used the ATM card most last month and who ate the last Fig Newton crop up where formerly it was "Darling," this and "Darling" that.

To avoid falling into the pattern of that couple who is always arguing at the table next to you at the local bistro, why not try spicing up your romance with a few of the following tips?

AVOID RUT-A-RAMA

Sunday is traditionally a day of rest, but that doesn't mean that you and your lover have to fall into the usual Sunday paper over brunch, a couple loads of laundry in the afternoon, and *60 Minutes* at supper that has defined your last two hundred Sundays together! Sure, no one wants to go into work on Monday morning with a raging hangover or having stayed up all night talking about their inner child, but you can at least break the mold and do something different on Sunday night for a change.

How about a nice stroll by the lake as the sun sets? Mike Wallace won't mind. How about a visit to one or two of the places you used to love when you first met, like that cozy park on the other side of town or that little bistro up the street? You don't have to spend a lot of money or go very far to break out of your end-of-the-week blahs, and if you're jonesing that badly for your Ed Bradley fix, there's always the VCR.

TOP 20 MOST ROMANTIC MOVIES EVER MADE

20 Ever After
19 Sabrina
18 My Best Friend's Wedding
17 Hope Floats
16 While You Were Sleeping
15 Dirty Dancing
14 The Bridges of Madison County
13 Somewhere in Time
12 Love Story
11 You've Got Mail

10 City of Angels
9 Romeo and Juliet
8 An Affair to Remember
7 Ghost
6 When Harry Met Sally...
5 Pretty Woman
4 Casablanca
3 Gone With the Wind
2 Titanic
1 Sleepless in Seattle

FUN NIGHT

If your date night consists of drive-thru Taco Bell on the way to the local laundromat, the romance hasn't just left your life—it has vanished. But it doesn't have to be forever. It's often a simple jumble of the equation that allows romance to creep back into a languishing couple's love life, and one way to do that is to have some fun. A good laugh helps you remember why you liked each other in the first place.

For starters, why not skip dinner altogether? Okay, okay, eat something, but why does a restaurant have to be the focal part of your "date?" A snack will do, as long as you're on your way somewhere

Heart's Haven

Sometimes she is a child within mine arms,
Cowering beneath dark wings that love must chase,—
With still tears showering and averted face,
Inexplicably fill'd with faint alarms:
And oft from mine own spirit's hurtling harms
I crave the refuge of her deep embrace,—
Against all ills the fortified strong place
And sweet reserve of sovereign counter-charms.

And Love, our light at night and shade at noon,
Lulls us to rest with songs, and turns away
All shafts of shelterless tumultuous day.
Like the moon's growth, his face gleams through his tune;
And as soft waters warble to the moon,
Our answering spirits chime one roundelay.

—Dante Gabriel Rossetti (1828-1882)

fun, such as that performance-art comedy with the ferrets. What ever makes you both laugh will rekindle those sparks. Romance has neither a price tag nor a time limit, and if you look back on some of your favorite, most romantic dates of all, chances are few of them had to do with five-star restaurants or airplane tickets.

SING FOR YOUR SWEETIE

There's nothing sexier than a sultry serenade, and if a new guitar, not to mention lessons and a pick, are out of your price range, why not try a little karaoke on for

> "We cannot really love anybody with whom we never laugh."
>
> —Agnes Repplier

size? Grab a quick bite to eat one night and surprise your lover by stopping in at one of the many bars, lounges, or clubs featuring karaoke these days.

Okay, it's corny, but before your lover can back out, sign both of you up for a romantic duet such as "I Got You Babe" or "Baby, It's Cold Outside!" Who cares if either of you can sing? Talent is irrelevant at these places, and when you're staring into each other's eyes, sharing the spotlight, and pouring out your hearts to each other in front of a dozen inebriated barflies, it might be the start of a really great night.

8
ROMANCE BY THE (DATE) BOOK

Nothing says romance quite like a holiday. Or least the two should be linked in some kind of hot embrace. But you're probably immune to the usual day-or-two-off, quick-trip-to-the-Hallmark-store, bottle-of-bubbly-to-celebrate routine. Shouldn't there be just a tad more romance in your next holiday?

From greeting cards to flowers, from candy to sexy stocking stuffers, lovers just can't help but get gushy at those special days on the calendar. But don't just stop at Valentine's Day. What about New Year's Eve and Christmas? And don't forget anniversaries and birthdays. So when your love life needs a boost, just look to the calendar for a little relief.

But don't wait for a holiday. After reading this chapter, you'll know how to make your lover feel romantic any day of the year.

WHY VALENTINE'S DAY
REALLY *IS* THE MOST
ROMANTIC DAY
OF THE YEAR

Well, it's supposed to be anyway. But thanks to the high saturation of greeting card company products, not to mention every mall, drugstore, and grocer putting out those heart-shaped boxes of candy the day after Christmas, Valentine's Day has gotten a bad rep.

Women complain that it puts too much pressure on them to find a date. Guys complain that the flowers and the candy and the presents and the arrangements and the dinner and the dancing puts such a dent in their wallet that they can't afford to go out again until Easter!

Now really, is all of this grumbling and groaning what Bishop Valentine defied the very emperor of Rome for way back when? According to legend, marriage had been outlawed by the emperor of Rome, Claudius II, around 270 AD. Claudius, believing that married men made poor soldiers because they regretted being torn away from their spouses in times of war, had recently issued this bummer of a decree.

Meanwhile, a man named Valentine was the bishop

during this period of matrimonial oppression. The good bishop disagreed with Claudius' decree, and believed that people should be free to marry, soldier or no. Valentine secretly invited the young couples of the area to visit him. When they did, in droves, Valentine married the couples on the sly.

Eventually, good sir Valentine was caught and brought before the emperor. The crafty Claudius overcame his anger and believed that Valentine had conviction and drive that were rare. In exchange for a pardon for violating the emperor's order, Valentine was offered a post in the Roman empire to use his influence over Rome's youth for the betterment of society.

However, St. Valentine held to his faith and did not repent. As a result, an enraged Claudius issued a three-part execution: Valentine would be beaten, then stoned, and finally, decapitated. Good thing getting stoned came first.

While in prison, waiting to be executed, it is

reported that Valentine fell in love with the jailer's daughter. Before being delivered to his trilogy of terror, Valentine sent his jailhouse love a final farewell note. And he signed the note . . . how? "From Your Valentine." He died on February 14th, 270 AD.

So, now who wants to bitch and moan about Valentine's Day, huh? All thoughts of decapitation and stoning aside, unless you bring your date to a Wes Craven movie, that is, why let a perfectly good opportunity for romance fall by the wayside just because the rest of the gang at the water cooler is whining over the high price of Valentine's Day cards?

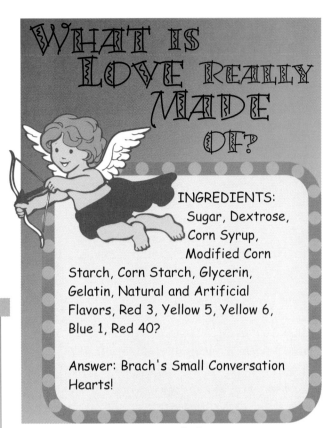

WHAT IS LOVE REALLY MADE OF?

INGREDIENTS: Sugar, Dextrose, Corn Syrup, Modified Corn Starch, Corn Starch, Glycerin, Gelatin, Natural and Artificial Flavors, Red 3, Yellow 5, Yellow 6, Blue 1, Red 40?

Answer: Brach's Small Conversation Hearts!

Passionate Poetry

Astrophel and Stella

With how sad steps, O Moon, thou
    climb'st the skies!
How silently, and with how wan a face!
What, may it be that even in
    heav'nly place
That busy archer his sharp arrows tries!
Sure, if that long-with love-acquainted eyes
Can judge of love, thou feel'st a
    lover's case,
I read it in thy looks; thy languish'd grace
To me, that feel the like, thy state descries.
Then, ev'n of fellowship, O Moon, tell me,
Is constant love deem'd there but want
    of wit?
Are beauties there as proud as here
    they be?
Do they above love to be lov'd, and yet
Those lovers scorn whom that love
    doth possess?
Do they call "virtue" there - ungratefulness?

—Sir Philip Sidney (1554-1586)

Most Popular Conversation Heart Sayings

My Cutie	Kiss Me
I M Sure	Mad 4 U
Dare Ya	U R Bad
Too Hot	Dare Ya
Don't Tell	Be True
You Rule	See Ya
Hello	Just One
No Way	Too Cool
First Kiss	Email Me
Got Love?	My Hero
U R Mine	

Anyone can celebrate Valentine's Day. But why not treat the most romantic day of the year with just a little more respect. Everybody knows about the 12 Days of Christmas and it's the rare dieter who doesn't break into that Halloween candy long before October 31. So why is there only one day of the year set aside for the hopeless romantic in all of us? After all, aren't there really 14 Days of Valentine's? Why not.

To make Valentine's Day last all month long, or at least for two solid weeks of non-stop sexiness, why not try a few of the tips to follow in this 14 part series of simple sweet nothings. They won't cost you a lot of money, but the payoff could just be your best Valentine's Day yet. After all, there's nothing sexier than thoughtfulness!

ON THE FIRST DAY OF VALENTINE'S . . . MUSTN'T SEE TV!

This one's easy, doesn't cost a lot, and could just start a weekly tradition that lasts your entire (love) life!

On the first night of February, why not celebrate Valentine's Day a little early by turning off the TV and turning on the charm. Skip the evening news, forego those goofy game shows, and forget about *Survivor* (or whatever "reality" show is on that night), this night's for you and yours and a little simple romance that could just be lacking from your workaday week.

Dust off those Barry White and Marvin Gaye CDs and set the volume on low as you treat your lover to a candlelight dinner at an actual, honest-to-goodness table. You remember where that is, don't you? Right there under that two-week pile of junk mail, the sewing machine, and all those Christmas "thank-you" cards you never got around to writing. Clear that stuff off, set two places, and light those tapered candles you've been saving for a special occasion.

If you're overworked and underskilled, don't worry about cooking. After all, you get to celebrate Valentine's Day a little early, too! Order some take-out from your favorite restaurant and serve it up on two of your best plates. (Just wait until the delivery guy's gone to slip into your sexy lingerie!) Enjoy the simple silence of romantic tunes and flickering candles as you forget all about the canned laughter, well-timed jokes, or soap opera emergency room shenanigans you're missing. This may not be the most original idea out there, but it's one that often gets passed over in the rush to forget about the workaday world in front of the boob tube. Get back to the basics and discuss your day, the good, the bad, the boring. Remember what your lover's eyes look like as you stare into them longingly over take-out Chinese and a weeknight glass of wine. Who knows, you might even go to bed early for a change!

ON THE **SECOND** DAY OF VALENTINE'S . . .
THE HEAT IS (REALLY) ON

As the winter months blanket most of the country with snow, and the rest with at least chillier weather than usual, why not turn your arctic abode into a tropical paradise with just a few quick and inexpensive ideas!

The next time your lover is out battling the frosty February weather, crank up the heat to a comfortable

temperature and lay out his or her favorite pair of swimming trunks or bikini. Rearrange the living room furniture (temporarily anyway) and drag out the beach or lawn chairs and drape them with your plushest beach towel. Put away the Christmas CDs and find a little Bob Marley or your favorite steel drum band and fire them up on the living room stereo. Rearrange whatever plants have survived the winter to set off your living room oasis and, while you're at it, why not inflate a beach ball or two. (You never know when they'll come in handy later on in the evening!)

Forego the hot chocolate for a nice cold beer or some frozen drinks courtesy of the blender, and whip up a spicy snack like corn chips and salsa. You may not need any cocoa butter or sunscreen, but what lover wouldn't be surprised when you whip out the coconut scented massage oil for a quick backrub while spread out on those fuzzy beach towels.

Either way, this is one hot tip that's likely to turn a regular old February evening into a Valentine's Day appetizer that's sure to go down hot and spicy.

ON THE **THIRD** DAY OF VALENTINE'S . . . JUST JOCK

When it comes to Valentine's Day, nothing gets the heart pumping like good, old-fashioned, hard-breathing, sweat-producing, hot and heavy—exercise! From teenagers in the dizzy throes of puppy love to senior citizens falling in love all over again, you're never too young or too old to get out there and feel the sun on your face, the wind in your hair, and the chewing tobacco in your back pocket.

Oh, well, whatever your choice of sports, make your prelude to Valentine's Day this year involve a little S & R. Sports and recreation, that is.

For a sweaty pre-Valentine's date that's sure to get the endorphins flowing, why not grab some balls and head down to the local driving range or batting cage (make sure it's heated!). It's the perfect treat for an after-work date, and neither destination requires you to be the next Tiger Woods or Derek Jeter. And just think, no fancy duds, no reservation required, and while all of those other boors are out winning and dining each other in preparation for the big day, you'll more than likely have the place to yourself.

For starters, why not show up at your lover's door with one of those cheesy do-it-yourself T-shirts that says something corny like "Sexy Slugger" or "She's #1" and insist he or she put it on before slipping into jeans and sneakers and grabbing a favorite ball cap and sunglasses, not to mention a generous helping of Ben Gay!

Don't forget dinner on the way. What would a rousing game of batting cage blunders or driving range dings be without swinging by a hot dog stand to stay in character? Not only does this help you save up money for the big day to come, but nothing says "I love you" like ketchup in the shape of a big, red heart!

Besides, you'll need all that beef in your system as you knock those balls around and spend a fun-filled evening giggling over missed shots or bad form. And if neither of you is a major jock, don't worry. After all, there's nothing like a little one-on-one coaching, up close and personal, of course, to break the ice. Especially if your pre-Valentine's Day outing just happens to be one of your first dates!

You may not hit a home run, but chances are pretty good you'll at least get to first. How's *that* for romantic?

ON THE **FOURTH** DAY OF VALENTINE'S . . . ARE YOU GAME?

As the days of February race on by and you find yourself pressed for time, but still wanting to continue your 14 Days of Valentine's, try this tip that takes less time than an actual "date" date, but which can often be twice the fun!

Why not show your date your childish side and visit the local arcade for a challenging change of pace? It may not be the days of wine and roses, but it's the perfect pick-me-up when you and your lover are starting to feel those winter blahs.

For starters, zip by the bank and trade in a few twenty-dollar bills (hey, we didn't say this was a cheap date, just a different one!) for several rolls of quarters. Slip them into a Valentine's Day gift bag and warn your date to dress casually. (*Really* casually!)

Show up at your lover's door with a pack of fresh bubble gum and your favorite retro '80s CD blaring Culture Club or Duran Duran to get them in the whole junior-high, skipping-school kind of mood.

Be forewarned, your date, unless the spontaneous type, might just have a few nose crinkles and eye rolls in store for you on the way, especially as she stares longingly out the window at all of those fancy restaurants you're passing up on your way to the "fun" side of town! Once you get into it, however, you're sure to find that the jingling bells, clinking quarters, and neon lights can't help but get her into the mood.

Test your skill at the free-throw shooting hoops game and challenge your lover to a rousing game of NFL Blitz. Let your date win a few, and hopefully she won't be the only one to "score!" There's nothing like the feeling of snatching one of those cheesy stuffed animals at the crane game, and it's the rare game room that doesn't have a snack bar offering all of those tempting carnival foods you know aren't good for you.

You may have to share the game room with a dozen or more pimply teenagers in love, but what better way to recapture the heady days of puppy love than to get high score on Tekken!

ON THE FIFTH DAY OF VALENTINE'S . . .
DOLLAR DAZE

Since you're probably still saving up for that grand finale to this wonderful two weeks worth of Valentine's Day splendor, try out the following budgetary measures to give your wallet a break, and your sweetheart a sexy surprise!

At least you can rest easy that you are not the only penny pincher in town! Today's frugal consumers have given new meaning to the term dime store, although inflation has renamed them "dollar" stores. Chances are, you can find several similarly named budget boutiques within driving distance of your workplace or home, from Dollar Tree to Dollar General, and though you may have never dared enter these penny-pinching portals in your life, they should be your first stop on the road to reduced-price romance!

Most dollar stores are laid out by section: house and home, bath and beauty, school and office, etc. Amble up any of these aisles and you're sure to find something that your lover needs, all for the price of a cup of coffee or a candy bar or two. For instance, is he a fishing fanatic? Grab several boxes of hooks, weights, or bobbers, top them off with a bag or two of Gummi fish, and hide them all away in a gift bag covered with, naturally, fish. Talk about catching a big one when you get home!

Or perhaps she's a feline fiend. Wander through the pet aisle and stock up on rubber balls, fish-flavored snacking treats, or even a skein or two of yarn for your female's feline friend. Add a cheap cat calendar or cat-covered pencils and erasers and you've got one *purr-fect* gift. What's that you say? The dollar store doesn't have a gift bag covered with cats? Don't despair. Just draw whiskers on a regular sack!

As you can see, the dollar store is full of thoughtful gifts just waiting to be left on your lover's desk, nightstand, or litter box for one sexy pre-Valentine's surprise. So what are you waiting for? Break open your piggy bank, check under those seat cushions, clean out your car's ashtray, and get in there!

restaurant or drive-thru, and try to beat him home to have it all laid out for that all-important surprise factor.

Even if your date's a light drinker, there's nothing more romantic than the sight of a chilled bottle of champagne, followed by the undoing of the foil, the popping cork, the fizzy fuzzing, and the flowing bubbly. Even if your lover only tastes a sip or two, the thought was there and you can always add the leftovers to a sauce for stir-fry or a glass of OJ for Sunday morning, or even to a running bath to add a little bubbly to your bubbles!

And hey, nothing classes up a bag of Monday night tacos like a bottle of champagne.

ON THE SIXTH DAY OF VALENTINE'S . . .
PREMATURE POPPAGE

Who says you have to wait until New Year's Eve, or even the *real* Valentine's Day, to spring for a little bubbly? Perk up your average weeknight with a bottle of the good stuff. Okay, maybe just the *okay* stuff.

But hey, champagne's champagne!

These days you can find decent champagne everywhere; most grocery stores have a good selection. Take advantage of this by picking up a reasonably priced bottle of bubbly for your unsuspecting lover. If you're feeling generous and have the time, stop into a real liquor store and grab two champagne glasses while you're at it. They're usually under three bucks each, and will make a great keepsake of your pre-Valentine's Day date!

If there's time, and enough money leftover from the bubbly, surprise your lover with take-out food from her favorite

ON THE SEVENTH DAY OF VALENTINE'S . . .
STUFF YOURSELF

Who says you have to be grown-up about Valentine's Day? Find the inner you—and all for under $5—when you explore the kiddy section in your local department store!

Relive your youth on this long, winding Seventh Day of Valentine's by swinging by your local department store and picking up the cheesiest, lamest, cutest, plushest, corniest most adorable stuffed animal you can find. You know the kind, an elbow-sized stuffed bee holding a plush, red heart that says "Bee Mine!" The cheesier the better!

It helps if you deposit your stuffed treat somewhere surprising so that your lover finds it quite unexpectedly, such as beneath her pillow just before bedtime or sitting on her towel when she goes to take her morning shower! You might also want to beef up your gift with supplemental treats, such as Reese's peanut butter cups shaped like hearts and a cheesy, goofy Valentine's Day card the likes of which most fourth graders present each other with. (If you can still find one, the Power Rangers cards are the best!)

Don't be afraid that your lover will think you're cheap. The simple delight of receiving something warm, fuzzy and corny when, and hopefully where, you least expect it will fill your lover's heart with joy!

And even if it doesn't, how much can a stuffed animal hurt when she throws it back at you?

Ladies, you can try getting your man WWF wrestling trading cards, or just regular old baseball cards. That'll put a smile on his face.

ON THE EIGHTH DAY OF VALENTINE'S . . .
SEXY STROLL

Who says you have to spend Valentine's Day on your duff at some stuffy restaurant feeding your face? Treat your lover's heart to a little fresh air and exercise with this simple way to celebrate the Eighth Day of Valentine's.

If at all possible, beat your lover home to make the most of this heart-healthy idea. Change into your favorite pair of sweats and lace up those sneakers so you can be ready to go when your lover finally walks through the front door after another long day at work. Make sure to have a fresh bottle of water to bring along, and perhaps a can of soda for a quick pick-me-up if your date's dragging. Greet your lover with a gentle bear hug and urge him or her into the bedroom to change into some comfortable active wear.

Next, take a simple stroll around the block. It may be the last thing either of you want to do on some generic weeknight, but once you get your feet to stepping and your heart to beating, you might just find it hard to stop. Sip your water liberally and hold hands lovingly as you stroll around your block, track, or park.

Let the rest of the country vegetate to Must See TV as the two of you enjoy the peace and quiet of a simple, sexy stroll together. Talk about your day or simply let the stress of the work week slowly fade away through the souls of your sneakers as you parade around with smiles on your faces and love in your hearts.

Who knows, it could become a nightly routine.

ON THE NINTH DAY OF VALENTINE'S . . .
MUNCHING MATINEE

So, let's see. So far you've shared game room tokens, stuffed animals, No- TV night, and a sexy stroll. What's next? Well, for a new twist on an old idea, forget dinner and a movie and have dinner at the movies!

This idea requires just a little planning to pull off, but is well worth it once you're there. For starters, grab the morning paper on the way to work and scour the movie section for a romantic double feature. Take heart, this doesn't mean two sappy romantic comedies, unless you want it to, that is. Any two movies will do, as long as your lover hasn't seen them and they don't involve Pauly Shore.

Find a theater that's either in between your two jobs, or drive your lover to work and promise to pick him up a little bit early. Coordinate your afternoons so that you can get to the first movie by five and the second movie by seven thirty, which seem to be the most popular show times for theaters big and small these days.

For a sexy treat, bring along a silk scarf and blindfold your lover as you navigate through rush hour traffic to arrive at what will most likely be a mostly empty movie theater. Buy your tickets in advance and head straight to the concession stand to purchase whatever your hungry lover so desires.

Whether it's double-buttered popcorn or fat-free Twizzlers, the treat is on you! It may seem corny at first, since most of us haven't attended an actual double-feature since *Star Wars* was still in the theaters, but by the time the house lights dim and the previews get started, you and your lover will be cozying up like two teens in the balcony on Saturday night.

Munch and crunch away as you enjoy dinner at the movies, and don't worry about the calories or the gratuitous violence. After all, what are double-features for?

ON THE TENTH DAY OF VALENTINE'S . . .
ROCKY MATING HIGH

As your prelude to Valentine's Day reaches double digits, steer clear of the road most traveled and drive straight to the latest trend in daring dating: rock climbing!

Don't worry, this type of rock climbing involves more plastic than peril and more rubber than rappelling. Everywhere from gyms to theme parks, clubs to game rooms all seem to have some type of rock-climbing outfit going on, and all that competition is good for you.

First, find out the prices and times that are best for you and yours. Then show up with an extra-strength Power Bar wrapped up in a bow and announce the big surprise. After a little initial hesitance, drag, dupe or carry your lover to the car and zip to the rock climbing destination before you miss your reservation.

After gearing up in the latest safety equipment, you and your lover and a few other hearty souls will embark on some heart-pounding excitement as you struggle up the beginner, intermediate, or just plain crazy "mountain," which actually looks more like a child's colorful finger-painting. Well-positioned hand-holds accompany you both all the way up the mountain of your choice, and even if you slip and fall, a series of slings and pulleys escort you safely to the ground.

It may not be Tom Cruise in *Mission: Impossible 2*, but it's the closest you can get without a stunt double.

ON THE ELEVENTH DAY OF VALENTINE'S . . .
POTTERY PLEASE!

If slings and pulleys, hand grips and helmets aren't your thing, let alone your lover's, take your daring hat off and come in for something a little more tame as you celebrate your countdown to Valentine's Day with dinner and—a souvenir?

Just as trendy as fake rock climbing and twice as safe, unless you poke your eye out with the paintbrush, that is, Painting Your Own Pottery is quickly replacing dinner and a movie as today's funky new date night of choice. But don't wait till the crowds of Valentine's Day catch on, beat the rush when you make a date to design and paint your own pottery.

This one involves little planning except for the obligatory coordination of schedules and a possible reservation if the 11th Day of Valentine's happens to fall on a weekend night. After those haggling details are out of the way, simply show up at your lover's door and whisk her away to a fun-filled night of munchies and making things.

You'll be able to get drinks and appetizers to accentuate your appetite for all that artsy stuff you'll be doing with the cups, plates, birdhouses, etc, that your pottery painting establishment has to offer. Let your lover see your formerly hidden creative side as you dazzle them with a personalized coffee cup that turns into a sexy souvenir of your creative night together. Not bad for a Valentine's Day countdown.

Passionate Poetry

To ——

One word is too often profaned
For me to profane it,
One feeling too falsely disdained
For thee to disdain it;

One hope is too like despair
For prudence to smother,
And pity from thee more dear
Than that from another.

I can give not what men call love,
But wilt thou accept not
The worship the heart lifts above
And the heavens reject not,——

The desire of the moth for the star,
Of the night for the morrow,
The devotion to something afar
From the sphere of our sorrow?

——Percy Bysshe Shelley (1792-1822)

ON THE TWELFTH DAY OF VALENTINE'S . . .
BLOCKBUSTER NIGHT

As the big day dawns, why not slow things down a bit with a sexy night at home? After all, neither you nor your lover is probably used to all these off-the-wall activities, unless you're 15 that is, and you could both probably use a break.

This may not be the most original idea in the series, but make it one by skipping the new releases and picking out your lover's favorite movie. Chances are, your constant companion has let it slip that she just can't live without seeing *Sleepless in Seattle* once a year, or perhaps it's *Brian's Song* for your ex-jock boyfriend.

Either way, skip the special effects and sexy stars of today's latest releases and reach for that cheesy copy of *Endless Love* or, gulp, *Fame*, and watch your lover's eyes light up as she expects yet another Schwarzenegger or Rambo romp! Don't forget the Milk Duds and the Raisinettes and be sure to beat your lover home to set the mood.

You can easily personalize the evening by sliding a sentimental Valentine's Day card under the popcorn bowl or surprising her with a heart-shaped ice cream cake or other dessert to seal the deal on one sweet night.

ON THE THIRTEENTH DAY OF VALENTINE'S . . .
SEXY SLEEPWEAR

Sure they're hokey, sure they're goofy, sure they're cheesy—but isn't that what romance is all about? So why not celebrate Valentine's Day Eve with a sexy souvenir that your lover will want to wear all year long?

Take another spin through one of the stores (try to make it earlier rather than later, as they tend to get crowded with last-minute shoppers such as yourself) and make a beeline for the sleepwear section, where you are sure to find a colorful collection of Valentine's Day sleepwear for him or her.

You might even get lucky and find things half-price already, or at least priced to move since there is only one shopping day left until the big day. If so, stock up for next year or give your lover a double-whammy with a two-for-one gift that is twice as sweet.

If you're feeling generous, why not zip over to the panties aisle and grab a 3-pack of heart-shaped panties in her size to top it all off. Toss in some ridiculous fuzzy slippers for just the right "over the top" feel.

For the gents, you'll want to invest in a pair of those adorable, puckered up lipstick covered boxer shorts, or if he's vain, a pair or two of similarly adorned bikini briefs. (Good gawd!) You might get lucky and find a T-shirt just as cheesy to top it all off with, and once you've made your selection for him or her, toss them in a cheery gift bag and race home to display it on your bed as if it was the finest piece of jewelry you could find.

You may not get squeals of delight at first, but once the cheese meter reaches a high enough velocity and the

effect of all those bright Valentine's Day colors hits your lover, you're bound to be appreciated for your thoughtfulness and bravery.

After all, who else but a thoughtful lover would actually buy this stuff!

ON THE FOURTEENTH DAY OF VALENTINE'S . . . WRITE ON!

Well, it's finally here: the most romantic day of the year. And after the 13 fun-filled days leading up to the biggie, we hope you don't get that all-the-Christmas-presents-have-been-opened-and-it's-only-8 a.m. feeling now that February 14th has finally dawned.

Of course, we've pulled out all the stops, so what you do on the big day is up to you. Whether it's a romantic dinner or a sunset cruise, a romantic getaway to somewhere exotic or a trip to that cozy little bed and breakfast right up the street, we wish you both the best time ever! So here's one last tip to help you seal the deal.

Now that you've decided where you're going, what you're doing, and who you're doing it with, it's time to put pen to paper and tell your lover, old or new, what you really think. Doesn't matter if it's in the borders of that fancy seven-dollar Hallmark greeting card or on the cocktail napkin from your favorite bar, the time has come to let it all hang out.

Whether it's a tongue-in-cheek limerick full of every inside joke the two of you share, or a heartfelt ode to how she's made you the man you always wanted to be, skip the flash and the dash and let your lover know, honestly, just how you really feel. There's nothing more romantic than honest heart-felt emotion, and what better day to pour your heart out than Valentine's Day? You don't have to be a poet, you don't even have to spell everything correctly, but as long as you speak from the heart, your lover will be able to understand that, yes, you do love her. And what better Valentine's Day present is there than that?

HAVE AN ANNIVERSARY THAT'S OFF THE CHART!

Anniversaries are a wonderful time to celebrate the hidden (or not so hidden) romantic inside of you. Why, they even have a handy chart to tell these lucky folks what gifts to give: Silver for the 25th anniversary, rust for the 26th, etc.

Of course, new twists on an old variation have allowed for more freedom than the charts of old provided. Where it used to be anniversary faux pas to give pearls when the chart clearly said copper, today there is more leeway in interpreting the chart. For instance, many jewelers and fine gift shops now have two versions of the chart, traditional and modern. Lucky you. Now instead of giving your lover a silver chastity belt, you can give her a pearl chastity belt.

But when the hipster in you revolts against being told what to give to your beloved, let alone what color crepe paper to hang, look to your heart for a more personal way to say "I love you" to the light of your life.

OPEN FOR INTERPRETATION

Okay, so let's say your lover is the traditional type and prefers to go by the charts of old, or even new, for that matter. Does that mean you have to go broke trying to live up to the accomplishments of your more romantic, not to mention more flush, ancestors? Heck no. All you need is a little creativity and not much more cash to turn that chart of old into a modern version just perfect for your pocketbook.

Okay, so traditionally your second anniversary gift is cotton. Cotton? Who thought up that hot number? Eli Whitney? Of course, back when the chart was dreamed up by a lot of leisurely women in white gloves chomping on finger cakes at their afternoon tea down on the plantation, cotton was a big deal. What they were probably shooting for with this one was lavish cotton tablecloths for their mile-long dinner tables, or fresh new sheets for their love nests, or possibly a year's supply of gloves so they didn't dirty their fingers eating all those dainty little sandwiches.

But cotton's come a long way, baby, and so have you. Why not tempt your lover with some sexy

Happy Anniversary Darling! I LOVE YOU

panties? Today's cotton is as soft as a baby's butt and lasts a lot longer. So after your little second-year anniversary celebration, unlike a tablecloth or pair of gloves, your little lady will be able to enjoy her comfortable anniversary gift again and again.

And who says even the big gifts, like gold or diamonds, have to be taken so literally? A golden picture frame containing your favorite Polaroid makes a sexy gift for her nightstand, as does a weekend getaway to the Golden Gate Bridge. (Which, of course, will come quite in handy, not to mention inexpensively, for our San Francisco readers.) Not to mention, a trip to those famous "golden arches" for dinner. Okay, there's no need to interpret things that cheaply, but a new era deserves new anniversary presents, and you're just the couple to do it!

CHART YOUR OWN COURSE

Who wrote this famed anniversary chart, anyway? Miss Manners? Dear Abby? Mr. Blackwell? Richard Simmons? Who are they to tell you what to give your loved one on the most special day of the year? Why not sit down with a little stationery of your own and come up with a chart that makes your sweetie happy, and not the jeweler down at the mall?

Take an evening, order in, and cozy up with your favorite pens and a bottle of wine as you chart out your next sixty years! Okay, so you've only been together sixty days, lovers can dream, can't they? Start smaller and rewrite the gifts for years one through five. For instance, after one glorious year together, why not agree to go someplace fun? Pencil in a trip to your favorite tropical island or bustling city, and start planning for it now! Not only will this give you something to look forward to for the next ten months together, but when your anniversary day finally arrives, you'll know that your lover got what he really wanted. And so did you!

Make the gift for two years together be something special as well. Forget the traditional cotton and turn your second-year gift into a flat screen TV or a furniture upgrade for when you both move in together. (Hint, hint.) Not only is this a useful gift, but you can save together and get each other exactly what you want.

Complete your chart and set it aside. Check it periodically to see how your vacation and TV funds are coming along, or update and change it as necessary. Just be sure not to change it when you're fighting. After all, scratching out "dinner at the best restaurant in town" for your third-year gift and changing it to "hire a hit-man!" might just come back to haunt you when you make up all nice and cozy. (Or when your case comes to trial—whatever.)

CALENDAR DAZE

Today's hipsters don't readily stand on ceremony, so why wait a whole year before throwing your anniversary bash? Don't forget about the yearly shindig, of course—unless you don't want to celebrate one next year—but take some time to stop and smell the roses all year long.

Maybe this coming Saturday is your six-month anniversary. What better way to celebrate than to grab a regular anniversary card and pencil in references to the six-month mark. After all, a surprise treat a whole half-a-year early will go a long way toward softening the blow of that big gift you won't be able to afford by then!

Studies show that the most romantic couples celebrate their anniversaries all year long. Not with silver or gold, paper or pearls, but with kindness and patience, love and honor, romance and passion. Who needs a calendar when you've got a heart?

"In the arithmetic of love, one plus one equals everything, and two minus one equals nothing."

—Mignon McLaughlin

WHAT ARE THE TRADITIONAL ANNIVERSARY GIFTS FOR EACH YEAR?

Anniversary	Traditional	Modern
First	Paper	Clocks
Second	Cotton	China
Third	Leather	Crystal/Glass
Fourth	Fruit/Flowers	Appliances
Fifth	Wood	Silverware
Sixth	Candy/Iron	Wood
Seventh	Wool/Copper	Desk Sets
Eighth	Bronze/Pottery	Linens/Lace
Ninth	Pottery/Willow	Leather
Tenth	Tin/Aluminum	Diamond Jewelry
Eleventh	Steel	Fashion Jewelry
Twelfth	Silk/Linen	Pearls
Thirteenth	Lace	Textiles/Furs
Fourteenth	Ivory	Gold Jewelry
Fifteenth	Crystal	Watches
Twentieth	China	Platinum
Twenty-Fifth	Silver	Silver
Thirtieth	Pearl	Diamond
Thirty-Fifth	Coral	Jade
Fortieth	Ruby	Ruby
Forty-Fifth	Sapphire	Sapphire
Fiftieth	Gold	Gold
Fifty-Fifth	Emerald	Emerald
Sixtieth	Diamond	Diamond

Passionate Poetry

O Mistress Mine

O Mistress mine, where are you roaming?
O, stay and hear; your true love's coming,
That can sing both high and low:
Trip no further, pretty sweeting;
Journeys end in lovers meeting,
Every wise man's son doth know.

What is love? 'Tis not hereafter;
Present mirth hath present laughter;
What's to come is still unsure:
In delay there lies not plenty;
Then, come kiss me, sweet and twenty,
Youth's a stuff will not endure.

—William Shakespeare (1564-1616)

BIRTHDAY BLUNDERS

Birthdays offer the thoughtful lover a wonderful way to be romantic. But beware of creating a monster.

DO-IT-YOURSELF DOOM

You went into a dime store, just because it was the only place you knew of that still printed do-it-yourself T-shirts. And so, like a nerdy boyfriend eagerly hoping for major brownie points, you bought a $4 yellow T-shirt, knowing she would only wear it once, that had the words, "HAPPY BIRTHDAY, HONEY!" printed in all pink capital letters, with the exclamation point in the shape of a burning candle.

The old woman behind the counter, wheezing from a quick smoke break that only kept you waiting for three whole minutes, croaked, "Aw, ain't that sweet. Now, tell me, is this for a girl... or a boy?"

Blushing, you assured her with shaky hands that, most definitely, the intended was a female of the girl variety. "Sure she is," she muttered, ironing your letters onto your shirt with a huge, handled waffle iron while tiny hoodlums stole licorice whips and cheap digital watches in the aisles behind you. "Sure she is."

Your girlfriend, of course, loved it. With a capital "L"! She wore it not once, not twice, but for two entire months solid. Traipsing around your two bedroom apartment in matching yellow, cotton panties each night and singing you both to sleep with a blissful, lullaby rendition of "Happy Birthday to Me."

Then, of course, all hell broke loose the day some good-hearted neighbor stole your basket from the laundry room downstairs, complete with her now faded birthday shirt tucked neatly inside!

"I can't believe it!" she ranted for days, until you told her you'd buy her another one.

"But that's not the point," she said pointedly. "They stole my favorite shirt. I have to do something to get them back. Quick, what's the address of the place you had it made.

I want to pay them a personal visit myself."

The very next night you had to help your girlfriend in from the car, so laden down was she with still warm self-made shirts. "Honey," you queried, hoping she'd gone grocery shopping on the way home as well. "What got into you?"

"I don't know," she gushed, tossing pink, blue, orange, and yellow shirts onto the bed like so many postcards after a month-long vacation. "I just got carried away."

"I see that," you said admiringly, as she paraded around (one benefit, she kept changing her top) the apartment in her new, slogan-filled shirts.

"Thou shalt not steal," read the first, original shirt, intended solely for laundry duty just in case the offending party should be washing clothes with her some fateful Saturday morning and made to suffer a massive guilt trip, if nothing else.

"I like it," you said, not knowing the rest of your evening would be spent uttering the same exact line until she'd exhausted the entirety of her new line of "controversial clothing."

"Meat Is Murder," read another T-shirt, red capital lettering on a bleak white background, which she vowed to wear every time you took her to Wendy's or McDonald's. Of course, you struck both such establishments off of your "places to take girlfriend" list immediately.

"Make Love Not War," read another, which you wholeheartedly supported, all the while wondering if she had brought her "cliché handbook" along with her to the T-shirt store.

All week long, day after day, her T-shirts brought stares, dirty looks, thrown food and, more than once, thrown punches, as in the occasion when she chose to wear her "Organized Religion Is for LOSERS" T-shirt to church with you one nice, normal Sunday morning gone terribly, horribly wrong.

Back at the apartment, nursing a black eye with filet of sole instead of a porterhouse due to her new "Meat Is Murder" T-shirt, you pushed aside the pain and gathered her weeks' worth of slogan-filled shirts and tossed them all into the laundry basket.

While she was out strutting around in her "Mean People Suck!" T-shirt, walking in the park and fending off said mean people for herself for a change, you dumped the entire load in the dumpster down the street and then sat idly in the apartment, enjoying the healing powers of a nice, cold beer and preparing your "alibi" of yet another laundry room larceny.

What other option did you have besides breaking up with her? Besides, all of those cheap, raised letters were starting to give her chest a nasty red rash.

Passionate Poetry

Take, O Take Those Lips Away

Take, O take those lips away,
That so sweetly were forsworn;
And those eyes, the break of day,
Lights that do mislead the morn:
But my kisses bring again,
bring again,
Seals of love, but seal'd in vain,
seal'd in vain.

—William Shakespeare (1564-1616)

DECEMBER DESIRES

With the chilly winter months, not to mention the candlelight and hypnotic Winter Solstice CDs that have become part of today's romantic holiday season, comes the unlimited potential for cozy fireside snuggling and December desires. Or does it?

BOXING DAY

Although your girlfriend of seven months is constantly informing you that you are the most "in touch with your feminine side" man she's ever dated (which you still haven't decided is a compliment yet), you once again find yourself racing around at the last minute on Christmas Eve filling the trunk of your Toyota Camry with last-minute gifts.

Of course, it's all *her* fault. You were under the entirely male understanding that, since you'd both decided to give each other the gift of a romantic New Year's Eve getaway in a secluded mountain cabin, that physical gifts were "off limits." There was even an agreement. A verbal one, mind you, but an agreement just the same.

Instead, stopping by her place after work several nights earlier, you noticed a pile of presents beneath her tabletop fiber optic tree bearing your name. Big presents. Boxes. Bags. Sacks. Tubs. Crates. Lots of them. Much more than just the card and Christmas tree shaped bath beads you currently had hanging in her stocking back at your place.

And so, like every other man on the planet (sensitive or not) you find yourself with a trunk load of Santa slippers, slinky negligees, cheap jewelry, and several household appliances spilling out of your trunk at four in the afternoon on Christmas Eve.

Forget the crowds, the overdrawn bank account, the waiting in line, the overflowing bladder, the parking at the mall, you're finally done with all of that.

However, merely a block from your home, you stop at a red light only to realize that you don't have a shred of wrapping paper at your place because, after all, you weren't supposed to be exchanging presents that, therefore, didn't need to be wrapped in the first place!

Fortunately, as you scan the deserted intersection, frantically searching for a 24-hour gift wrapping store, (why aren't there more of those, anyway?) you spot a blinking neon sign for Spanky's Pub that boasts, "Holiday Special: FREE gift wrapping with two drink minimum!"

"Perfect," you shout as you make a U-turn and pull into the nearly deserted parking lot of a sketchy looking pub you'd never dared enter before, owing to the bars on the windows and, on most nights, a plethora of pick-up trucks with gun racks dotting the sand-and-gravel parking lot.

Still, the hour is growing late, and you are most definitely desperate. Opening the black spray-painted door to a tinkling of cow jingle and sleigh bells, you hear country Christmas carols blaring inside and search for a place to rest your towering pile of hastily purchased presents.

A gaunt man under a stained and dilapidated Santa hat greets you just inside the door and guides you to a hastily assembled "wrapping station," where a harried woman in a matching, and just as disgusting, cap is already loaded down with a table full of unwrapped presents. A rolled up carpet-sized wheel of snowman wrapping paper stands at her side as she rips off sheet after sheet. Mr. Claus sticks the number 6 on each of your presents, then hands you the same number as he explains that, this way, none of your presents get mixed up with the other patrons.

Judging from the pile of Popeil Pocket Fisherman and Swiss army knives currently spread across the wrapping station, however, you don't see this as much of a problem. You thank them both and head toward the circular bar with only a few backward glances at your teetering pile of presents. Settling in for your two obligatory drinks, you revel in one of the largest

screwdrivers you've ever seen outside of a James Bond movie and reflect on your good fortune. Not only are you able to relax with a couple of drinks after a long, stressful day of last-minute shopping, but you're getting your presents wrapped to boot!

As you sip your bowl of orange juice and vodka, admiring the blinking Christmas lights adorning the beer taps and pickled pigs feet behind the bar and enjoying yet another Dolly Parton Christmas carol, you watch as Spanky's slowly fills up with men from all walks of life.

The front door next to the wrapping station opens again and again to welcome men in grease jockey overalls, nurse scrubs, lawyer's suits, and fast food uniforms. By the time you finally get Mr. Claus to make that all important second drink, the last minute male shoppers like a modern day pilgrimage are bunched at the bar elbow to ankle and you've given up checking on the status of your presents because to look behind you only reveals a wall of expectant and thirsty male faces just waiting for you to vacate your coveted barstool.

And, since you've got one of the best (and only) seats in the house, you stay put, listening as each newcomer to the bar reports on the horrible experiences he had while last minute shopping at the mall. You listen intently, corroborate conspiratorially, and, before you know it, find yourself full of the holiday spirit, ordering drinks for several of your new friends, only to find the favor returned time and time again.

Before you know it the Christmas lights behind the bar (which seem to have mysteriously doubled) are brighter than ever and your watch reads 10 p.m.! Realizing that you have a big day of giving (and receiving) presents ahead of you tomorrow, you fumble for the number Mr. Claus gave you earlier, much earlier, that afternoon.

Now, where could it be? It was right there on the bar between your neighbor's Long Island iced tea and the beer nuts. It was a—nine, right? Or was it a six? Oh, well, you find a soggy "9" sitting on the bar first, so that must be it.

Turning in your ticket to the frustrated Mrs. Claus, whose roll of wrapping paper is now quite thin, she points you to a pile of presents that seems somehow smaller than you recall. Still, the hand-printed numbers seem to match, and that's what really matters. Right?

Somehow wrestling them all into a waiting taxi (no sense in driving home), you take a nap while the driver finds his way to your house. There, of course, you promptly pass out beneath the Christmas tree, only to awake there the next morning to hear your girlfriend's persistent knocking at the front door. Happy (sort of) to be already dressed for the occasion, you manage to answer the door without vomiting all over your girlfriend's too-perky Christmas sweater.

When her face collapses into a mountain of worry, you mention something about the holiday flu and revel as she whips into action, brewing you a fresh pot of coffee and neutralizing it with a shot of eggnog from the fridge. Half a pot and two Christmas albums later,

you settle at opposite ends of the couch feeling *almost* human and dig into your presents.

The ties and socks, nose hair clippers and Kenny G CDs she gives you (you can't believe you were so worried) pale in comparison to the elegant cashmere sweater and diamond tennis bracelet your girlfriend sheds copious tears over. Suddenly realizing that your number was indeed a #6 and most definitely not a #9, you gratefully reflect that the real holder of #9 was most likely that chubby lawyer who took the seat next to you somewhere in between your fifth and ninth mountainous screwdriver. Thank goodness you stayed put so long. The guy he took the seat from was the assistant manager of Taco Bell, and you're quite sure your girlfriend's surprise gifts this morning might not have been quite so…plush. And it is better to give than to receive, especially when someone else is paying.

Passionate Poetry

Music, When Soft Voices Die

Music, when soft voices die,
Vibrates in the memory—
Odours, when sweet violets sicken,
Live within the sense they quicken.

Rose leaves, when the rose is dead,
Are heap'd for the beloved's bed;
And so thy thoughts when thou are gone,
Love itself shall slumber on.

—Percy Bysshe Shelley (1792-1822)

WHAT ARE YOU DOING NEW YEAR'S EVE?

5, 4, 3, 2, 1—smooch! Is there anything more romantic than a midnight kiss on New Year's Eve? This holiday tradition is recognized the world over as the universal symbol of love, warmth, and happiness. So why is it that you always get stuck kissing cousin Ernie over by the cheese dip on the last night of every year? Don't worry, you're not alone. It is estimated that over half of all New Year's Eve kisses are wasted on distant cousins, waiters, minor acquaintances, and Stan, that jerk from accounting, every single year. That's a whole lot of wasted lip time. But are you really surprised?

Think about it: You and your date are enjoying the party, and want to make sure you have a full glass of fresh champagne to toast that auld lang syne. So, you send him off to the bar, underestimating that every other guest had the same idea, at the same time. So those ten minutes you had

to spare before the big countdown quickly slip by as you search high and low for your date, not to mention that belated bubbly.

Meanwhile, your date has finagled an entire bottle of champagne from a well-compensated busboy, only to struggle like a salmon upstream through the hundreds of partygoers still clustered at the bar. As the ball drops, the orchestra plays, and the countdown begins, you find yourself pinned between a loving couple who has already started smooching and good, old cousin Ernie.

Happy New Year!

To avoid your yearly nod to inbreeding, why not heed the following tips, all of which are designed to help you ring in next New Year's the right way.

BE A PARTY POOPER

The key to a romantic evening is to think outside of the champagne bottle. After all, who ever said that you *had* to go to a big, loud, rowdy, noisy party on New Year's Eve? Probably the same person that told you guys love Old Spice or girls love sports bars.

When you get right down to it, there are basically three kinds of New Year's Eve parties: the intimate evening with friends, the polite party, and the drunken bash. While some are more romantic than others, few afford the loving couple any quality time under that famous dropping ball.

Take the intimate evening with friends. Here you have a collection of civilized couples and snooty singles gathered around a blazing fire telling war stories of New Year's past or playing a rousing game of Trivial Pursuit. There are several imported bottles of wine on the counter, the pate is all gone, and Dick Clark's mouth may be moving, but no one can hear him because the TV is muted in favor of the host's collection of light jazz CDs.

The ball drops, the couples kiss, and you sneak the last bit of pate before anyone gets wise.

Likewise, the polite party is another gathering of friends and acquaintances, with the emphasis on the latter. You got the invitation from a coworker, a neighbor, a customer, or a boss, and either couldn't refuse, or waited too long for your date to set up something romantic and, when she didn't, had to take this option out or stay home and eat frozen dinners while nipping at the last of the Christmas brandy. You don't really know anybody, but you're all dressed up and, finally, have somewhere to go.

Lastly, the drunken bash is exactly what it sounds like. So even if things do turn out romantically, you either won't remember how to repeat the experience next year, or who to repeat it with. Either way, none of these three options is exactly off the romantic charts.

So forget the traditionally tired and try starting a brand new tradition for a brand new year.

PLAN AHEAD

A New Year's Eve to remember often takes a considerable bit of planning that most couples would rather soon forget. Unless you have a personal assistant or a time machine, it's not something you can just think about the day after Christmas.

Try a little closer to Thanksgiving. Many hotels, resorts, airlines, and travel agencies begin advertising their New Year's Eve specials before you've even had a chance to flip the calendar from November to December. So once you've digested all that turkey, spend a few quiet hours in your easy chair alternately napping and cruising through the Travel section of your local paper.

Even if you're not going out of town, many of your favorite restaurants will be booked up in advance if you don't act soon, so get out your handy red pen and circle your top five favorites. Then let your fingers do the walking as you start making those calls. Just remember, a quiet romantic New Year's Eve dinner could just be the difference between dropping the ball, and having one!

GET LOST!

Is a quiet dinner not romantic enough to ring in the New Year? Why not splurge a little and take advantage of a weekend getaway in honor of the occasion. Chances are you'll have New Year's Day off, so why not get a mini-vacation in while you're at it. In these hectic days of e-mails and cell phones, nothing's more romantic than some downtime with your lover. A weekend away is sure to be romantic in itself, so anything you do on top of that will be worth sexual favors.

Try to find a reasonable package that's not too expensive, not too far away, but not too shabby either. Try to find a chain hotel or a bed and breakfast that's in town or in the neighboring city so you know what you'll be getting into. (There's nothing romantic about staying at a roach motel, no matter how many days you're off!) Then set about adding your own frills by having flowers delivered to the room, ordering room service, or bringing along special soaps and bath beads for a little New Year's Eve soak that's bound to counterbalance the fact that your view is of the parking lot instead of the Pacific Ocean.

Passionate Poetry

Loving in Truth

Loving in truth, and fain in verse my love to show,
    That she, dear she, might take some pleasure of my pain:
Pleasure might cause her read, reading might make her know,
Knowledge might pity win, and pity grace obtain,
I sought fit words to paint the blackest face of woe,
Studying inventions fine, her wits to entertain:
Oft turning others' leaves to see if thence would flow
Some fresh and fruitful showers upon my sun-burn'd brain.

But words came halting forth, wanting Invention's stay,
Invention, Nature's child, fled step-dame Study's blows,
And others' feet still seem'd but strangers in my way.
Thus great with child to speak, and helpless in my throes,
Biting my trewand pen, beating myself for spite,
Fool, said my Muse to me, look in thy heart and write.

—Philip Sidney (1554-1586)

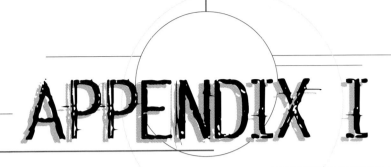

A Year of Holidays

Even amid the proliferation of commercial holidays, there are always a few more obscure observances throughout the year—even if most people don't observe them, or even know they exist. There's a celebration just waiting to happen for every single day of the year if you follow our fun-filled guide to some of the more obscure holidays. Plan something romantic or just plain fun in honor of Wear Your Underwear Inside-Out Day or National Frozen Yogurt Day. Enjoy!

JANUARY

January 1 – First Foot Day
January 2 – Run Up the Flagpole and See if Anyone Salutes it Day
January 3 – Festival of Sleep Day
January 4 – Trivia Day
January 5 – Bird Day
January 6 – Bean Day
January 7 – Old Rock Day
January 8 – Man Watcher's Day
January 9 – Play God Day
January 10 – Peculiar People's Day
January 11 – Smoking May Be Hazardous to Your Health Day
January 12 – Work Harder Day
January 13 – Make Your Dream Come True Day
January 14 – National Dress Up Your Pet Day
January 15 – Hat Day
January 16 – National Nothing Day
January 17 – Cathedral Day
January 18 – Winnie the Pooh Day
January 19 – National Popcorn Day
January 20 – National Buttercrunch Day
January 21 – National Hugging Day
January 22 – National Brownie Day
January 23 – National Handwriting Day
January 24 – Eskimo Pie Patent Day
January 25 – Opposite Day
January 26 – Australia Day
January 27 – Thomas Crapper Day
January 28 – Clash Day
January 29 – National Cornchip Day
January 30 – Escape Day
January 31 – Child Labor Day

FEBRUARY

February 1 – Serpent Day
February 2 – Purification Day
February 3 – Cordova Ice Worm Day
February 4 – Create a Vacuum Day
February 5 – Disaster Day
February 6 – Lame Duck Day
February 7 – Charles Dickens Day
February 8 – Kite Flying Day
February 9 – Toothache Day
February 10 – Umbrella Day
February 11 – White T-shirt Day
February 12 – National Plum Pudding Day
February 13 – Get a Different Name Day
February 14 – Ferris Wheel Day
February 15 – National Gum Drop Day
February 16 – Do a Grouch a Favor Day
February 17 – Champion Crab Races Day
February 18 – National Battery Day
February 19 – National Chocolate Mint Day
February 20 – Hoodie-Hoo Day
February 21 – Card Reading Day
February 22 – Thinking Day
February 23 – International Dog Biscuit Appreciation Day
February 24 – National Tortilla Chip Day
February 25 – Pistol Patent Day
February 26 – National Pistachio Day
February 27 – International Polar Bear Day
February 28 – Public Sleeping Day

MARCH

March 1 – National Pig Day
March 2 – Old Stuff Day
March 3 – I Want You to Be Happy Day
March 4 – Holy Experiment Day
March 5 – Multiple Personalities Day
March 6 – National Frozen Food Day
March 7 – National Crown Roast of Pork Day
March 8 – Be Nasty Day
March 9 – Panic Day
March 10 – Festival of Life In the Cracks Day
March 11 – Worship of Tools Day
March 12 – Plant a Flower Day
March 13 – Jewel Day
March 14 – National Potato Chip Day
March 15 – Buzzard's Day
March 16 – Everything You Do Is Right Day
March 17 – Submarine Day
March 18 – Supreme Sacrifice Day
March 19 – Poultry Day
March 20 – Proposal Day
March 21 – Fragrance Day
March 22 – National Goof-Off Day
March 23 – National Chip and Dip Day
March 24 – National Chocolate Covered
             Raisins Day
March 25 – Waffle Day
March 26 – Make Up Your Own Holiday Day
March 27 – National Joe Day
March 28 – Something On A Stick Day
March 29 – Mirrors Day
March 30 – I Am In Control Day
March 31 – National Clams on the Half-Shell Day

APRIL

April 1 – One-Cent Day
April 2 – National Peanut Butter and Jelly Day
April 3 – Tweed Day
April 4 – Tell a Lie Day
April 5 – Go For Broke Day
April 6 – Sorry Charlie Day
April 7 – No Housework Day
April 8 – All Is Ours Day
April 9 – Name Yourself Day
April 10 – Golfer's Day
April 11 – Eight-Track Tape Day
April 12 – Look Up at the Sky Day
April 13 – Blame Somebody Else Day
April 14 – National Pecan Day
April 15 – Rubber Eraser Day
April 16 – National Stress Awareness Day
April 17 – National Cheeseball Day
April 18 – International Jugglers' Day
April 19 – National Garlic Day
April 20 – Look Alike Day
April 21 – Kindergarten Day
April 22 – National Jelly Bean Day
April 23 – Read Me Day

April 24 – National Pigs in a Blanket Day
April 25 – National Zucchini Bread Day
April 26 – Richter Scale Day
April 27 – Tell A Story Day
April 28 – Great Poetry Reading Day
April 29 – National Shrimp Scampi Day
April 30 – National Honesty Day

MAY

May 1 – Save the Rhino Day
May 2 – Fire Day
May 3 – Lumpy Rug Day
May 4 – National Candied Orange Peel Day
May 5 – National Hoagie Day
May 6 – No Diet Day
May 7 – International Tuba Day
May 8 – No Socks Day
May 9 – Lost Sock Memorial Day
May 10 – Clean Up Your Room Day
May 11 – Twilight Zone Day
May 12 – Limerick Day
May 13 – Leprechaun Day
May 14 – National Dance Like a Chicken Day
May 15 – National Chocolate Chip Day
May 16 – Wear Purple for Peace Day
May 17 – Pack Rat Day
May 18 – Peace Day
May 19 – Frog Jumping Jubilee Day
May 20 – Eliza Doolittle Day
May 21 – National Memo Day
May 22 – Buy a Musical Instrument Day
May 23 – National Taffy Day
May 24 – National Escargot Day
May 25 – National Tap Dance Day
May 26 – Gray Day
May 27 – Body Painting Day
May 28 – National Hamburger Day
May 29 – End of the Middle Ages Day
May 30 – My Bucket's Got a Hole Day
May 31 – National Macaroon Day

JUNE

June 1 – Dare Day
June 2 – National Rocky Road Day
June 3 – Repeat Day
June 4 – Old Maid's Day
June 5 – Festival of Popular Delusions Day
June 6 – Teacher's Day
June 7 – National Chocolate Ice Cream Day
June 8 – Name Your Poison Day
June 9 – Best Friend's Day
June 10 – National Yo-Yo Day
June 11 – King Kamehameha Day
June 12 – Machine Day
June 13 – Kitchen Klutzes of America Day
June 14 – Pop Goes the Weasel Day

June 15 – Smile Power Day
June 16 – National Hollering Contest Day
June 17 – Watergate Day
June 18 – International Panic Day
June 19 – World Sauntering Day
June 20 – Ice Cream Soda Day
June 21 – Cuckoo Warning Day
June 22 – National Chocolate Eclair Day
June 23 – National Pink Day
June 24 – Museum Comes to Life Day
June 25 – Log Cabin Day
June 26 – National Chocolate Pudding Day
June 27 – National Columnists Day
June 28 – Paul Bunyan Day
June 29 – Camera Day
June 30 – Meteor Day

JULY

July 1 – Creative Ice Cream Flavor Day
July 2 – Visitation of the Virgin Mary Day
July 3 – Stay Out of the Sun Day
July 4 – National Country Music Day
July 5 – Workaholics Day
July 6 – National Fried Chicken Day
July 7 – National Strawberry Sunday Day
July 8 – Video Games Day
July 9 – National Sugar Cookie Day
July 10 – Clerihew Day
July 11 – National Cheer Up the Lonely Day
July 12 – National Pecan Pie Day
July 13 – Fool's Paradise Day
July 14 – National Nude Day
July 15 – Respect Canada Day
July 16 – International Juggling Day
July 17 – National Peach Ice Cream Day
July 18 – National Caviar Day
July 19 – Flitch Day
July 20 – Ugly Truck Contest Day
July 21 – National Tug-of-War Day
July 22 – Ratcatcher's Day
July 23 – National Vanilla Ice Cream Day
July 24 – Amelia Earhart Day
July 25 – Threading the Needle Day
July 26 – All or Nothing Day
July 27 – Take Your Pants for a Walk Day
July 28 – National Milk Chocolate Day
July 29 – Cheese Sacrifice Purchase Day
July 30 – National Cheesecake Day
July 31 – Parent's Day

AUGUST

August 1 – Friendship Day
August 2 – National Ice Cream Sandwich Day
August 3 – National Watermelon Day
August 4 – Twins Day
August 5 – National Mustard Day

August 6 – Wiggle Your Toes Day
August 7 – Sea Serpent Day
August 8 – Sneak Some Zucchini Onto
        Your Neighbor's Porch Night
August 9 – National Polka Day
August 10 – Lazy Day
August 11 – Presidential Joke Day
August 12 – Middle Child's Day
August 13 – Blame Someone Else Day
August 14 – National Creamsicle Day
August 15 – National Relaxation Day
August 16 – Bratwurst Festival
August 17 – National Thriftshop Day
August 18 – Bad Poetry Day
August 19 – Potato Day
August 20 – National Radio Day
August 21 – National Spumoni Day
August 22 – Be an Angel Day
August 23 – National Spongecake Day
August 24 – Knife Day
August 25 – Kiss and Make Up Day
August 26 – National Cherry Popsicle Day
August 27 – Petroleum Day
August 28 – World Sauntering Day
August 29 – More Herbs, Less Salt Day
August 30 – National Toasted Marshmallow Day
August 31 – National Trail Mix Day

SEPTEMBER

September 1 – Emma M. Nuitt Day
September 2 – National Beheading Day
September 3 – Skyscraper Day
September 4 – Newspaper Carrier Day
September 5 – Be Late for Something Day
September 6 – Fight Procrastination Day
September 7 – Neither Rain Nor Snow Day
September 8 – Pardon Day
September 9 – Teddy Bear Day
September 10 – Swap Ideas Day
September 11 – No News is Good News Day
September 12 – National Chocolate Milkshake Day
September 13 – Defy Superstition Day
September 14 – National Cream-Filled Donut Day
September 15 – Felt Hat Day
September 16 – Collect Rocks Day
September 17 – National Apple Dumpling Day
September 18 – National Play-Doh Day
September 19 – National Butterscotch Pudding Day
September 20 – National Punch Day
September 21 – World Gratitude Day
September 22 – Dear Diary Day
September 23 – Dogs in Politics Day
September 24 – National Comic Book Day
September 25 – National Good Neighbor Day
September 26 – National Pancake Day
September 27 – Crush a Can Day
September 28 – Ask a Stupid Question Day
September 29 – Poisoned Blackberries Day
September 30 – National Mud Pack Day

OCTOBER

October 1 – Magic Circles Day
October 2 – Name Your Car Day
October 3 – Virus Appreciation Day
October 4 – National Golf Day
October 5 – National Storytelling Festival
October 6 – Come and Take It Day
October 7 – National Frappe Day
October 8 – American Tag Day
October 9 – Moldy Cheese Day
October 10 – National Angel Food Cake Day
October 11 – It's My Party Day
October 12 – International Moment of
　　　　　　　Frustration Scream Day
October 13 – National Peanut Festival
October 14 – Be Bald and Free Day
October 15 – White Cane Safety Day
October 16 – Dictionary Day
October 17 – Gaudy Day
October 18 – No Beard Day
October 19 – Evaluate Your Life Day
October 20 – National Brandied Fruit Day
October 21 – Babbling Day
October 22 – National Nut Day
October 23 – National Mole Day
October 24 – National Bologna Day
October 25 – Punk for a Day Day
October 26 – Mule Day
October 27 – Sylvia Plath Day
October 28 – National Chocolate Day
October 29 – Hermit Day
October 30 – National Candy Corn Day
October 31 – Increase Your Psychic Powers Day

NOVEMBER

November 1 – Plan Your Epitaph Day
November 2 – National Deviled Egg Day
November 3 – Sandwich Day
November 4 – Waiting for the Barbarians Day
November 5 – Gunpowder Day
November 6 – Marooned Without a Compass Day
November 7 – National Bittersweet Chocolate
　　　　　　　With Almonds Day
November 8 – Dunce Day
November 9 – Chaos Never Dies Day
November 10 – Forget-Me-Not Day
November 11 – Air Day
November 13 – National Indian Pudding Day
November 14 – Operation Room Nurse Day
November 15 – National Clean Out Your
　　　　　　　Refrigerator Day
November 16 – Button Day
November 17 – Take a Hike Day
November 18 – Occult Day
November 19 – Have a Bad Day Day
November 20 – Absurdity Day
November 21 – False Confessions Day
November 22 – Start Your Own Country Day

November 23 – National Cashew Day
November 24 – Use Even If Seal is Broken Day
November 25 – National Parfait Day
November 26 – Shopping Reminder Day
November 27 – Pins and Needles Day
November 28 – Make Your Own Head Day
November 29 – Square Dance Day
November 30 – Stay at Home Because You're
　　　　　　　Well Day

DECEMBER

December 1 – National Pie Day
December 2 – National Fritters Day
December 3 – National Roof-Over-Your-Head Day
December 4 – Wear Brown Shoes Day
December 5 – National Sacher Torte Day
December 6 – Mitten Tree Day
December 7 – National Cotton Candy Day
December 8 – Take It In the Ear Day
December 9 – National Pastry Day
December 10 – Festival For the Souls of
　　　　　　　Dead Whales
December 11 – National Noodle Ring Day
December 12 – National Ding-a-Ling Day
December 13 – Ice Cream and Violins Day
December 14 – National Bouillabaisse Day
December 15 – National Lemon Cupcake Day
December 16 – National Chocolate
　　　　　　　Covered Anything Day
December 17 – Underdog Day
December 18 – National Roast Suckling Pig Day
December 19 – Oatmeal Muffin Day
December 20 – Games Day
December 21 – Look at the Bright Side Day
December 22 – National Date-Nut Bread Day
December 23 – Roots Day
December 24 – National Egg Nog Day
December 25 – National Pumpkin Pie Day
December 26 – National Whiners' Day
December 27 – National Fruitcake Day
December 28 – Card Playing Day
December 29 – Pepper Pot Day
December 30 – National Bicarbonate of Soda Day
December 31 – Unlucky Day

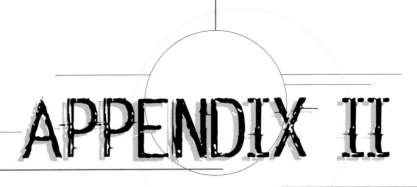

APPENDIX II

Hotels in Romantic Destinations

Are you and your lover planning a romantic getaway together? If so, you'll need a nice place to stay, a room that you hopefully may not even leave very often! The following is a listing of some hotels and bed & breakfasts in some likely romantic destinations.

Hawaii

The Royal Hawaiian
Island of O'ahu
2259 Kalakaua Avenue
Honolulu, Hawaii 96815-2578
808-923-7311
www.royal-hawaiian.com

The Orchid at Mauna Lani
Island of Hawai'i
One North Kaniku Drive
Kohala Coast, Hawaii 96743
808-885-2000
www.orchid-maunalani.com

Princeville Resort
Island of Kaua'i
5520 Ka Haku Road
Priceville, Kauai, Hawaii 96722-3069
800-826-4400
www.princeville.com

The Manele Bay Hotel
Island of Lana'i
1233 Fraser Avenue
Lanai City, Hawaii 96763
800-321-4666
www.manelebayhotel.com

Kapalua Bay Hotel
Island of Maui
One Bay Drive
Kapalua, Hawaii 96761-9099
808-669-5656
www.kapaluabay.com

Las Vegas, Nevada

Luxor Resort and Casino
3900 Las Vegas Boulevard South
Las Vegas, Nevada 89119
888-777-0188
www.luxor.com

The Mirage
3400 Las Vegas Boulevard South
Las Vegas, Nevada 89109
800-374-9000
www.themirage.com

The Aladdin Resort and Casino
3667 Las Vegas Boulevard South
Las Vegas, Nevada 89109
800-634-342
www.aladdincasino.com

MGM Grand Hotel and Casino
3799 Las Vegas Boulevard South
Las Vegas, Nevada 89109
800-646-7787
www.mgmgrand.com

New York New York Hotel & Casino
3790 Las Vegas Boulevard South
Las Vegas, Nevada 89109
800-NY FOR ME
www.nynyhotelcasino.com

Golden Nugget
129 East Fremont
Las Vegas, Nevada 89125
800-634-3454
www.goldennugget.com

Treasure Island Hotel and Casino
3300 Las Vegas Boulevard South
Las Vegas, Nevada 89109
800-288-7206
www.treasureisland.com

Bally's Hotel and Casino
3645 Las Vegas Boulevard South
Las Vegas, Nevada 89109
800-644-0777
www.ballyslv.com

Barbary Coast
3595 Las Vegas Boulevard South
Las Vegas, Nevada 89109
888-227-2279
www.barbarycoastcasino.com

The Bellagio
3600 Las Vegas Boulevard South
Las Vegas, Nevada 89109
888-987-6667
www.bellagiolasvegas.com

Binion's Horseshoe
128 Fremont Street
Las Vegas, Nevada 89101
800-634-6811
www.binions.com

Caesars Palace
3570 Las Vegas Boulevard South
Las Vegas, Nevada 89109
800-223-7277
www.caesars.com/palace

Circus Circus
2880 Las Vegas Boulevard South
Las Vegas, Nevada 89109
800-634-3450
www.circuscircus-lasvegas.com

Excalibur
3850 Las Vegas Boulevard South
Las Vegas, Nevada 89109
800-937-7777
www.excalibur-casino.com

Harrah's Hotel and Casino
3475 Las Vegas Boulevard South
Las Vegas, Nevada 89109
800-427-7247
www.harrahs.com

Las Vegas Hilton
3000 South Paradise Road
Las Vegas, Nevada 89109
800-774-1500
www.lv-hilton.com

Mandalay Bay
3950 Las Vegas Boulevard South
Las Vegas, Nevada 89119
877-632-7000
www.mandalaybay.com

Monte Carlo
3770 Las Vegas Boulevard South
Las Vegas, Nevada 89109
800-311-8999
www.motne-carlo.com

Paris Las Vegas
3655 Las Vegas Boulevard South
Las Vegas, Nevada 89109
888-266-5687
www.parislasvegas.com

Stardust Hotel and Casino
3000 Las Vegas Boulevard South
Las Vegas, Nevada 89109
800-824-6033
www.stardustlv.com

Stratosphere Hotel Casino and Tower
2000 Las Vegas Boulevard South
Las Vegas, Nevada 89104
800-998-6937
www.stratlv.com

The Venetian
3355 Las Vegas Boulevard South
Las Vegas, Nevada 89109
888-283-6423
www.vebetian.com

Niagara Falls

Niagara Falls Courtyard
5950 Victoria Avenue
Niagara Falls, Ontario L2G3L7
800-695-8284
www.courtyard.com

Niagara Falls Marriott Fallsview
6740 Fallsview Boulevard
Niagara Falls, Ontario L2G3W6
888-501-8916
www.niagarafallsmarriott.com

Old Stone Inn
5425 Robinson Street
Niagara Falls, Ontario L2G7L6
800-263-6208
www.oldstoneinn.on.ca

Quality Hotel Near the Falls
5257 Ferry Street
Niagara Falls, Ontario L2G1R6
905-356-2842

Imperial Hotel and Suites
5851 Victoria Avenue
Niagara Falls, Ontario L2G3L6
800-263-2553
www.imperialniagara.com

Renaissance Fallsview Hotel
6455 Buchanan Avenue
Niagara Falls, Ontario L2G3V9
800-468-3571
www.renaissancehotels.com

The Inn on the Niagara Parkway
7857 Niagara River Parkway
Niagara Falls, Ontario L2G6R5
800-263-2552

The Oakes Inn Fallsview
6546 Buchanan Avenue
Niagara Falls, Ontario L2G3W2
800-263-7134

Lion's Head Bed & Breakfast
5239 River Road
Niagara Falls, Ontario L2E3G9
905-374-1681

Cascade Inn
5305 Murray Street
Niagara Falls, Ontario L2G2J3
800-663-3301

Inn by the Falls
5525 Victoria Avenue
Niagara Falls, Ontario L2G3L3
800-263-2571
www.fallscasino.com./inbyfall

Sheraton Fallsview Hotel
6755 Oaks Drive
Niagara Falls, Ontario L2G3W7
905-374-1077
www.fallsview.com

An's House
745 Fourth Street
Niagara Falls, New York 14301
716-285-7907

Olde Niagara House
610 Fourth Street
Niagara Falls, New York 14301
716-285-9408

Fallsview Travelodge Hotel
201 Rainbow Boulevard
Niagara Falls, New York 14303
800-876-3297
www.niagarafallstravelodge.com

Holiday Inn Select
Third & Old Falls Street
Niagara Falls, New York, 14303
800-465-4329
www.basshotels.com/holiday-inn

San Francisco, California

The Archbishop's Mansion
1000 Fulton Street
San Francisco, California 94117
800-543-5820
www.archbishopsmansion.com

Dockside Boat and Bed
C Dock
San Francisco, California 94133
415-392-5526
www.boatandbed.com

Hotel Bohème
444 Columbus Avenue
San Francisco, California 94133
415-433-9111
www.hotelboheme.com

The San Remo Hotel
2237 Mason Street
San Francisco, California, 94133
800-352-7366
www.sanremohotel.com

The Bed and Breakfast Inn
4 Charlton Court
San Francisco, California 94123
415-921-9784
www.1stb-bsf.com

The Hyde Regency
1531 Hyde Street
San Francisco, California 94109
415-552-7555
www.hyderegency.com

The Nob Hill Hotel
835 Hyde Street
San Francisco, California 94109
877-662-4455
www.nobhillhotel.com

Hotel Triton
342 Grant Avenue
San Francisco, California 94108
800-433-6611
www.hotel-tritonsf.com

Hotel Metropolis
25 Mason Street
San Francisco, California 94102
800-553-1900
www.hotelmetropolis.com

Hotel Union Square
114 Powell Street
San Francisco, California 94102
415-397-3000
www.hotelunionsquare.com

Hotel Diva
440 Geary Street
San Francisco, California 94102
415-885-0200
www.hoteldiva.com

Kensington Park Hotel
450 Post Street
San Francisco, California 94102
800-553-1900
www.kensingtonparkhotel.com

The Steinhart Hotel
952 Sutter Street
San Francisco, California 94109
415-928-3855
www.steinharthotel.com

The Red Victorian Bed, Breakfast & Art
1665 Haight Street
San Francisco, California 94117
415-864-1978
www.redvic.com

Artists Inn
2231 Pine Street
San Francisco, California 94115
800-854-5802
www.artistsinn.com

Clebia's Place
767 San Bruno Avenue
San Francisco, California 94107
415-648-0135
www.clebiasplace.com

El Drisco Hotel
2901 Pacific Avenue
San Francisco, California 94115
415-346-2880
www.eldriscohotel.com

The Hotel Rex
562 Sutter Street
San Francisco, California 94102
415-433-4434
www.thehotelrex.com

Miyako Inn
1800 Sutter Street
San Francisco, California 94115
415-921-4000

The Phoenix Hotel
601 Eddy Street
San Francisco, California 94109
800-248-9466
www.thephoenixhotel.com

The Chancellor Hotel
433 Powell Street
San Francisco, California 94102
800-428-4748
www.chancellorhotel.com

New Orleans, Louisiana

The Bourbon-Orleans Hotel
717 Orleans Street
New Orleans, Louisiana 70116
504-523-2222
www.bourbonorleans.com

Hotel de L'Eau Vive
315 Tchoupitoulas Street
New Orleans, Louisiana 70130
504-592-0300
www.hoteldeleauvive.com

The Inn On Bourbon
541 Bourbon Street
New Orleans, Louisiana 70130
800-535-7891
www.innonbourbon.com

Hotel Inter-Continental
444 St. Charles Avenue
New Orleans, Louisiana 70130
504-525-5566
www.neworleanshotel.com

International House Hotel
221 Camp Street
New Orleans, Louisiana 70130
504-553-9550
www.ihhotel.com

The Lafayette Hotel
600 St. Charles Street
New Orleans, Louisiana 70130
800-270-7542
www.nolacollection.com/lafayette

Hyatt Regency New Orleans
Poydras Plaza at Loyola Avenue
New Orleans, Louisiana 70113
504-561-1234
www.hyatt.com

New Orleans Marriott
555 Canal Street
New Orleans, Louisiana 70130
504-581-1000
www.marriott.com

Royal Sonesta Hotel
300 Bourbon Street
New Orleans, Louisiana 70130
504-586-0300
www.sonesta.com/neworleans_royal

Chateau Sonesta
800 Iberville Street
New Orleans, Louisiana 70112
504-586-0800
www.sonesta.com/neworleans_chateau

Rue Dumaine Guesthouse
517 Rue Dumaine
New Orleans, Louisiana 70116
800-9-DUMAINE
www.ruedumaine.com

Windsor Court Hotel
300 Gravier Street
New Orleans, Louisiana 70130
888-596-0955
www.windsorcourthotel.com

The Ambassador
535 Tchoupitoulas Street
New Orleans, Louisiana 70130
888-527-5271
www.clients.neworleans.com/ambassador

Ashton's Mechling Bed & Breakfast
2023 Esplanade Avenue
New Orleans, Louisiana 70116
800-725-4131
www.ashtonbb.com

The B&W Courtyards Bed & Breakfast
2425 Chartres Street
New Orleans, Louisiana 70117
800-585-5731
www.bandwcourtyars.com

Bienville House
320 Decatur Street
New Orleans, Louisiana 70130
800-535-9603
www.bienvillehouse.com

Chateau Dupré Hotel
131 Rue Decatur
New Orleans, Louisiana 70130
800-256-0135
www.nolacollection.com/chateau

Dauphine Orleans Hotel
415 Dauphine Street
New Orleans, Louisiana 70116
800-508-5554
www.dauphineorleans.com

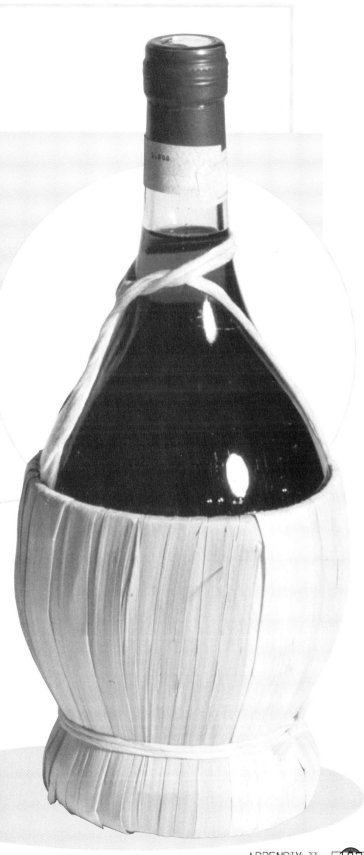

The Frenchmen
417 Frenchmen Street
New Orleans, Louisiana 70116
888-365-2775
www.clients.neworleans.com/lamothe/frenchmen

French Quarter Landmark Hotel
920 Rampart Street
New Orleans Louisiana 70116
877-791-1312
www.nolahotels.com/landmarkfq

The Historic French Market Inn
501 Rue Decatur
New Orleans, Louisiana 70130
800-256-9970
www.nolacollection.com/frenchmarket

The Lamothe House
621 Esplanade Avenue
New Orleans, Louisiana 70116
888-696-9575
www.clients.neworleans.com/lamothe

Le Pavillon Hotel
833 Poydras Street
New Orleans, Louisiana 70112
800-535-9095
www.lepavillon.com

Maison Dupuy Hotel
1001 Rue Toulouse
New Orleans, Louisiana 70112
504-586-8000
www.maisondupuy.com

The Hotel Monteleone
214 Rue Royale
New Orleans, Louisiana 70130
800-321-6710
www.hotelmonteleone.com

The Parc St. Charles
500 St. Charles Avenue
New Orleans, Louisiana 70130
800-272-4373
www.nolacollection/stcharles

The Pelham Hotel
444 Common Street
New Orleans, Louisiana 70130
800-272-4583
www.nolacollection.com/pelham

Place d'Armes
625 St. Ann Street
New Orleans, Louisiana 70130
800-366-2743
www.placedarmes.com

The Ponchartrain
2031 St. Charles Avenue
New Orleans, Louisiana 70140
800-777-6193
www.grandheritage.com

Prince Conti
830 Conti Street
New Orleans, Louisiana 70130
800-366-2743
www.princeconti.com

Hotel Provincial
1024 Rue Chartres
New Orleans, Louisiana 70116
800-535-7922
www.hotelprovincial.com

The Queen & Crescent Hotel
344 Camp Street
New Orleans, Louisiana 70130
800-975-6652
www.queenandcrescenthotel.com

Royal Street Inn and R Bar
1431 Royal Street
New Orleans, Louisiana 70116
800-449-5535
www.royalstreetinn.com

St. Ann Marie Antoinette Hotel
717 Rue Conti
New Orleans, Louisiana 70230
888-367-7281
www.hotelstlouis.com/saintann

The Saint Louis
730 Rue Bienville
New Orleans, Louisiana 70130
888-367-7281
www.hotelstlouis.com

The St. Peter House Hotel
1005 St. Peter Street
New Orleans, Louisiana 70116
888-604-6226
www.clients.neworleans.com/lamothe/stpeter

Hotel Storyville
1261 Esplanade Avenue
New Orleans, Louisiana 70116
866-STORVIL
www.hotelstoryville.com

The Sully Mansion
2631 Prytania Street
New Orleans, Louisiana 70130
800-364-2414
www.sullymansion.com

Miami Beach, Florida

The Alexander
5225 Collins Avenue
Miami Beach, Florida 33140
888-287-3390
www.alexanderhotel.com

Blue Moon Hotel
944 Collins Avenue
Miami Beach, Florida 33139
800-724-1623
www.bluemoonhotel.com

Boulevard Hotel
740 Ocean Drive
South Miami Beach, Florida 33139
305-532-0376

Breakwater Hotel
940 Ocean Drive
Miami Beach, Florida 33139
800-454-1220
www.breakwater-hotel.com

The Carlton Hotel
1433 Collins Avenue
Miami Beach, Florida 33139
305-538-5741
www.carltonmiamibeach.com

Casablanca
6345 Collins Avenue
Miami Beach, Florida 33141
800-813-6676
www.florida.com/casablanca

The Catalina resort Hotel
1732 Collins Avenue
Miami Beach, Florida 33139
800-292-9252
www.catalinahotel.com

The Chesterfield Hotel
855 Collins Avenue
Miami Beach, Florida 33139
305-531-5831
www.thechesterfieldhotel.com

The Clarion Miami Beach
6985 Collins Avenue
Miami Beach, Florida 33141
305-865-9555
www.clarionmiamibeach.com

Crown Hotel
4041 Collins Avenue
Miami Beach, Florida 33140
305-531-5771
www.crownmiamibeach.com

Delano Hotel
1685 Collins Avenue
Miami Beach, Florida 33139
305-672-2000

Dezerland Beach Resort Hotel
8701 Collins Avenue
Miami Beach, Florida 33154
305-865-6661

The Dorchester
1850 Collins Avenue
Miami Beach, Florida 33139
800-327-4739
www.dorchesterhotel.net

Eden Roc Resort & Spa
4525 Collins Avenue
Miami Beach, Florida 33140
800-327-8337
www.edenrocresort.com

The Franklin
860 Collins Avenue
Miami Beach, Florida 33139
305-531-5541
www.franklinhotelmb.com

Hideaway Suites
751 Collins Avenue
Miami Beach, Florida 33139
305-531-2464
www.hideawaysuites.com

The Impala
1228 Collins Avenue
Miami Beach, Florida 33139
305-673-2021
www.hotelimpalamiamibeach.com

La Flora Hotel
1238 Collins Avenue
Miami Beach, Florida 33139
305-531-3406
www.laflorahotel.com

The Lorraine Hotel Beach Resort
2601 Collins Avenue
Miami Beach, Florida 33140
800-545-3905

The Marseilles Hotel
1741 Collins Avenue
Miami Beach, Florida 33139
800-327-4739
www.marseilleshotel.com

Miami Beach Ocean Resort
3025 Collins Avenue
Miami Beach, Florida 33140
800-550-0505
www.mbor.com

The National Hotel
1677 Collins Avenue
Miami Beach, Florida 33139
800-327-8370
www.nationalhotel.com

Ocean Surf Hotel
7436 Ocean Terrace
Miami Beach, Florida, 33141
800-555-0411
www.oceansurf.com

The Pelican Hotel
826 Ocean Drive
Miami Beach, Florida 33139
800-7PELICAN
www.pelicanhotel.com

Penguin Hotel
1418 Ocean Drive
Miami Beach, Florida 33139
305-534-9334
www.penguinhotel.com

Raleigh Hotel
1775 Collins Avenue
Miami Beach, Florida 33139
800-848-1775
www.raleighhotel.com

Hotel Riu
3101 Collins Avenue
Miami Beach, Florida 33140
305-673-5333
www.riu.com

Roney Palace
2399 Collins Avenue
Miami Beach, Florida 33139
800-432-4317
www.roneyplaza.com

The Shelborne Beach Resort
1801 Collins Avenue
Miami Beach, Florida 33139
800-327-8757
www.shelborne.com

The Hotel Shelley
844 Collins Avenue
Miami Beach, Florida 33139
800-414-0612
www.hotelshelley.com

Sherbrooke All Suites Hotel
901 Collins Avenue
Miami Beach, Florida 33139
305-532-0958
www.thesherbrooke.com

South Seas
1751 Collins Avenue
Miami Beach, Florida 33139
800-345-2678
www.southbeachhotels/southsea

Waldorf Towers
860 Ocean Drive
Miami Beach, Florida 33139
800-933-2322
www.travelbase.com/destinations/miami-
beach/waldorf-towers

Wyndham Miami Beach Resort
4833 Collins Avenue
Miami Beach, Florida 33140
305-532-3600
www.wyndham.com

Paris, France

Ritz Paris
15, place Vendome
75041 Paris, France
Tel: (33) (0) 1 43 16 30 30
www.ritz.com

Hotel Vernet
25, rue Vernet
75008 Paris, France
Tel: (33) (0) 1 44 31 98 00
www.hotelvernet.com

Hotel Intercontinental Paris
3, rue de Castiglione
75001 Paris, France
hotels.paris.interconti.com/parfra

La Grand Hotel
2, rue Scribe
75009 Paris, France
Tel: (33) (0) 1 40 07 32 32
www.hotels.paris.interconti.com/paragra

Hotel Royal Monceau
37, avenue Hoche
75009 Paris, France
Tel: (33) (0) 1 42 99 88 00
www.royalmonceau.com

Hotel Sofitel
17, boulevard Saint-Jacques
75014 Paris, France
Tel: (33) (0) 1 40 78 79 80

Normandy Hotel
7, rue de l'échelle
75001 Paris, France
www.hotel-normandy.com

Villa Pantheon
41, rue des Ecoles
75005 Paris, France
Tel: (33) (0) 1 53 10 95 95
www.villapanteon.com

Villa Eugénie
167, rue de Rome
75017 Paris, France
Tel: (33) (0) 1 44 29 06 06
www.villa-eugenie.com

Villa Opera Drovot
2, rue Geoffroy Marie
75009 Paris, France
Tel: (33) (0) 1 48 00 08 08
www.villa-opera-drovot.com

La Villa Luxembourg
121, boulevard du Montparnasse
75006 Paris, France
Tel: (33) (0) 1 43 35 46 35
www.villaluxembourg.com

Hotel Bourgogne & Montana
3, rue de Bourgogne
75007 Paris, France
Tel: (33) (0) 1 45 51 20 22
www.bourgogne-montana.com

Hotel Buci
Buci, 22 rue de Buci
75006 Paris, France
Tel: (33) (0) 1 55 42 74 74
www.bucihotel.com

Relais-Christine
3, rue Christine
75006 Paris, France
Tel: (33) (0) 1 40 51 60 80
www. relais-christine.com

Villa Beaumarchais
5, rue des Arquebusiers
75003 Paris, France
Tel: (33) (0) 1 40 29 14 00
www.villa-beaumarchais.com

Four Seasons Hotel
George V
75008 Paris, France
Tel: (33) (0) 1 49 52 70 00
www.fourseasons.com/paris

La Villa Allessandra
9, place Boulnois
75017 Paris, France
Tel: (33) (0) 1 56 33 24 24
www.villa-alessandra.com

Hotel Concorde Saint-Lazare
108, rue Saint-Lazare
75008 Paris, France
Tel: (33) (0) 1 40 08 44 44
www.concordestlazare-paris.com

Villa Montparnasse
2, rue Boulard
75014 Paris, France
Tel: (33) (0) 1 56 80 34 34

Terrass Hotel
12, rue Joseph-de-maistre
Montmartre, 75018 Paris, France
www.ila-chateau.com/terrass

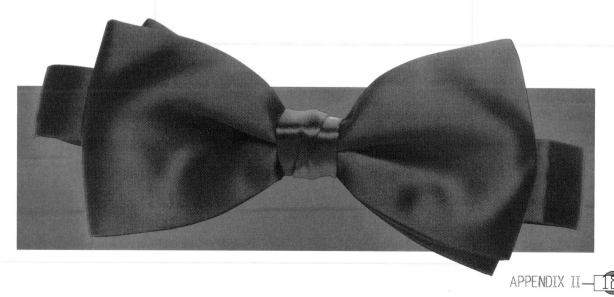

Hotel de Longchamp
68, rue de Longchamp
75116 Paris, France
Tel: (33) (0) 1 44 34 24 14
www.hotel-longchamp.com

Hotel de Louvre
place André Malraux
75001 Paris, France
Tel: (33) (0) 1 44 58 38 38
www.hoteldelouvre.com

Tulip Inn Aida Opera
11, rue Richer-17 rue de Conservatoire
75009 Paris, France
Tel: (33) (0) 1 45 23 11 11
www.aida-opera.com

TimHotel
216-218, avenue Jean Jaures
75019 Paris, France
Tel: (33) (0) 1 53 38 40 00
www.timhotel.com

Rome, Italy

De la Ville Inter-Continental Rome
Via Sistina 67/69
Rome 00187
Italy
Tel: +39 06 67331
rome.interconti.com

Hotel de Russie
Via del Babuino 9
00187 Rome
Italy
Tel: +39 06 32 8881
www.rfhotels.com/italy/rome/derussie/hotels_derussie

Hotel Zara
Via Quattro Fontane, 37 - 00184 Rome
(corner Nazionale Street)
Tel: +39-6-4814847/4870436
www.venere.com/it/roma/zara

Hotel Turner
Via Nomentana, 29 (Porta Pia)
00161 Rome
Tel: 06-44-25-00-77
www.hotelturner.com

Hotel Quirinale
Via Nazionale 7
Rome 00184
Italy
Tel: +39 6 4707
www.srs-worldhotels.com/italy/rome/hotel_romqui

Hotel Dei Console
Via Varrone, 2/D - angolo via Cola di Rienzo -
Rome, Italy
Tel +39 06-68892972
www.venere.com/it/roma/deiconsoli

Hotel Medeci
Via Flavia, 96- 00187
Rome, Italy
Tel. +39-06 48 27 319
www.venere.com/it/roma/medici

Casa Howard
Via Capo Le Case 18
Rome, Italy
tel +39 06 69 924555
www.casahoward.com

Hotel Savoy
Piazza della Repubblica 7
50123 Florence
Italy
Telephone: +39 (0)55 27 351
www.rfhotels.com/italy/florence/savoy/hotels_savoy

Hotel Morandi Alla Crocetta
Via Laura, 50
50121 Florence, Italy
Tel: 055/2344747
www.hotelmorandi.it

Hotel City
Via Sant'Antonino, 18
50123 Florence-Italy
www.abaka.com/Italy/City

Hotel Sampaoli
Via S. Gallo, 14
50129 Firenze
www.abaka.com/Italy/Cellini

Relais Hotel
Via Taddea 6
50123 Florence, Italy
www.abaka.com/Italy/Relais

Athens, Greece

Areos: Park Hotel Athens
Leoforos Alexandras 10
10682, Athens, Greece
Tel: 01 643 7302

Makrygianni: Ira
Falirou 9
11742, Athens, Greece
Tel: 01 923 5618

MakrygianniL Royal Olympic
Athanasiou Diakou 28-32
11743, Athens, Greece
Tel: 01 923 6832

Omonoia: Dorian Inn
Peiraios 15-19
10552, Athens, Greece
Tel: 01 523 9782

Neos Kosmos: Athenaeum Inter-Continental
Leoforos Anrea Syngrou 115
11745, Athens, Greece
Tel: 01920 6000

Syntagma: Grande Bretagne
Plateia Syntagmatos
10263, Athens, Greece
Tel: 01323 0251

Syntagma: Athens Plaza
Vasileos Georgiou
10564, Athens, Greece
Tel: 01 325 5301

Satorini, Greece

El Greco Hotel
Fira, 847 00
Santorini, Greece
Tel: +30 286 24946
www.agn.gr/hotels/elgreco/elgreco

Aigialos Luxury Traditional Houses
Fira, 84 700
Santorini, Greece
Tel: +3 0286 25191 5
www.agn.gr/hotels/aigialos/aigialos

Artemis Villas
Santorini, Greece
Tel: + 30 286 22712
www.agn.gr/hotels/artemis/artemis

Kouros Village
Perissa, 847 00
Santorini, Greece
Tel: +30 286 81972
www.agn.gr/hotels/kourosv/kourosv

Mediterranean Beach Hotel
Vothonas, 847 00
Santorini, Greece
Tel: +30 286 31167
www.agn.gr/hotels/mediter/mediter

Santorini Palace Hotel
Fira Santorini, 84700 Greece
Tel: +30 0286 22771
www.agn.gr/hotels/santorinipalace/santorinipalace

Spiliotica Traditional Villas
Imerovigli
Santorini, Greece
Tel: +30 286 24767
www.agn.gr/hotels/spilio/spilio

Hotel Zephyros
Kamari, 84 700
Santorini, Greece
Tel: +3 0286 31990
www.agn.gr/hotels/zephyros/zephyros

Hotel Galini
Firostefani - Santorini, 84 700, Greece
Tel: (0030 286) 22095
www.agn.gr/hotels/galini/galini

Mykonos, Greece

Hotel Belvedere
Rohari, 846 00
Mykonos, Greece
Tel: +30 289 25122 5
www.agn.gr/hotels/belveder/belveder

Kivotos Clubhtel Deluxe
Ornos Bay
Mykonos, 84600 Greece
Tel: +30 289 25795/6, 24094
www.agn.gr/hotels/kivotos/kivotos

Maki's Place
Tourlos, 846 00
Mykonos, Greece
Tel: +30 289 25118
www.agn.gr/hotels/maki/maki

Villa Giovani
School of fine arts
Mykonos Town - 846 00
Tel: +30 289 23485
www.agn.gr/hotels/giovani/giovani

Kouros Apartment Hotel
Tagu, 846 00 Mykonos
Summer - Tel: +30 289 25381/3
Winter - Tel: +30 1 899 0032
www.agn.gr/hotels/kouros/kouros

Casa Delfino Suites
Old Town of Chania
9 Theofanous str. - 731 00 Chania - Crete, Greece
Tel: +30 821 87400
www.agn.gr/hotels/delfino/delfino

Crete

The Marina Hotel
GR-700 14 Gouves
Heraklion, Crete
Tel: (0030) 897 41362
www.agn.gr/hotels/marina/marina

Kydon Hotel
Sofoklis Venizelou Sqr., Chania, Crete, Greece
Tel: (0821) 52280 4
www.agn.gr/hotels/kydon/kydon

King Minos Palace Hotel & Bungalows
70014 Limin Hersonissou, Heraclion, Crete
Tel: 0897 22781 4
www.agn.gr/hotels/kingminos/king

Villa Naias - Exclusive Apartments
Daskalogianni str.
Chrisi Akti
Chania, Crete
Tel: +30 821 33008

Minos Palace Hotel
GR 721 00 Ag. Nikolaos,Crete,Greece
Tel: +30 841 23 801
www.agn.gr/hotels/minospalace/minos

Bahamas

The Flamingo Bay Yacht Club & Marina Hotel
P.O. Box F-43819
Freeport, Grand Bahama Island
Bahamas
888-311-7945
www.flamingobayhotel.com

The Ritz Beach Resort
P.O. Box F-43819
Freeport, Grand Bahama Island
Bahamas
242-373-9354
www.ritzbeach.com

Freeport Resort & Club
P.O. Box F-42514
Freeport, Grand Bahama Island
Bahamas
877-699-9474
Local: 242-352-8425

Bermuda

Horizons & Cottages
33 South Shore Road
Paget, PG04, Bermuda
800-468-0022
Local: 441-236-0048
www.bermudasbest.com

Waterloo House
PO Box HM 333
Hamilton HM BX, Bermuda
800-468-4100
Local: 441-295-4480
www.bermudasbest.com

Coral Beach & Tennis Club
P.O. Box PG 200
Paget PGBX, Bermuda
441-236-2233
www.bermudasbest.com

Pompano Beach Club
36 Pompano Beach Road
Southampton SB 03 Bermuda
441-234-0222
www.bermuda.com/pompano/contact.html

Newstead Hotel
27 Harbour Road
Paget PG 02
Bermuda
800-468-4111
Local: 441-236-6060

St. John, U.S. Virgin Islands

Caneel Bay: Rosewood Hotels & Resorts
St. John, U.S. Virgin Islands 00831-0720
340-776-6111
www.caneelbay.com

Garden by the Sea Bed & Breakfast
Cruz Bay, St. John
U.S.V.I. 00831
340-779-4731
www.gardenbythesea.com

The Inn at Tamarind Court
St. John, U.S.V.I. 00831
800-221-1637
www.tamarindcourt.com

Estate Lindholm
St. John, U.S. Virgin Islands 00831
800-322-6335
Local: 340-776-6121
www.estatelindholm.com

St. Thomas, U.S. Virgin Islands

Renaissance Grand Beach Resort
Smith Bay Road, Rte 38
ST. Thomas, 00802
United States Virgin Islands, US Virgin Islands
340-775-1510
renaissancehotels.com

The Crystal Palace
St. Thomas, US Virgin Islands 00801
340-777-2277
crystalpalaceusvi.com

St. Croix, U.S. Virgin Islands

Carringtons Inn St Croix
4001 Estate Hermon Hill
St Croix, VI 00820
877-658-0508
Local: 340-713-0508
www.carringtonsinn.com

Pink Fancy Hotel
27 Prince Street
Christiansted, St. Croix VI 00820
800-524-2045
www.pinkfancy.com

Cormorant Beach Club and Hotel
4126 La Grande Princesse
St. Croix, 00820, U.S. Virgin Islands
800-548-4460
Local: 340-778-8920
www.triple1.net/R/Resorts-In-St-Croix

Inn Paradise Bed & Breakfast
1-E Golden Rock, PO Box 428
Saint Croix, Virgin Islands 00821
866-800-9803
www.innparadisestcroix.com

The Inn at Pelican Heights
4201 Estate St. John
Christiansted, St. Croix, USVI 00820-4491
888-445-9458
www.innatpelicanheights.com

Key West, Florida

Alexander Palms Court
715 South Street
Key West, Florida 33040
305-296-6413
www.alexanderpalms.com

Andrews Inn
0 Whalton Lane
Key West, Florida 33040
305-294-7730
www.andrewsinn.com

The Banyan Resort
323 Whitehead Street
Key West, Florida 33040
305-296-7789
www.banyanresort.com

Blue Marlin Resort Hotel
1320 Simonton Street
Key West, Florida 33040
305-294-2585

Blue Skies Inn
630 South Street
Key West, Florida 33040
305-295-9464
www.blueskiesinn.com

Center Court Historic Inn & Cottages
915 Center Street
Key West, Florida 33040
305-296-9292
www.centercourtkw.com

Chelsea House
707 Truman Avenue
Key West, Florida 33040
305-296-2211
www.redroosterinn.com

The Colony Exclusive Cottages
714 Olivia Street
Key West, Florida 33040
305-294-6691
www.thecolonykeywest.com

The Cuban Club Suites
1108 Duval Street
Key West, Florida 33040
305-296-0455
www.elmesondepepe.com

Cypress House Bed & Breakfast
601 Caroline Street
Key West, Florida 33040
305-294-6969
www.cypresshousekw.com

Frances St. Bottle Inn
535 Frances Street
Key West, Florida 33040
305-294-8530
www.bottleinn.com

Heron House
512 Simonton Street
Key West, Florida 33040
305-294-9227

Key Lime Inn
725 Truman Avenue
Key West, Florida 33040
305-294-5229
www.heronhouse.com

La Casa de Luces
422 Amelia Street
Key West, Florida 33040
305-296-3993
www.elmesondepepe.com

La Pensione
809 Truman Avenue
Key West, Florida 33040
305-292-9923
www.lapensione.com

Lightbourne Inn
907 Truman Avenue
Key West, Florida 33040
305-296-5152

The Palms Hotel
820 White Street
Key West, Florida 33040
305-294-3146
www.palmshotelkeywest.com

Pegasus International Hotel
501 Southard Street
Key West, Florida 33040
305-294-9323
www.pegasuskeywest.com

Pier House Resort & Caribbean Spa
One Duval Street
Key West, Florida 33040
305-296-4800
www.pierhouse.com

Southernmost Motel in the U.S.A.
1319 Duval Street
Key West, Florida 33040
305-296-6577
www.oldtownresorts.com/southernmost

Watson House
525 Simonton Street
Key West, Florida 33040
305-294-6712
www.oldeisland.com/watsonhs

Westwinds
914 Eaton Street
Key West, Florida 33040
305-296-4440

Wyndham Casa Marina Resort & Beach House
1500 Reynolds Street
Key West, Florida 33040
305-296-3535
www.casamarinakeywest.com

Chattanooga, Tennessee

Baymont Inn and Suites
3540 Cummings Highway
Chattanooga, Tennessee 37419
423-821-1090

Best Inn
7717 Lee Highway
Chattanooga, Tennessee 37421
423-894-5454

Chanticleer Inn
1300 Mockingbird Lane
Chattanooga, Tennessee 37419
423-820-2015

Chattanooga Clarion
407 Chestnut Street
Chattanooga, Tennessee 37402
423-758-5150
www.chattanoogaclarion.com

Chattanooga Marriott
2 Center Plaza
Chattanooga, Tennessee 37402
423-758-0002
www.marriotthotels.com

Country Hearth Inn
7638 Lee Highway
Chattanooga, Tennessee 37421
423-510-0088
www.countryhearth.com

Fairfield Inn
2350 Shallowford Village Drive
Chattanooga, Tennessee 37421
423-499-3800
www.fairfieldinn.com

Guesthouse International Inn
2201 Park Drive
Chattanooga, Tennessee 37421
423-510-0800

Homewood Suites
2250 Center Street
Chattanooga, Tennessee 37421
423-510-8020

Kings Lodge
2400 Westside Drive
Chattanooga, Tennessee 37404
423-898-8944

MainStay Suites
7030 Amin Drive
Chattanooga, Tennessee 37421
423-485-9424

Rodeway Inn
2000 East 23rd Street
Chattanooga, Tennessee 37404
423-622-8053

Adams Hilborne Mansion Inn
801 Vine Street
Chattanooga, Tennessee 37403
423-265-5000

Country Inn & Suites
3725 Modern Industries Boulevard
Chattanooga, Tennessee 37419
423-825-6100

McElhattan's Owl Hill B & B
617 Scenic Highway
Chattanooga, Tennessee 37409
423-821-2040

Microtel Inn
7014 McCutcheon Road
Chattanooga, Tennessee 37421
423-510-0761
www.microtelinn.com

Wingate Inn
7312 Shallowford Road
Chattanooga, Tennessee 37421
423-890-7400

Martha's Vineyard

Harbor View Hotel
131 North Water Street
Edgartown, Massachusetts 02539
800-225-6005
www.harbor-view.com

Clarion Martha's Vineyard
227 Upper Main Street
Edgartown, Massachusetts 02539
800-922-3009
www.clarionmv.vom

Hob Knob Inn
128 Main Street
Edgartown, Massachusetts 02539
800-696-2723
www.hobknob.com

Martha's Place B & B
114 Main Street
Vineyard Haven, Massachusetts 02568
508-693-0253
www.marthasplace.com

Beach Plum Inn
50 Beach Plum Lane
Menemsha, Massachusetts 02552
877-645-9454
www.beachpluminn.com

The Crocker House Inn
12 Crocker Avenue
Vineyard Haven, Massachusetts 02568
800-772-0206
www.crockerhouseinn.com

The Doctor's House
60 Mt. Aldworth Road
Vineyard Haven, Massachusetts 02568
866-507-6670
www.thedoctorshouse.net

The Hanover House
28 Edgartown Road
Vineyard Haven, Massachusetts 02568
800-339-1066
www.hanoverhouseinn.com

The Inn at 148 Main Street
148 Main Street
Edgartown, Massachusetts 02539
508-627-7248

Island Inn
Beach Road
Oak Bluffs, Massachusetts 02557
800-462-0269
www.islandinn.com

The Kelley House
23 Kelley Street
Edgartown, Massachusetts 02539
800-225-6005
www.kelley-house.com

The Pequot Hotel
19 Pequot Avenue
Oak Bluffs, Massachusetts 02557
800-947-8704
www.pequothotel.com

The Point Way Inn
Main Street and Pease's Point Way
Edgartown, Massachusetts 02539
888-711-6633
www.pointway.com

The Shiretown Inn
44 North Water Street
Edgartown, Massachusetts 02539
800-541-0090
www.shiretowninn.com

GLOSSARY

Naturally, the world of romance and seduction has a language all its own. From the poetry of Shakespeare to the lingo on urban city streets, there are different words used to describe the emotions and actions that go along with the pursuit of happiness, romance, love, and sex, not necessarily in that order.

A

Abstinence: To refrain from having sex.

Affair: When a person seeks sex and/or romance outside of a pre-existing monogamous relationship.

Androgyny: Having both masculine and feminine characteristics.

Asexual: To be without sexual attributes.

Attraction: A desire to be in the presence of a specific person; an admiration of someone's physical appearance.

Aphrodisiac: A drug that is designed to stimulate sexual arousal and desire.

Autoeroticism: Sexual acts done to oneself.

B

Beefcake: A man with a lot of sex appeal.

Birth control: Pills taken by a woman to prevent pregnancy.

Bisexual: One who is attracted to both men and women.

Brothel: A whorehouse.

C

Condom: Latex covering for the penis, used to prevent conception and spread of sexually transmitted diseases.

Cyber sex: The act of writing sexual messages and descriptions in a private forum online.

E

Easy: A man or woman who will engage in sexual activity with nearly anyone with few prerequisites.

Erection: Rigid state of the penis, indicating arousal and preparedness for sexual activity.

F

Fetish: A non-sexual body part or object that causes extreme sexual arousal in a person.

Flirt: Playful behavior intended to arouse romantic interest.

Foreplay: Acts of a sexual nature which begin arousal and lead to intercourse.

Frigid: Description of a person who does not desire sex, or has a fear of intercourse.

French kiss: An open mouth kiss in which tongues come into contact with each other.

H

Horny: To be in a state of sexual arousal.

Hug: A tight embrace.

I

Impotence: Being unable achieve an erection.

Infatuation: A temporary fascination with another person, usually based on looks, which feels similar to love.

Intimate: Very close in friendship or affection.

J

Jacuzzi: A bubbling tub usually large enough to accommodate several people.

Jail bait: Someone under the age of 18.

K

Kiss: A caress with the lips.

L

Libido: A person's sexual appetite.

Love at first sight: When people believe they fall in love with someone upon their first interaction.

Lust: A strong sensual and/or sexual attraction to another person.

M

Matchmaker: Someone who brings two people together for the purpose of starting a romantic relationship.

Marriage: The act of two people committing themselves romantically to each other for the span of their lives.

Massage: Kneading and rubbing parts of the body to promote relaxation, and often causing romantic and sensual arousal.

Monogamy: The practice of selecting one exclusive sexual mate.

N

Nibble: Gentle biting in a sensuous manner.

Nymphomaniac: A derogatory term used to describe a person who seeks out excessive sexual encounters on a regular basis.

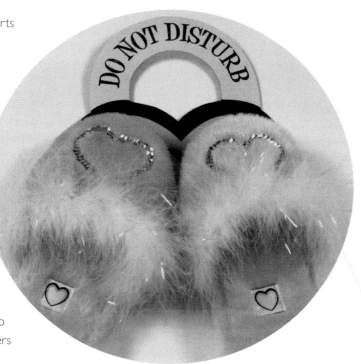

O

One-night stand: A sexual encounter without the bonds of a romantic relationship, taking place only once between specific people.

One-way: Someone who will only engage in one type of sexual activity.

Orgasm: The climax of a sexual encounter.

P

Pervert: Someone who receives gratification from bizarre and unusual sexual activities.

Petting: Touching and/or fondling the genitals of another person.

Pick-up line: A short sentence used to initiate a conversation with another person.

Phallic symbol: Any object that resembles a penis, being longer than it is wide.

Phone sex: The act of having a telephone conversation in which the participants describe sexual acts and situations.

Polygamy: The practice of having two or more wives or husbands at the same time.

Pro: A prostitute.

Q

Quicky: A short sexual encounter.

R

Romance: A relationship between two lovers and the feelings shared between them.

S

Score: To achieve any step toward seduction of a person.

Seduction: The process of arousing romantic, sensual, and/or sexual interest in another person.

Sensuality: Desire for pleasures of the senses.

Sex symbol: A celebrity who is seen as the highest standard of attractiveness and sexuality.

Sexually transmitted disease: Any one of several viruses that are contracted through sexual contact with an infected person.

Soul-mate: One whose soul is believed to be spiritually connected to another.

Stalker: Someone who secretly follows and watches the intimate activities of another.

Sweetheart: Term of affection for a loved one.

T

Tease: To lead a person into sexual arousal and leave them off without fulfillment; one who engages in such behavior.

U

Unconditional Love: Affinity that is not withheld due to any circumstances.

V

Voyeur: Someone who receives sexual gratification by watching others perform sex acts on themselves or with others.

X

Xanadu: An idyllic, beautiful place.

A

Adams, Bryan
  "Everything I Do, I Do It For You," 106
  "I Finally found Someone," 11
adult bookstores, 53
Adventures of Don Juan, the, 49
Advil, 62
Affair to Remember, an, 142
affairs, 26-27
Aguilera, Christina ("What a Girl Wants"), 11
All for One ("I Swear"), 106
American Beauty, 107
"American Pie" (song), 72
Andes (candy), 30
Anniversaries, 159-161

Anthony, Mark ("You Sang to Me"), 11
AOL, 20, 22
Apple Jacks, 103
Armstrong, Louis ("What a Wonderful World"), 11
Ashford Collection, the, 85
Asshur (Phoenician God), 90
Atlantic City, 74
autoreply, 14

B

Baby Ruth, 102
Bacchanalian Festivals, 44
Bahamas, 2
Barbie, 32

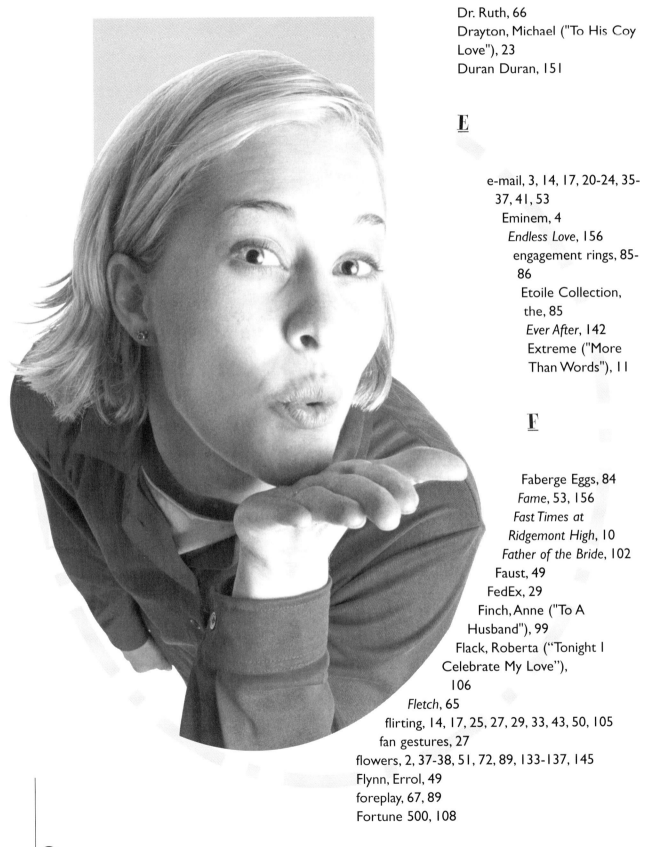

Dr. Ruth, 66
Drayton, Michael ("To His Coy Love"), 23
Duran Duran, 151

E

e-mail, 3, 14, 17, 20-24, 35-37, 41, 53
Eminem, 4
Endless Love, 156
engagement rings, 85-86
Etoile Collection, the, 85
Ever After, 142
Extreme ("More Than Words"), 11

F

Faberge Eggs, 84
Fame, 53, 156
Fast Times at Ridgemont High, 10
Father of the Bride, 102
Faust, 49
FedEx, 29
Finch, Anne ("To A Husband"), 99
Flack, Roberta ("Tonight I Celebrate My Love"), 106
Fletch, 65
flirting, 14, 17, 25, 27, 29, 33, 43, 50, 105
fan gestures, 27
flowers, 2, 37-38, 51, 72, 89, 133-137, 145
Flynn, Errol, 49
foreplay, 67, 89
Fortune 500, 108

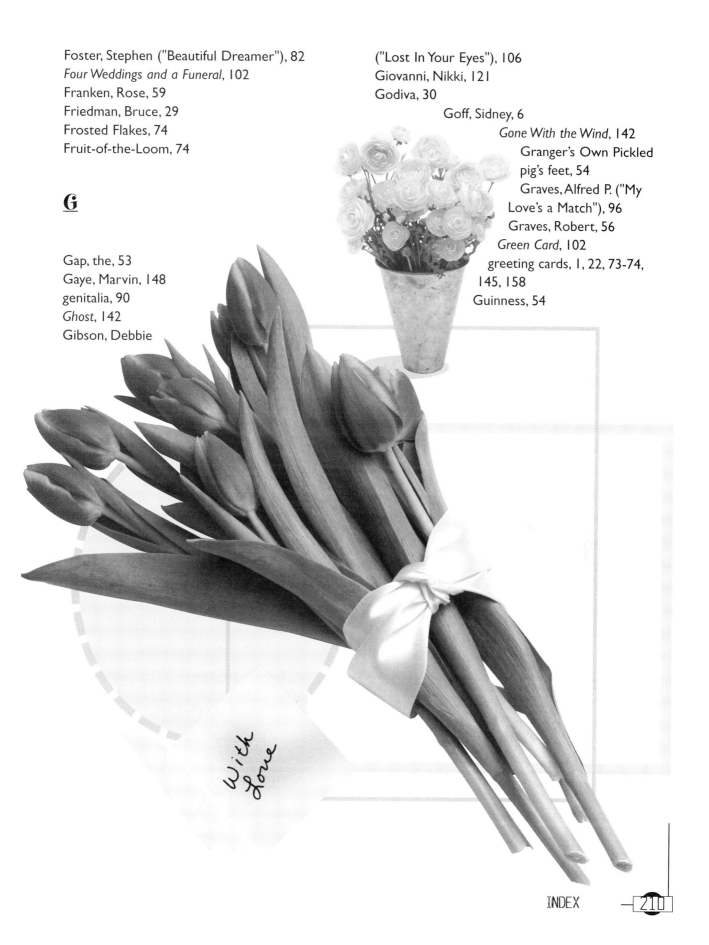

J

K

L

M